Michael Denneny, General Editor

Stonewall Inn Editions

Buddies by Ethan Mordden
Joseph and the Old Man by Christopher Davis
Blackbird by Larry Duplechan
Gay Priest by Malcolm Boyd
Privates by Gene Horowitz
Taking Care of Mrs. Carroll by Paul Monette
Conversations with My Elders by Boze Hadleigh
Epidemic of Courage by Lon Nungesser
One Last Waltz by Ethan Mordden
Gay Spirit by Mark Thompson
As If After Sex by Joseph Torchia
The Mayor of Castro Street by Randy Shilts
Nocturnes for the King of Naples by Edmund White
Alienated Affections by Seymour Kleinberg
Sunday's Child by Edward Phillips
The God of Ecstasy by Arthur Evans
Valley of the Shadow by Christopher Davis
Love Alone by Paul Monette
The Boys and Their Baby by Larry Wolff
On Being Gay by Brian McNaught
Parisian Lives by Samuel M. Steward
Living the Spirit by Will Roscoe, ed.
Everybody Loves You by Ethan Mordden
Untold Decades by Robert Patrick
Gay and Lesbian Poetry in Our Time by Carl Morse and Joan Larkin, eds.
Reports from the holocaust: the making of an AIDS activist by Larry Kramer
Personal Dispatches by John Preston, ed.
Tangled Up in Blue by Larry Duplechan
How to Go to the Movies by Quentin Crisp
Just Say No by Larry Kramer
The Prospect of Detachment by Lindsley Cameron

Stonewall Inn Mysteries

Death Takes the Stage by Donald Ward
Sherlock Holmes and the Mysterious Friend of Oscar Wilde by Russell A. Brown
A Simple Suburban Murder by Mark Richard Zubro

Also by Quentin Crisp:

HOW TO GO TO
THE MOVIES

Quentin Crisp

ST. MARTIN'S PRESS
NEW YORK

Library of Congress Cataloging-in-Publication Data

Crisp, Quentin.
    How to go to the movies / Quentin Crisp.
        p.   cm.
    Reprint. Originally published: 1988.
    ISBN 0-312-05444-0 (pbk.)
    1. Motion pictures.   2. Motion pictures—Reviews.   I. Title.
[PN1994. C695   1991]
791.43—dc20   90-49955
                                                                      CIP

First U.S. Paperback Edition.
10 9 8 7 6 5 4 3 2 1

*Most of the material in this book appeared previously, in slightly different form, in *Christopher Street* magazine.

To Mr. Steele, Editor of *Christopher Street* magazine.

CONTENTS

Thanks to Thomas Keith for help in preparing the manuscript and to my editor, Michael Denneny, and my agent, Connie Clausen.

I

THE FORGETTING CHAMBER

INTRODUCTION

In his wonderful novel *The Child Buyer*, Mr. Hersey makes an anxious citizen inquire what will happen to the little boy who is being purchased by a vast business concern. The kindly reply is that he will be well treated. Then this disturbing phrase is added: "Of course, he will have to go into the forgetting chamber."

For me, this was the story's moment of true poetry.

At the very end of the book, as he is being led away from his home forever, the victim asks, "What will happen to my dreams?" This is the question that all of us might well ask ourselves.

Apparently, it has been scientifically established that to forget real life for a few hours every night is not enough—that people become more psychotic when forced to go without their dreams than when deprived of sleep. I seldom remember my dreams, but I recall every frame of every movie I see and my fantasy life used to be lived chiefly in the cinema. However, a regular diet of celluloid is fast becoming difficult to obtain.

In the 1950s, it was prophesied that television would kill the movies; it didn't, but it helped to drive the industry mad. I am not an economist and cannot account for what has gone wrong, but, like the rest of the world, I have no difficulty in seeing that the trend has been away from a steady flow of seldom first rate but very acceptable pictures to a few productions upon which so much money has been squandered and on which so many expectations ride that a kind of financial hysteria has set in. The producers, the actors, and the audiences have all been led to believe that each new release will be the greatest ever. It is as though every sexual union between a husband and his wife must be the most shattering experience ever or the marriage will fail. As Dr. Westheimer would be the first to point out, it is the accumulated understanding by each partner of the other's needs that is the foundation of a successful relationship; and it is the continuous appreciation of a director's work or an actress's performances that are the deepest joy of moviegoing.

As a child, I was totally absorbed in each picture I saw and so was everybody I knew. In factories, laundries, kitchens where the faithful were gathered together, the conversation was about nothing except the week's releases. Every sentence began with the words "Didn't you love the bit where . . . ?" Between the years 1926 and 1930, all the women in England looked like Miss Garbo (or wished they did). Then *The Blue Angel* burst upon their group consciousness; they ran home to curl their hair and shave off their eyebrows in order to redraw them wantonly across their foreheads and look like Miss Dietrich.

In spite of the intensity of her interest, the average movie maniac knew little about the mechanics of filmmaking. Only a highbrow critic would have spoken of a powerful sequence in *Anna Karenina* in which, though the count forbade his wife to leave their house, she defied him. The rest would have said, ". . . and that Basil Rathbone, he shouted at her, but you know our Greta; she didn't take a blind bit of notice." It didn't matter that in one picture an actress might be wearing an Empire dress and in the next, a preruined raincoat; each movie was seen as another day in the life of its star. These great ladies were not exactly our friends, because friends are people with whom you get stuck; they were what the word *star* implies—distant, permanent, dazzling icons who evoked from us a loyalty and an adoration that only a fool would have lavished upon a lover or a member of her family.

The cinema—at least the American cinema—was then a phantasmagoric realm in which feelings ran higher than elsewhere, sentiments were purer, human beings were capable of greater nobility or degradation, and yet we took this other world completely for granted, like daylight. Reciprocally, the big film companies felt equally sure of their audiences. They even gave us serial films of which each episode ended with the words "Come next week and see another installment of this exciting adventure." Such pictures counted on our fidelity; they assumed we would never leave our hometown. They fulfilled exactly the same function as the soap operas of modern television, except that now the whole world is everybody's hometown.

At that time, movies, some of which are not the subjects of scholarly theses, were deemed to be entertainment for the masses. My mother did not consider herself to be a mass, and only accompanied me to the cinema in that spirit of ostentatious condescension with which the British middle classes now treat television. If questioned closely, they say, "Well, yes, we do have a television set but, of course, we never watch it."

The early moviemakers were fully aware of the lowliness of their audiences; they catered to it; they wallowed in it and, accordingly, kept cinema seats well within the financial reach of almost everybody.

When I lived in London, a woman who occupied the room behind mine nagged me into consenting to read a book entitled *The Children of Sanchez*. She was excruciatingly Russian and wished to rub my powdered nose in the excrement of the world. This vast tome described in monotonous and squalid detail the tribulations of one poor Mexican family. In my cotenant's presence, I opened the book at random. Immediately, my disdainful gaze fell on the sentence "My mother went to the movies almost every afternoon." Thus was confirmed my conviction that people—especially women—are prepared to make do without the barest necessities but not without the cinema.

This law does not only prevail in Mexico. By the time I was as adult as I am ever likely to be, there were three movie "circuits" in Britain. They were the Odeon, the Gaumont, and the A.B.C. Throughout the length and breadth of the land, in throbbing cities, in smug towns, in marooned villages, each of these cinema chains exhibited a different double feature every week of the year, come rain or come shine, as Miss Garland would have said. This meant that with a little luck, a lot of ingenuity, and a total disregard for domestic duties, it was possible for everyone to spend three and a half hours on three nights a week away from the inclement world. Almost all the films shown in those days were American, until a "quota" system came into force, which compelled each cinema manager to foist upon his clientele a certain number of English pictures as part of their weekly fare of illusion. As Mr. Korda says in his fascinating book about his famous uncle, *Charmed Lives*: "when this law came into effect the British public went mad as though it had been asked to do without bread." This extreme reaction was due not only to the self-evident inferiority of the home product; it was also occasioned by the fact that to the British, British films did not constitute a visit to the forgetting chamber; they were as boring as life in England really is. Serious crime, which is the staple diet of scriptwriters, seemed to be a daily occurrence in Chicago and New York but was almost unknown in Manchester or Wigan. There, if he played his cards right, a murderer could stay on the front page of the *Daily Telegraph* for weeks. Who wants art to reflect his own humdrum existence?

The years of the double feature were the happiest days of their lives not only for audiences; they were also the golden age of actresses.

Today, when people speak of the seven-year contract, they do so with curled lips. Now that everyone thinks he has rights, that arrangement is considered to have been too heavily loaded in favor of the employer. It has become yet another area in which the unions have raised their ugly heads; but, as Miss Kerr has pointed out, in fact it provided a stable atmosphere in which an actress could perfect her skills with at least some assurance that they would be used. Her studio would carry her through at least one flop, and by the time her contract was well under way, she had usually acquired her own secretary, her own makeup artist—in some cases, her own cameraman. (Mr. Daniels photographed almost all of Miss Garbo's movies.) In other words, a leading lady became a kind of queen bee attended by five or six drones who had no other function than to enhance her assets and conceal her defects. No wonder so many of them became permanent stars. What keeps a woman young and beautiful is not repeated surgery but perpetual praise. They were the eternal mistresses of their public. In deference to the art directors of their films, they changed their costumes occasionally, but only as ballerinas wear tights and tutus to remind us that they are first and foremost classical dancers but, if spoken to nicely, will don a turban to show that for the moment they are the playthings of cruel Turks. A movie star never deprived her public of the thrill of instant recognition at her first appearance on the screen.

This happy predictability no longer prevails. Now, every new picture is a desperate gamble, deafeningly publicized, with its mounting costs broadcast like news of a forest fire. If a film fails, even though its star may have been judged by the critics to have been the only good thing in it, when her name is mentioned, some movie mogul will growl, "Isn't that the broad that cost us thirty-four million dollars?" In these circumstances, actresses have decided to be different people in different roles; they have taken to acting—a desperate measure indeed.

Though television has wrought all this havoc in Hollywood, it is no real substitute for the movies. It has its star; it has Miss Collins, who remains through all vicissitudes of plot the last of the "vamps." If she ever appeared on any screen, large or small, as a nice home girl, the world would come to an abrupt and ignominious end. In general, however, the effect of television upon our lives has been pernicious. Big was beautiful. Television diminishes the scale of our fantasies, but it does worse than that; it domesticates them. It does not compel us to give it our whole attention. We can sip our instant decaffeinated coffee while being thrown out of the fortieth-floor windows of an expensive hotel; we can file our nails while being raped by hooded intruders. We see television on our own mundane turf. It is as injurious to the soul as fast food is to the body.

We should vacate our homes and go to a movie for the very reason that this exodus will force us to take the occasion seriously, to abandon everyday life, to place ourselves for a while where there are fewer distractions, where the telephone bell cannot toll for us. We ought to visit a cinema as we would go to church. Those of us who wait for films to be made available for television are as deeply under suspicion as lost souls who claim to be religious but who boast that they never go to church. As Mr. Godard has said, such people are as wholly to be condemned as the Philistines who say they are art lovers but who never step inside a gallery, preferring instead merely to buy picture postcards of famous paintings.

The way to go to the movies is incessantly. The more often we visit the cinema, the more exciting the experience becomes, not the more boring, as one might have expected. Films teach us how to see them; they are written in a language that we must learn. If, some fifty years ago, the average audience had been shown a film as complicated as *Charade* or *Arabesque*, it would have tottered out into the light of day completely bewildered. Now, in a carefully constructed, well-told movie, we can perceive and interpret the slightest tremor of the camera, the most fleeting glance of an actor. We must go to the movies so often that, while remaining distant, the stars become calculable to us, allowing us to recognize and dote upon their gestures, the tones of their voices, their every idiosyncrasy. After a while, even the unseen presence of our favorite directors will become traceable.

The way to go to the movies is reverently. We must be prepared to believe in the most improbable hypothesis, provided that it is presented to us with sufficient conviction, enough passion. We must surrender our whole beings to whatever reaction the story demands—gasping, laughing, weeping, wincing, sighing with utter abandonment. Thus we shall be spared the appalling likelihood of giving way to indecorous emotion in real life. Audiences who consider themselves sophisticated do not always understand this. When *Last Tango in Paris* was first shown in London, journalists, their microphones erect, lurked outside the cinema like rapists, waiting to pounce upon the female members of the clientele. "What did you think of it?" they inquired. "We liked it," the girls replied somewhat nonplussed. Never known for their delicacy in such matters, the reporters then asked, "What did you think of the sexy bits?" To this onslaught on their maidenly modesty, the girls then answered, "Oh, we just laughed"—not, you will note, "we laughed" but "we *just* laughed," meaning that they felt no more involving emotion. Why? If we are prepared—nay, eager—to be shot by Mr. Robinson or to be driven at breakneck speed through busy narrow streets by Mr. McQueen, why do we not long to be defiled by Mr. Brando? This thin-lipped response is typically English and must be cured.

The way to go to the movies is critically. That is to say, we must take to each cinema two pairs of spectacles. While we plunge into each picture as though it were happening to us, we must also watch it from a distance, judging it as a work of art. Thus, to seeing a film will be added an extra pleasure that can never be derived from real life, which has no plot and is so badly acted. This dual vision is especially beneficial when watching a movie made in a different era. In these productions, their old-fashioned clothes and morality render them superficially ludicrous, but their quaintness must not blind us to the skill with which they have been made.

If we go to the movies often enough and in a sufficiently reverent spirit, they will become more absorbing than the outer world, and the problems of reality will cease to burden us.

This is the state of affairs toward which so many of us unsuccessfully strive. Opium is the religion of the people, or it was until very recently when cocaine came back into fashion, but we are told by heaps of teenagers that the ecstasies of crack only last about a quarter of an hour—hardly as long as a travelogue or an animated cartoon. A first feature lasts eight times as long. No toxic substance is a real answer. Comrade Dostoyevsky said that without tobacco and alcohol, life for most men would be intolerable, but he had never been to a double feature. It is true that movies are as addictive as dope, but they are far less injurious to health and they ought not to be as expensive.

Clearly, the salvation of the Western world is in the hands of the film industry.

In order that the poorest among us may once again go to the

movies several times a week, someone must find a way to lower the price of cinema seats. The unions must be crushed and there must be a return to the making of low-budget pictures so as to provide us with longer programs.

The world is pining for a steady diet of celluloid; it desperately needs an alternative life to that through which it drags itself at the office or, worse, at home. This other existence need not be prettier, but it must be richer; it must have the power to use those capacities for love and courage for which we can find no worthy object in real life.

For me, it was in middle age that mundane activities claimed so much of my time. For my own sake and for the sake of other people's survival, I tried to take part in real life. In old age, as in childhood, I have been lucky; I have felt less need to keep my feet on the ground; I have begun to float into other realms. For some people, this higher plane is mysticism or reincarnation or worse; for me, it has been the cinema.

For the chance to indulge this passion, I have to thank *Christopher Street* magazine and especially its editor, Mr. Steele. I would like to think that the reviews in this book show that, even when I have found fault with some particular film, I have enjoyed watching it. I also hope that I have been able to impart to my readers a little of the pleasure that I have experienced in the forgetting chamber.

STARDOM

It is difficult for anyone who has had the misfortune to be born into this age of appalling equality to imagine how brightly shone the stars on younger and happier nights.

Time is the great leveler—the irreversible homogenizing agent—and, in the past fifty years, it has been performing its evil work at an ever-increasing pace. Since the First World War, almost all the distinctions that once kept civilized society in place and made it so variously interesting have vanished. The differences between nationalities, between classes, between age groups, and even between the sexes have all disappeared. As these barriers crumble, the area in which stardom can flourish does not increase; it diminishes. Our capacity for worship and for wonder fades. The place of these agreeable reactions is taken by contempt and envy.

During the first two decades of this century, holidays abroad, which are now a commonplace, were the privilege of the daring and the rich. The arrival of a foreigner anywhere was as exciting as a visit from a Martian would be now. As rumor reached the outer world that in Hollywood fame grew on trees, all the adventurous women from Central Europe, if they thought of themselves as in any way alluring, set out for California; and it must be remembered that in Europe almost all women think they are beautiful. Those who arrived in Los Angeles knew they had the extra asset of being foreigners. On the screen, it was the age of what Mr. Brownlow calls the Golden Silence. Therefore, a broken accent was no disadvantage; indeed, it was taken to be a guarantee of great artistry. How could anyone with a name such as Lya de Putti, Alla Nazimova, or Pola Negri possibly fail to be a wonderful actress? Now, such a woman is known as a displaced person and would be an object not of admiration but of the deepest suspicion.

It is no longer possible to be exotic.

While the glamour of being a foreigner was evaporating, so was the prestige of coming from the upper classes, which, especially in the United States, have always been vaguely connected with wealth, education, and glamour. As the movies quickly passed from a mere mechanical wonder to being a whole library of novels that you could enjoy without being able to read, they became almost entirely a lower-class pastime. Audiences were dazzled by glimpses of the lifestyle and the imperious antics of the well-born and the well-heeled and the well-endowed, of which they knew absolutely nothing. The upper classes, to show that they could spell, plodded on with the novel from time to time, alleviating the boredom of this occupation by making fun of the cinema.

> I wish I hadn't broke that cup;
> I wish I was a movie star.
> I wish there weren't no washing-up
> and life was like the movies are.
> I don't have adventures in the street;
> Bill don't register emotion when we meet.

This song was sung in an English highbrow revue in the late twenties or early thirties. It contains all the required ingredients of condescension. The deliberate grammatical errors grade this prototypical film fanatic as illiterate. The reference to the breaking of a cup designates her as a housemaid—even as a scullery maid, that very symbol of abjection; and the phrase *register emotion* betrays her half-understood fascination with film jargon. Most denigrating of all is the evidence that in the mind of this devotee, the life of the actress is blended with that of the tempestuous character on the

12

screen to whom the star lends her glorious presence. This confusion was almost universal.

In fact, not all of the early Hollywooden dolls had adventures in the street or anywhere else except at parties with their own kind. Even there, they were careful not to associate—let alone fornicate—with anyone whose salary was inferior to their own. Their managers, their agents, and their publicists saw to that. This fact was hardly known to the earliest moviegoers.

It was the harrowing great divide between the sexes that dealt, most surprisingly of all, the most severe blow to stardom.

When recently the late Mr. Welles was asked the question "What is a star?" he replied without a tremor of hesitation, "A star is a woman." Pressed for further Delphic utterance, he added, "If there are now no stars, it is because there are now no women." I imagine that by this remark, he meant that in modern life there are no mysterious creatures who weep and yearn and carry on in a way that no mere man expects or wishes to understand. There are also no superior beings who either urge there mates on to greatness or bring them social, financial, and physical ruin. In other words, there are no more goddesses and no more vamps. Indeed, as far as I know, that expression has disappeared from the vernacular of the United States. The American vamp was the counterpart of the French femme fatale. Neither of the descriptions have a synonym in British usage, because in Britain the idea of a man taking any woman seriously is too ridiculous to contemplate. Something went wrong with the notion of victory through cosmetics, and some twenty-five years ago, women abandoned the idea, adopting instead the strategy of victory through work, which they called liberation. Thus was the final nail hammered into the coffin of stardom.

Until this disastrous turn of events, not only were the times propitious, the place was also right. After a few false starts, the movie industry shifted from the East Coast of the United States to Hollywood. The reasons given for this change of venue were two. Firstly, the new terrain brought within easy reach of cameramen a staggering variety of scenery—mountains, deserts, the shore; secondly, the clarity of the atmosphere was ideal for long-distance photography. What really turned out to be the locality's most valuable asset was its isolation. In those days, Hollywood was only a few wooden huts leaning against each other in a wilderness some distance from Los Angeles. It became an oasis where there were no conversations, only captions, no people, only actresses. In that earthly paradise, life with its many-colored dome of compromise could not stain the white radiance of the movies.

Moreover, this geographical remoteness was a two-way stretch. On the one hand, it enabled scriptwriters and directors to maintain the purity of their vision; on the other, it prevented audiences from knowing too horribly much about their screen idols. They learned only what Mr. Mayer wished them to know or what the yellow press could discover or invent. These two sources of information, though opposite in intention, had something in common—the extremity of their moral postures. Between them, they arranged that to the outer world—the lower world—the stars seemed always either to be sitting innocently holding hands with a fiancé (secretly hired from Central Casting) in expensive restaurants or else they were engaged in the wildest orgies. The important thing was that nothing reported about them was ever humdrum.

This romantic situation could not last. As soon as gossip columnists discovered that their readers would gladly devour absolutely anything written about Hollywood, they started to describe even the utmost trivialities.

In recent years, the veil of romance has been rent asunder still further. The invention of the tape recorder has made it possible for anyone who can put two words (or two actors) together to tell her life story. We now know not only that actresses are ordinary but also that they do not have the grace to be ashamed of the fact.

The result of all these banal details being too freely given has not been to make the world like the stars more; it has made it question their greatness. If actresses do not hold their exalted position by some mysterious otherness, why, we ask, are they stars? We begin to resent their status or, more crudely, their salaries.

If publishing firms or the visual arts had moved their head-quarters from farthest east to farthest west of the continent, it would have made very little difference to their histories, but the cinema turned out to have a unique aptitude for perpetuating personal myths—for deploying the physical idiom of the human animal. This largely depended on the enchantment that distance lends to everything.

This is something that the theater can never do. By comparison with the movies, the stage is as intimate as a football field. Our vision of a play is telescopic. We can hardly tell whether the leading lady is smiling or frowning. This handicap seduces her into multiplying her every gesture, her every word by the seating capacity of the theater. She embraces us with semaphore gestures and tells us her secrets in the voice of a town crier while we, anxious to communicate our appreciation, clap and cheer out of all proportion to the price of the seat we have been given.

On television, the situation is reversed. The scale of the image tends to belittle the performer; and the fact that, on the Mahomet principle, she goes to her people rather than graciously granting them an audience in her temple means that we watch her with half an eye and treat her with that contempt we usually reserve for our families.

In between these two media, the cinema holds a unique position. It allows us an intimate glimpse of a woman's soul that could never be obtained in real life. There our scrutiny would cause its object either to pretend to be shocked or to give way to hideous exhibitionism. In a movie house, we are totally absent from the action being shown on the screen, but at the same time we are immersed in it.

It was when the movie industry discovered that it had this special pleasure to offer to the masses—an experience for which they had been waiting since the beginning of the world—that it decided to consolidate its position by inventing the "star system."

In modern times, when people utter this phrase, they curl their lips. The complaints leveled at this ploy are two in number—one aesthetic, the other legal.

People—or rather critics—say that stars are discouraged from acting. This is true, but the statement ought to be praise rather than blame. The word *act* has two meanings. A performer may adopt a set of gestures, a way of speaking, and a makeup that help to persuade her and her audience that she seems to be someone other than she is off the screen. The knack of being able to do this convincingly raises the practitioner to the level of an artiste and is useful to small-part players. A star acts in this sense only to the very slightest degree. She may wear her hair in a plait round her head to suggest she is a peasant or in a bun to tell us she is a schoolmistress, but nothing was ever done to cheat her audience out of instant recognition. She "acted" in a quite different sense. She spoke and moved in such a way that her entire being was transfused with the emotion that she, the actress, would herself feel if she were really in the fictitious situation in which the script places her. Her art is therefore not one of concealment but of revelation. As the late Mr. Cagney said, "Technique consists of allowing nothing to come between you and your audience."

It is also mentioned from time to time that this kind of performance tends to create bad films. This only means that a star shines most brightly in pictures with simple narrative lines. This objection falls into the error of likening movies to prose, where a complicated plot might be awaiting. A film is a poem. Mr. Shakespeare's entire sonnet sequence only tells us he loved Mr. H. more than Mr. H. loved him—a notion which, if judged as mere information, is banal if not actually disgusting to most people. What entrances the reader of those verses is the ideas, the images, and even the puns that the poet brings to bear on this simple central theme. In the same way, a star vehicle can be about some tawdry woman killing herself for love but can be elevated to the level of a masterpiece by the intense application of the images that the director chooses—by the skill with which he prepares the story for the screen and the intensity with which the star embodies his idea. Not only is it fatal for a star to act, it is unwise for her to be known even to have acted in her entire life. It is difficult to rise to stardom from the ranks. Mr. von Sternberg informed us that Miss Dietrich had been in nine films before he put her into *The Blue Angel*. The lady herself told a slightly different story. It was wise of her to do this because what mattered was that her past should be shrouded in mystery—that, like Mr. Botticelli's little friend, she should arise naked out of a sea of confusion. We know now that Miss Garbo appeared in a movie called *Joyless Street*, where she did not even play the leading part, but when she appeared in *The Temptress* in Hollywood, she seemed to the whole world to be untouched by even a vestige of a past.

The second objection to the star system was that it was unfair. It often was absolutely binding upon the actress to give options to the production, but she could be taken up or dropped upon a whim.

Thus was created a kind of Gilded Cage—a structure that came in for a lot of criticism but that, deep down, is the only environment in which the soul of a woman can ever feel at home. There, she is simultaneously a tyrant and a slave. There, she possessed and is possessed by a lover, a mentor, or a director who had the power to destroy her but had so far not brought himself to do so.

The public cannot make a star. It is she who creates her own public. If this was not so, then a star would be no more wonderful than a human being. We ordinary mortals find it hard to imagine anything but a magnified image of our dreary selves. A star has to be someone we could not have invented if we had sat up all night. She can only be created by a genius whose imagination, so much vaster than our own, is ignited into a blaze that lights up the whole Californian sky by some aspect of an earthly woman and who can then transform her into an ideal of virtue or mystery or depravity. For days or even months, an old-fashioned impresario observed his protégé as a sculptor walks about a block of marble, thinking, dreaming, until he has decided what work of art will require the least amount of superfluous stone.

Beauty was never a woman; it was a man's idea of a woman.

In Hollywood, it was usually a Jewish man's idea of an Aryan woman, because this relationship preserved an element of the unknown so essential to romance.

While all this ferment was taking place, what did the star do? Practically nothing. However, it was not quite enough for her merely to follow the instructions of her creator; she needed to allow herself to be irradiated by his Pygmalian obsession with her. Even if she could never explain it, she had to sense throughout her body what it was that sustained his dream.

This was asking a lot, but we do not know that there are now no women and no directors capable of this process. We do not ask them to try. We reject, even mock them if they make the attempt. We have lost forever our capacity for reverence. As a life of luxury and unlimited sexual experience has come within the reach of every woman however gross, she has begun in her tawdry way to live the lives of a movie star and consequently to regard the graces of real stars as unwarranted arrogance. Therefore, do not ask why there are now no Garbos, no Dietrichs. The fault lies not in our stars but in ourselves.

There is no way back to Eden; we have eaten the bitter apple of equality to the very core, dragging the gods down to our own mean level. From now on, our lives will consist of a relentless, exhausting pursuit of pleasure instead of a quest for the Holy Grail of Happiness. Our talk will be of money and of sex—never of power or of beauty.

STARS

Some time ago, during a British radio program, a gentleman of great age was asked by an interviewer to what he attributed his longevity. After a brief hesitation, he replied, "To bad luck— mostly."

I would say the same of my own situation, but with reservations. I know that I am like a guest standing at my host's door, saying that I must go but not going—that I am still writing and speaking though I have nothing new to say, but being so old has given me an advantage over many other movie maniacs. I saw the silent movies with silent eyes.

Most of these masterpieces have perished; they were printed on celluloid, which has turned out to be a less durable substance than human memory. The early films that remain are occasionally exhibited at "art" houses, where they are viewed by special audiences out of antiquarian curiosity or amusement. However, I saw them as serious entertainment. Modern audiences go to the showing of a late silent film or an early talkie as anthropologists attend tribal rituals. I was a native. Though converted later, originally I believed in magic—in a world ruled solely by the power of personality. When, on one of the "culture" channels of television or at the Public Theater, I watch a picture directed by Mr. Griffith or Mr. Vidor, my pristine faith revives and I reenter that happier, more romantic world.

These are some of the stars that I most admired.

Miss Helm

When we hear a movie actress speak, she immediately acquires a nationality and, worse, a class. Her image becomes limited. She can no longer embody all our dreams, but in younger and happier days, when the films were silent, their stars had the power to wound the imagination beyond repair.

In the late 1920s, all the most exciting pictures were made in Germany, many of them by Mr. Lang. He liked his women fatal and processed his actresses to fit this ideal. His greatest discovery was Miss Helm, whom he put into *Metropolis*, the first science-fiction movie ever made. In this movie, the usual mad scientist captures her and with some rather glib use of electricity makes a robot in her likeness, except that the chromium Miss Helm has no soul and one eye never shuts.

In the original version of this story, the robot does a pseudo-Egyptian dance, but this episode was cut from later copies, presumably because it was thought too shocking. An alternative sequence was substituted, which, in fact, was infinitely more perverse.

An entirely male audience is seen staring intently at some silver theater curtains. Suddenly, Miss Helm insinuates herself between the curtains. She is wearing a black satin dress that reaches up to her ears, down to her knuckles, and trails along the ground behind her. She divides the slit in her skirt just enough to reveal one thigh, from which she snatches a diamente garter, which, with a darting cobralike movement, she flings at her audience. At once, a forest of hands springs up to catch it and the sequence is over. In all, it cannot have lasted more than a minute, but its impact was unforgettable. At that moment, Miss Helm looked like a large spider that had been dipped in melted sugar.

I cannot imagine anything more alluring.

Miss Crawford

Miss Crawford did not grow old as other women do, nor did she become a dehydrated version of her former self as other movie queens are apt to do. Age could not wither her nor custom stale her infinite monotony. Instead, her face appeared to undergo what geologists term a process of denudation. As the tides of youth receded, the implacable ambition upon which the critics remarked in her early films emerged slowly like a smoldering volcano arising from the sea. The cheeks became more hollow, the eyes more prominent, and the mouth took on the permanent curve of lips that are determined not to cry. Toward the end of her life, she looked like a hungry insect magnified a million times—a praying mantis that had forgotten how to pray. Even her springy posture started to resemble the stance of a brave soldier facing death.

The mystery of a Garbo or a Dietrich is a veiled glimpse of delights that, out of indifference or sheer perversity, they withhold from us. In Miss Crawford's gaze we read the mystery that we are to her. Apparently, our presence wounds or angers or terrifies her. Her method of dealing with the menace of human relationships was to become a star—to be unassailable. In this ambition, she was abetted by Mr. Mayer, of whom, unlike so many actresses of her day, she never spoke badly. They were, for many years, in almost total agreement. He told her that it was her duty to him to live every moment of her public life as a star, and this, using her nearly inexhaustible fund of self-discipline, she did. The strain must always have been considerable and in time, if the grim tales told by her daughter are to be believed, it became unbearable.

We shall never know what wild impulse sent Miss Crawford out on those two fatal shopping sprees from which she returned home with four children. A marriage can sometimes become a way to stardom, but motherhood is the most starless role a woman can undertake. This actress and her family learned that the hard way.

It appears that she fell into the age-old error of being unable to relinquish all other aims for the most important. She seems to have wanted the best of everything, as in the film of that name—

to be an ordinary mortal at times and, on other occasions, to be a movie queen. She was not alone in her confusion. Many actresses have foolishly imagined that they could be great without being lonely. It is impossible. Only Miss Garbo seems to have realized this. She chose to have no husbands, no children, no friends—only fame.

In real life, Miss Crawford was inured, if not to anguish, at least to hardship and a certain amount of humiliation at a very early age. Her mother really did work in a laundry and she herself found employment in a department store at thirteen, but she never relinquished her hopes, and her persistence was rewarded. She was placed under contract by Mr. Mayer when she was sixteen. At first, in her professional life, she did not seem to be destined to be a tragedienne. Like Miss Harlow, who started out as the inevitable blonde in slapstick movies featuring Mr. Laurel and Mr. Hardy, and like Miss Monroe, who was originally chased around the set by the Marx brothers, Miss Crawford played opposite the comedian, Mr. Langdon. Without any natural gifts except for ballroom dancing, as Miss Crawford once said, she nagged herself into being a competent actress—not for love of the art but as means to becoming a celebrity. Even her fans were aware of her technical weaknesses. They did not think her successful when she played an English woman, nor as a French girl in *Reunion in France*, nor in a period piece called *The Gorgeous Hussy*. If she had any ability as an actress, it was never for pretending to be somebody else; it lay in transforming her face into a mask of fear or hatred or grief.

It was not until she was twenty-four that she was given a worthwhile part. This was in *Our Dancing Daughters*. In 1928, the most wicked thing that a girl could do—or at least be photographed doing—was taking off her dress in public. Miss Bankhead, who at that time represented sin on a grand scale, did it in a play on the London stage called *The Garden of Eden* and Miss Crawford did it in her picture of the Roaring Twenties, but, even in this comparatively lighthearted film, what she symbolized was not really naughtiness. It was desperation. She was later to play in several comedies, the best of which was *They All Kissed the Bride*, and her comedy acting was highly praised, but this underlying quality of being a troubled personality she was never to lose.

When, after the Second World War, Hollywood lost interest in her, Miss Crawford herself began to search for a movie that could match the face she had now acquired. She found *Mildred Pierce*. From that moment onward, the quest was over. Thereafter, she would always play desperate victims, as in *Sudden Fear*, or desperate tyrants, as in *Queen Bee*.

Finally, in real life, she became a member of the board of Pepsi-Cola. Her movie career and her life were welded together in the unquenchable furnace of her ambition.

Miss Harlow

Miss Harlow was largely a self-made star.

She was never given the glossy treatment lavished by producers and directors upon such superlative screen beings as Miss Dietrich and Miss Garbo. Almost at the outset of her career, she had the good fortune to be placed under contract by Mr. Hughes, but he does not seem to have valued her very highly, or not for long. Perhaps their personal relationship proved unsatisfactory to one or the other or both of them. After giving her the female lead in *Hell's Angels*, he did not process her as another impresario might have done. On the contrary, he loaned her to other studios so often that gossip writers referred to her as "the borrowed blonde." Such treatment is inevitably bad for an actress—especially if it occurs before she has learned to recognize her image, let alone gain control of it.

To be directed is merely to be told where to stand and what expression to wear; it is not an education in how to be.

When she was new to the public, even her publicity stills seem to have been carelessly taken. In them, her hair is chalky white, her lips, boot black, and her eyebrows are two penciled lines, varying neither in thickness nor in emphasis. Her postures, frequently with her terrible knees on view for all the world to see, are so awkward that they seem like parodies of glamorous attitudes. Her dresses, neither elegant nor daring, look like part of the wardrobe of a barman's daughter who has just won a lottery. Furthermore, they are rumpled as though she had but a moment ago narrowly avoided rape. One wonders what her studios thought that they were doing. Similar defects are noticeable in the early pictures of Miss Monroe, but, in her case, the result was less harmful because she was always presented to her admirers as the helpless victim of the world's crudities.

By contrast with that perpetual waif, Miss Harlow seems tough. In repose, her features appear sullen and greedy; she looks like the most popular girl in a remand home. When she finally came into her own, it was because Metro-Goldwyn-Mayer had at last settled for the fact that this was the message that she was born to deliver.

A Miss Tazelaar compared her acting in *Hold Your Man* to the work of Miss West, who undulated onto the screen at about the same time. The comparison is, of course, absurd. Miss West ruled the movie industry not with a scowl but with a lazy, self-indulgent tyranny. She took Hollywood by the throat or, rather, by the sensitive part of its anatomy and compelled it to display her on her own terms. She was so completely self-aware that she could afford a large amount of self-mockery. Miss Harlow's performances were full of mockery and even of contempt but rarely for herself.

Nevertheless, she eventually won over the critics who in her early films had not merely ignored her; they had stated that she didn't exactly get the hang of motion picture histrionics. By the time *Red-Headed Woman* was being distributed in 1932, she was being described as "what the tired business man likes." The press praised her "effortless vulgarity," a quality that most stars in those days tried to hide if they originally had possessed it. The general opinion was that her acting was improving, and, doubtless in a purely technical way, it was; she was becoming accustomed to the cameras and the lights, but the real change was that she was moving or being moved nearer to the heart of her screen image. She was one of the few stars who appeal to men. There are two types who can do this; one is the sweet but not too sweet girl next door and the other is the woman who is as coarse or nearly as coarse as a man. Miss Harlow fell into this second category. She was at her best in films where her playmates were sailors or fishermen, and my guess is that it was among such men as these that she was most popular.

She died at the age of twenty-six. Between *Hell's Angels* and *Saratoga* only seven years passed. That isn't a long time for a woman alone to travel from leading lady to stardom, but she succeeded. As a rule, it is a great advantage for movie actresses to die young, but in Miss Harlow's case, this was not so. In spite of her platinum hair, her appeal was not glamorous—still less exotic or mysterious. She was sexy in the coarsest way. This quality could have lasted into middle or even old age.

Miss Bankhead

Queen Elizabeth I was married to England. Several centuries later, Miss Bankhead lived in sin with it for eight hilarious years. The time, the country, and the women were made for each other. She had decided to become the patron saint of exhibitionists, and in the twenties, the British loved to be shocked. Nearly every issue of their oldest living magazine, *Punch*, contained a joke drawing depicting a short-skirted niece making pert replies to the homilies of an uncle so outraged that his spectacles could be seen flying from his nose. This made the role that the actress had chosen for herself too easy. Onstage the most daring gesture that the Lord Chamberlain ever allowed her was the flinging off of her wedding dress (not at the altar). She compensated for the comparatively restrained tone of her professional image with the riotousness of her private life—if you could call it private.

When, inevitably, her permit to work in London was not renewed, Miss Bankhead returned to America and made six movies whose stories must have been provided by fortune-tellers. "Because of your sensitive nature, you have suffered deeply, but in your tea leaves I see a dark stranger [Mr. March] who will understand you." In each of these pictures, she was cast as a victim of fate, when we all knew that in her ravenous hands fate was a pushover.

After that, nothing was ever quite the same. A day slowly dawned when it was difficult to prevent actors from stripping on-stage and when every filmscript writer used the shortest words for the longest things. Miss Bankhead had not foreseen this possibility and was at a loss. The press took to saying that she had become a parody of her former self, but how could a woman be blamed for scorning development if her past had been effortlessly perfect?

Maturity is the refuge of failures.

Miss Garbo

Miss Garbo had eye lids like rolltop desks.

According to the boring minimum standards imposed upon us by the Greeks, this would not have made her beautiful, but the moguls of the late silent films and the early talkies did not worry. She possessed a quality more subtle than beauty; she had glamour—the mysterious glow that warns the beholder that although all appears to be offered, not all is likely to be given.

In fact, few great vamps of the screen ever won popularity polls. They were worshiped chiefly by artists, who were the public-relations officers for the Tristan-and-Isolde racket, and by homo-sexuals, who in their hearts imitated the stars but, fearing the world's mockery, parodied them in public. Ordinary men and women wanted to get on with the job and therefore settled for a balanced diet of niceness and availability.

For glamorous women, there were many methods of dodging the horrible sexual payoff. The Garbovine way was exaltation. Watching her films, audiences asked themselves why the human relationships in which most of us dabble more or less contentedly were not good enough for her. In each picture that she reluctantly consented to make, Miss Garbo alone of all the cast seemed to have read the entire scenario. She knew things would turn out badly. When she smiled, it was always in a sickly fashion and merely to humor us.

Long ago in some now-extinct Swedish university, Miss Garbo must have majored in hopeless love. All that made her trashy films worth one-and-ninepence were the moments when the script permitted her to hold forth on her favorite subject. In *Romance*, for instance, on hearing her leading man sing "Annie Laurie," she murmured, "To me love is only a little light in all this darkness." In *Camille*, when Mr. Taylor tried against all odds to cheer her up, she replied, "It is better that I live only in your heart where nothing can stain our love."

It is precisely such lines as these that would cause a modern actress to groan and say, "Do I really have to say this rubbish?"

This is a pity. Romance was the style in sex.

Miss West

Miss West was a conspicuously round woman in a very square industry.

Nevertheless, at the start of the 1930s, she took to Hollywood like a duck to drakes. In that far-off age, there was still a noticeable difference between the sexes, and studio heads catered almost exclusively to what they considered to be women's tastes in entertainment. Sensual pleasure was veiled by prudery or sentimentality. Miss West was guilty of neither of these sins. Her sense of humor would at that time have been described as masculine; it was founded on superb detachment. In her day, the vogue was for making fun of intimate relationships between men and women by presenting one or both parties as hideous, old, or in some other way ill-equipped for love, but this unpleasant ploy only ridicules the unfortunate. Miss West struck with faultless aim at the very heart of the matter; she lampooned sex. Indeed, she sent up everything including herself.

Almost from the beginning of her movie career (short if you exclude the horrible *Myra Breckinridge*), she imposed upon her pictures not only her unique view of the human comedy but also her own method of photographing it. Before her reign, almost all wisecracks ended with an abrupt cut corresponding with the blackout that followed the punch lines of old-fashioned revue sketches. Miss West insisted that she be shown walking—nay, sailing—away from her deflated victims, thus producing a joke upon a joke.

Her success seems all the more remarkable if we remember that it occurred when Wall Street, when the entire Western world was tottering. Through those dark days, she kept Paramount solvent single-handedly, though doubtless the lady herself would say that hands were not all she employed.

Now that she is gone, we shall never be sure how she achieved her singularly personal triumph in a business where traditionally so many people have a finger in the pie, to say nothing of a hand in the cookie jar. If charisma is the ability to persuade without the use of logic, then probably it was by this elusive power that Miss West ruled with such apparent ease her chosen domain.

Miss Davis

I suspect that when Miss Davis began her career in Hollywood, the making of movies was even more chaotic than it is now—that a feature player might be in several pictures being produced simultaneously. To establish consistency in a character, an actress might feel the need to develop a series of mannerisms that an audience could easily recognize and from which it could quickly derive a sense of familiarity. Even when she became a star, Miss Davis continued to do this (the replacing of stray hair in the heroine's coiffure in *The Little Foxes*; the cigarette gestures in *All About Eve*). The compulsion to watch this kind of performance is stimulated not by its naturalism but by the attack with which even corny aphorisms are uttered and the command with which gestures are made. If a director or cameraman wishes to convert this method of acting into melodrama, nothing can prevent him.

Miss Davis knows this but I don't think she likes it.

Not long ago, she voiced her objection to the label "horror film." With invincible logic, she pointed out that hundreds of movies depicting antisocial behavior, including murder, have found their market without suffering the humiliation of this absurd trade description. *Hamlet*, for instance, does not end until more than half the cast is dead. (The English celluloid version of that story was indeed a horror, but that is another matter.)

If Miss Davis thinks—and, even in her sleep, the lady thinks—she will instantly realize that the word *horror*, when used to categorize a film is not a warning to the squeamish to stay away; it is an escape clause permitting audiences not to take seriously anything they see on the screen. As with pornography, so with violence in entertainment, what is immoral is not the disgusting relish for detail but the fact that the true consequences are never shown.

Dear Miss Davis, we hope that the impending television series prophesied for you by Mr. Fain will not be trivialized. We long to tremble when you glare at us; we hope to cringe when you threaten, and, when you shoot, do not miss. We know that we deserve to die.

Come to think of it, why not go for broke and play Lady Macbeth on Broadway. I'm sure Mr. Price would costar.

Miss Dietrich

Beauty is, as already noted, not so much a woman as a man's idea of a woman—preferably born of a different race from his own or into another class so as to add a pinch of unattainability. In the movie industry, enchantment was acquired by Aryan goddesses when seen through Jewish eyes.

The relationship that most perfectly embodied this eternal law was that which bound Mr. von Sternberg to Miss Dietrich. She had, in fact, made many films before; against all odds, he cast her as Lola Lola in *The Blue Angel*, but he was the first director to realize the full possibilities of her immaculate insolence. This characteristic, he made into her personal method of stretching to the requisite hour and forty-five minutes the time lag between her first meeting with her leading man and their traditional close-up, fadeout kiss.

Modern movies are not constructed on this principle. Delicious dalliance has gone out of fashion and the new film length of two and a quarter hours is deemed too long to wait just for a bit of you know what.

Miss Dietrich's early Hollywood movies were the most immoral ever generally released. She did not reveal any more of her body than other screen sirens of her day, nor was she seen behaving in an any more explicitly sexual way, but the plots of nearly all these pictures showed her living a life of total degradation. In *Shanghai Express*, for instance, she forever plied her trade back and forth from Shanghai to Peking until, after a great deal of mileage, to say nothing of footage, she remet her former fiancé quite by chance but without, one must add, the slightest sign of embarrassment. Here as elsewhere, her costar was chosen from among the most boring actors that the casting office could supply. This was done to make it clear that matrimony was inevitable.

Though on one occasion she sank so low as to wear a hat—the brim of which was weighted down with artificial cherries—Miss Dietrich never seemed to pay the smallest price for her sins, but perhaps I have read the message wrongly. It may be that the ultimate punishment for a lifetime of unremitting fornication is that you become too weak to defend yourself from marriage.

THE NEW
HOLLYWOOD

When the Portuguese explorers of old set out across the Atlantic Ocean, their publicly avowed intention was to find the Islands of the Blessed. They meant Hollywood, of course. Until I was almost seventy years of age, I was like those ancient mariners; I saw Hollywood only in my heart or, more exactly, in the cinema. In 1978, I visited the place in actuality. It was not quite as I had hoped. Since then, every time that I go there, I cannot help wondering whether I shall discover that yet another fragment of my dream has become detached and floated into oblivion. During my most recent trip to the West Coast, I tried to determine what has caused this gradual disintegration.

On the plane bound for Los Angeles, those passengers who were not trying to sleep off their gin lag were encouraged to watch *Star Wars*. I recalled that, in its day, this space epic was said to be the most profitable film ever made, though whether because more people went to see it or because cinema seats had become so much more expensive, I could not tell. Mr. Guinness (Sir Alec) made a valiant attempt to bestow upon the movie a saintly, El Greco halo, but the story remained paralyzingly monotonous. I longed for its incessant, violent motion to cease, but when the end title at last appeared and I was allowed to raise the eyelid of the porthole nearest to me, I found that nothing had changed. I was still in the movie—still in a hideous, hazardous object racing over a mountain range the color of despair and totally devoid of human life. It became suddenly obvious that, for some time past, art and life have been growing more and more unpleasantly alike. In a world where there is no longer anyplace that it is agreeable to tarry, perpetual motion is the only happy state. No wonder there is a drug that is colloquially called speed.

Emerging from the plane, I became aware that Los Angeles Airport, like so much in America, is in a chaos of improvement. I fled in a taxi. The very moment that I began to tell the driver how to reach my destination, I realized that I was uttering the first words of any Chandler thriller. "She has a place out on one of the canyons." This was exhilarating, but, at the same time, I noticed that one of the great myths of Hollywood was evaporating. The sky was clouded. The region is popularly supposed to enjoy perpetual sunshine. Like every traveler arriving at the end of his journey, I was being confronted not with the beautiful mirage of climate but with the horrible fact of weather. As we sped through the streets of Los Angeles, the sky became even more overcast and before long, a few drops of rain had fallen. These meteorological disturbances are said to be caused by the activities of an angry volcano situated on the borders of Mexico and Guatemala, but I interpreted them as symbols of the movie industry's disintegration.

My hostess lives in a house of moderate proportions by Hollywood standards. Like so many of the older homes in this neighborhood, it was built with the proverbially eternal sunshine in mind. As the sky at that moment was gray, the interior of her home was dark and even a little chilly.

By noon the following day, the weather had changed back to its traditional brilliance. For all the remaining days of my visit, it was as though Mr. Goldwyn had never died. The sun shone from dawn till dusk; a naked child whose entire body was the color of rosewood splashed in and out of the swimming pool; crimson flowers cascaded down the hillside; a butterfly as large as a bird did its ballet exercises on the edge of the breakfast table, and hummingbirds as small as insects hovered or darted among the branches of trees heavy with grapefruit and peaches.

There was no smog; I have never seen any. Smog is one of

the modern myths of the region. It is akin to the warning that all foreigners receive that it is impossible to get about Los Angeles without a car. This is untrue. While I was there, 4,600 bus drivers went on strike and the whole city was plunged into turmoil. If the transport system was really redundant, the strike would have passed unnoticed. In fact, it is only the rich who live in the canyons and have no intention of ever setting foot in a public vehicle, who claim that everyone must own a car. The rest of the inhabitants walk or travel by bus.

That's the trouble with history; it's always written by the upper classes, who have nothing better to do. The glories of Greece and the grandeurs of Rome would be considerably dimmed if they had been described by slaves.

The smog and the futilities of the rapid transport system are invented by the natives to ward off the envy of the gods. Americans in general have become afraid of their luck. Years ago, English and European magazines were full of joke drawings in which American tourists were depicted wearing long racoon coats and horn-rimmed glasses and boasting that everything was bigger and better "back home." Now the national image of the United States has passed from self-praise to self-doubt. Their prosperity and their power have become a burden to them because news has reached them from less fortunate areas of the earth. These craven fears of being great have even settled upon Hollywood.

I asked Miss Gish whether Mr. Griffith had ever bestowed star status upon her. Her reply was an emphatic "No." Then she added, "That was why we all felt so safe working for him." She went on to say that when she and her sister told their mother that they had been recognized in the street, her mother's only comment was that if all they wanted was to be stared at by strangers, they could go about with rings through their noses. That attitude of profound modesty did not prevail in Hollywood for long. Miss (Mary) Pickford saw to that. Yet even while hairdressers were pinning pretty ringlets to some of the most grasping heads in history, the stories of the movies remained as clear as a chapel bell, as simple as a sampler.

The people of Los Angeles have become excruciatingly conscious of living in the vicinity of the movie industry. The shop assistants are all acting at being shop assistants; waitresses act being waitresses. I accompanied my hostess to a shop on Rodeo Drive, which is hallowed ground because part of it is rumored to belong to Miss Garbo. I noticed at once how exotic the saleswoman looked, her fingernails so long that they hardly permitted her to write out a bill. After the shopping spree, I was taken out to lunch at a restaurant outside of which were parked four Rolls-Royces. As we had arrived in a less prestigious vehicle, it was taken to the car park behind the building, like a wrong hushed up. I would not have been at all surprised to learn that the Rollses were props hoping to be used in a location shot. Inside the restaurant, at the table next to ours, a woman was celebrating her birthday. The waiters clustered around her and sang "Happy Birthday" as though it were the big number to an operetta. It may have been their first audition in months.

Even the behavior of the Los Angeles police has lately become tinged with theatricality. The newest scandal started a while ago when two officers were caught carrying electronic equipment out of a warehouse and into their car. Thus far, the scenario had seemed like an Abbott and Costello comedy. Then the mood changed, as though Billy Wilder had been fired and Mr. Peckinpah called in. A Glen Ford courtroom drama began, in which the district attorney filed charges against six members of the force. Then the plot thickened into tragedy. One of the policemen involved was described as "somehow losing control of his pickup truck" and being hurled from the vehicle; he died on the freeway. On the day when I happened to turn the pages of the Los Angeles Times, I read that a prostitute had been murdered. She was to have been a key witness for the prosecution in a case that involved not only burglaries but also what journalists were calling "sexual escapades." The woman had already divulged the information that one officer "had transported her in his patrol car for no official purpose." What dialogue! Where are you, Mr. Spillane, when we need you? The effect of the movies on the outer world has been paralleled by the encroachment of the real or worse-than-real world upon Hollywood, but this is not immediately discernible. On the surface, the place still seems to be an unruffled suburb. The sprinklers still sparkle in the sunshine. As I sat by my host's swimming pool, I could hear the polite barking of well-bred dogs and the purring of lawn mowers. The segregation of the poor from the rich is absolute. We drove around quite extensively but we never caught sight of a down and out in Beverly Hills; when we stopped, no one offered to smear our windshield with a rag more greasy than the glass; we did not see a single old lady huddled in a doorway. Nevertheless, the presence of the world's grief is felt.

At a lunch party when I asked the guest beside me whether the earthly paradise in which we sat was real, she told me that there are four Hollywood suicide-prevention centers. Many volunteers man the telephones day and night, but there are still not enough of them. It is possible that you may try to tell somebody about your broken heart and be put on hold. I cynically assumed that these faceless cries for help came from the children of the rich. Apparently, this is not so. These youngsters form only ten percent of the total number of callers. More than a third of the remainder is Spanish-speaking and only slightly fewer are black.

Those who, unlike my compassionate fellow guest, do not engage with this problem, defend themselves from it. They live in palaces on the tops of hills surrounding Los Angeles, from which they look down with some misgiving at the neon-tinted valley below. One of these homes that I visited was built like a ranch with a huge room but low ceilings. Everything, even our host, seemed to be made of wood. Another was like a mixture of Greek temple and padded cell. To reach it, I was driven through the gauzy California dusk up winding roads that grew ever narrower, ever steeper until we came to a tiny plateau where stood the house surrounded by glassy cars. As is usual in these circumstances, it was a single-story building spreading outward rather than upward. I was led through pink rooms, over carpets as thick as pampas grass, to the edge of a rectangular pool that reflected the purple sky. The water was flanked by colonnades of classical white pillars running to the very brink of a precipice, down which on some disastrous rainy night the entire structure will fall like a raging cataract. All these palaces, of whatever architectural design, bristle with burglar alarms and some are patrolled night and day by guards with dogs.

Apart from the knowledge that, outside the gilded stockades, distress and even anger may lurk, there are other factors that contribute to the present unease of Hollywood.

It is in the nature of men that they become restless in the presence of vast sums of money. Where quite modest homes are advertised at 6 million dollars, temperatures run high. At the final party to which I was invited, I realized that almost all the men in Hollywood are lawyers and to be with them is like visiting a zoo just before feeding time. There are few exchanges of ideas; almost all conversations are deals. For this reason, the males tend to drift into one area of the available space while the women remain in another, though there is no such clearly defined arrangement as the old-fashioned ritual of sitting at a dinner table among the walnut shells while the ladies retire to the drawing room. When by mistake I drifted into the financial zone of the party, I found myself standing next to a man as tall as a tree and twice as shady. He was questioning his companion cautiously. "Have you seen anything of X lately?" This appeared to be a more or less innocent question likely at worst to provoke gossip, but it was no such thing. X had not been seen for some weeks and was not known to be engaged in any particular project. The next query was, "Do you think he would be willing to come with us as director?" This remark revealed that what the first question had really meant was, "Do you think that X has sunk so low that he would be willing to work for us for less?" In Hollywood—in show business in general in America—time moves so fast that if you haven't been actively—nay, ostentatiously—employed for the past six weeks, you have to make a comeback.

The rich, whom I found more often the managers of pop groups than moviemakers, look for cast-iron ways of securing their wealth, while the rest twist and turn in a frantic search for some gimmick, some property, some personality by means of which they will be able to catch a few of the dollars that at times seem to be falling from the sky. They are in the City of the Angels.

Men love money with a pure spiritual flame. It is an end in itself. To them, banks are like temples; they fondle their credit cards as though they were fetishes and, when they pray, they pray not with words but in numerals.

To fame, they are relatively indifferent. When the television series "Columbo" was first shown, I happened to be sitting beside a girl who was asking its star, Mr. Falk, whether he was enjoying his newly augmented celebrity. Of his reply, I caught only the phrase "It's pathetic." I was worried by this and made so bold as to point out the public's interest in him was a form of love, though on a broad front instead of disposed in depth. He complained that strangers always say the same thing. I consider this an advantage and suggested that the more often any question is asked, the more polished one's reply becomes. Mr. Falk remained disgruntled. "Where's yer raincoat?" he growled. "What am I supposed to say to that?"

This is a male reaction. I know actresses who would gladly answer some such inane question a hundred times a day.

With women, these masculine priorities are reversed. It is hard to say why. Now that the sexes have become so astonishingly alike that couples are not merely similarly clad but occasionally wear each other's clothes, the only remaining distinction between the male and the female of the species (apart from you know what) is that women remain primarily interested in activities from which some vestige of human relationship can be extracted. Consequently, they live for fame. A pinch of notoriety will do. To money, they are indifferent. Miss (Jayne) Mansfield's agent once drew her attention to the fact that very few of her admirers when asking for a signed photograph sent return postage money. This didn't matter a damn to Miss Mansfield. She simply wanted everybody in the world to own a picture of her no matter what the cost to herself.

Women tend to convert mere money into things—chiefly symbols of the pampered life, though less blatantly now than formerly. Miss Dietrich once wore a mink coat and a mink stole at the same time.

It is noticeable that in Hollywood women do not wear jeans. Their sense of style warns them that there would be something perverse about putting on clothes made of denim—a material more properly used for boiler suits and overalls—when they have not the slightest intention of ever doing a day's manual labor in their lives. They do, however, wear trousers most of the time, but baggy ones in soft fabrics. At a party attended by a large number of girls, the scene takes on the look of a harem. Unfortunately, this impression is seldom reinforced by odalisque figures. All the women in Hollywood are actresses or wish they were and all cherish the notion that to succeed it is necessary to be thin. While in one part of the house, the men are talking about money, in another, the girls are discussing what they don't eat. It was in vain that I tried to explain to them that women are lovable by the pound.

Although the female population of Hollywood is not driven mad by the smell of money that grows wild in this region, this does not mean that their souls are at peace. I think they are made uneasy by the ghosts of greatness that still haunt the place. In spite of the fact that so much has changed and a supermarket stands on the spot where Comrade Nazimova lived and fought with Mr. Valentino, the legends of Hollywood cannot be entirely uprooted. A map of the homes of the stars, printed only last year, still catalogues the last local address of Miss Dietrich, Miss Dunne, and even Miss Montez.

It is hard for women not to be aware that there was a time when they ruled the screen. In those days, except in Westerns and war films, men were supporting players. Now that regrettably sex seems to be here to stay, we refer to these screen goddesses as sex symbols. In the past, they were no such thing, for the simple reason that, in the era when they shone their best and brightest, no man went to the cinema merely to watch a movie. His purpose was to sit in the dark and fumble with his girl friend. (I speak of a long-lost time when nice girls lived at home or in boarding houses where male visitors were not permitted.) Women, on the other hand, went to the pictures in search of that exalted realm where they would not be subjected to precisely the humiliating smash-and-grab raid that was at that very moment being inflicted upon their persons. While they tried to prevent the buttons from being torn from their blouses, their tearful eyes scanned the screen for clues that would tell them why their own lives were so very different from those of their favorite stars. Was there no way, they silently asked them-selves, in which they could ever win respect, or even a little courtesy? There is a movie in which Mr. Navaro (foolishly) re-minded Miss Garbo that on the previous evening she had led him to believe that she loved him; she replied, "That was yesterday." Her devotees in the one-and-ninepennies were not slow to note that he did not punch her on the nose as their boyfriends would have done. This led women everywhere to suppose that if they plucked their eyebrows into single file or blacked their lashes until they looked as thick as chimney sweeps' brushes or adopted a foreign accent, they, too, would triumph over the squalor of the real world or, if they were defeated by it, at least they would die on a satin sheet with some man breathing deeply into their hair while allowing a maudlin aphorism to seep from their glossy lips.

The supremacy of the female stars depended entirely on the loyalty of their women supporters. From 1926 to 1930, every girl in the western world looked like Miss Garbo. Then *The Blue Angel* was released and they all looked like Lola Lola.

Apart from the erosion by guilt of America's pride in its power and its wealth, apart from the political shift from certainty to doubt, apart from fashion's trend from the bizarre to the ordinary, there have been two specific invasions of the kingdom of women. The first came from men. While there was a difference between the sexes, acting was not considered a suitable profession for men. At one time, stagehands considered all actors to be pansies—including Mr. Valentino. Mr. (Michael) Caine has frequently spoken of the difficulty he originally encountered while trying to persuade his male friends that he was not under suspicion just because he wanted to go into the movie industry. Presumably, he has that bother no more. If girls can become firepersons, boys can become actors. They may even become stars.

When Mr. Heston was asked to list the names that could be invoked to squeeze money from the pockets of movie moguls, except for Miss Streisand and Miss Dunaway, they were all men. That is, of course, why films have recently become so violent and why in many modern scenarios women are featured only as victims.

The second invasion of their territory was carried out by machines.

In a long-gone movie entitled *Dinner at Eight*, Miss Harlow prophesied that all the work that was now being done by human beings would one day be accomplished by machines. Miss Dressler replied, "That's a possibility you'll never have to worry about." She was wrong. The only movie I heard praised when I was last in Hollywood was *E.T.* The eulogy did not come from an actress but from a producer. That's natural enough. Lord knows that mechanical objects can be temperamental, but at least they don't demand a percentage of the profits. Science fiction is the long-awaited answer to the prayers of the front office. If Miss Louise Brooks is to be believed, the movie magnates hated the female stars almost from the beginning of time, chiefly, I imagine, because they depended on them so helplessly. How else could Miss Garbo, while her current contract had years to run, have suddenly demanded that it be torn up and that she be given another? Nothing like that can ever happen again. Producers no longer need women; they have robots.

I have not seen *E.T.* From what I have been told, I assume it is sort of a revised Peter Pan, a visitant from another world, half-glad and half-regretful at not being a member of the human race. I am quite prepared to find that, from now onward, there will always be showings of this film in one New York cinema or another during the Christmas school holidays, just as there are of Mr. Barrie's play in London. I am not in any way disparaging Mr. Spielberg's masterpiece. I am only saying that its success must be frightening to all the actresses in Hollywood.

Actors view this trend toward steel-and-glass heroes with less nervousness because of their love of everything mechanical. If, in a shopping center, you see a huddle of men in front of a window, it must not be assumed that there is a naked woman on display; it is more likely to be a tasteful arrangement of nuts and bolts. When the ultimate movie is made in which there is no sign of human life from beginning to end, actors will all agree that it couldn't happen to a nicer bunch of gadgets. Women will by then only be going to the pictures in the capacity of nannies.

As I returned to Los Angeles Airport prepared for yet another flight through space, I met a young man who had come to Hollywood especially for the Emmy ceremony. I asked him whether he had received one. He has won seven. This seemed like a debauch of recognition. When I gave expression to my amazement, the young man explained that he wrote for and acted in a program called "Sesame Street." To this information, he added the curious words "We don't think of it as being television."

In Hollywood, television is treated by performers as though it were a hideously demanding but rich wife, vigorously embraced but ridiculed behind her back; whereas in its heyday, the movie industry was at times a smiling sweetheart and at others an enigmatic mistress.

The Hollywood that is an estate agent's dream suburb is flourishing; indeed, it is bigger, more populous, and more expensive than ever, but the other Hollywood that was less a locality than a code word for limitless success, that Hollywood that was a lacquered pavilion of women, an exotic aviary of actresses, that Hollywood that was the Fort Knox of the heart, *that* Hollywood is dead.

II

GOING TO THE MOVIES

FRANCES/THE PIRATES OF PENZANCE

It was a great advantage to the American film industry that
after a few false starts on the East Coast, it took to the deserts of
Southern California. In those days, Hollywood seemed to be just
a few wooden huts leaning against one another several miles from
Los Angeles, which was then a comparatively small town. It was
an oasis where there was no conversation, only captions; no people,
only actresses. The benefits of this isolation were two. Firstly, the
imagination of screenwriters and directors was not trammeled by
unpleasant glimpses of reality; and secondly, the distant world knew
very little about the sordid lives of its screen idols.

Then there was Miss Farmer.

Things changed; ugly rumours trickled into our flapping ears.
Soon, since there was no traditional Dutch boy to put his hand in
the dike (you can hardly blame him), the trickle became a flood.
Now we are being inundated by the communication deluge; we
know all and worse than all about everybody, sometimes, as in the
case of Miss Farmer, from her own lips. The world has become
full of books about movie stars.

Of course, there must be film people who get up, go to work,
return home, write to their mothers, mend their socks—but no, I
am going too far—throw away their socks, and generally live like
the rest of us, but the histories of these well-behaved individuals

never reach the bookshops. Inevitably, we form the impression that, if her looks or her luck or the ambitions of her mother raise a girl to a level from which she can clearly see the lamp of fame, she will dash herself against it until she breaks her wings and falls to the depth of degradation unimaginable to the more fortunate among us who are born plain and boring.

Miss Farmer, whose story is somewhat sketchily told in *Frances* was one of these beautiful but doomed young women.

We first see her reading to a group of startled parents and teachers an end-of-term composition about the fact that there is no God. Even then, at the age of sixteen, she wears almost permanently the mocking—the desperate—smile of someone who at any moment may hit you.

She wins a prize and, later, a visit to Moscow and the disapproval of her hometown, Seattle. She is labeled a pinko and her troubles begin. In spite of this, she goes to Hollywood and a few frames later is put under a seven-year contract by Paramount. Her head filled with socialist rubbish preached by the detestable Mr. Odets and the Group Theatre, she apparently imagined that she would have some control over the subject matter of the films in which she appeared. When she finds that this is by no means the case, she leaves Hollywood but is forced back by her studio chiefs, who make an example of her by humiliating her in every possible way. Under this treatment, she becomes uncontrollable, strikes her dresser, resists arrest, and generally carries on in such a way that she ends up in a mental hospital.

A woman's place is in a home.

The film has been very carefully researched. The dialogue and the clothes are just right and I am told that the fights with the police are exactly like the newspaper photographs taken at the time of these incidents.

The picture is very obliquely directed, but occasionally, Miss Lange leaps out of the screen at you, as when she says to a gossip writer, "You're an intelligent man. Can't you find a way of earning a living that is less undignified?" In any case, she wins my personal Oscar because she spares herself nothing. If Miss Lange ever writes the story of her life, it will be a catalogue of sprains, bruises, and abrasions. For almost half the entire length of the film, she is screaming, fighting, cursing. It is a remarkable performance, scorning the love not only of her friends, her employers, and her jailers in the movie but also of the film's audiences. In this sense, *Frances* is quite a different matter from *The Snake Pit*. There Miss de Havilland, however bedraggled she became, retained the image of the butterfly on the wheel. (What would a butterfly be doing on the wheel?) By comparison, Miss Lange seems a clever, foulmouthed, and totally ungrateful hooligan. This means that the film is fascinating and horrifying but never sad.

In a way, its power is also its weakness. Except when she is with her father, we hardly ever see the heroine being polite, let alone kind. Therefore, we keep asking ourselves: What did she have that made her so instantly acceptable to the movie moguls? At that time, all the pretty girls in the world traveled to Southern California, so her mere appearance would never have been enough to recommend her. Did she make audiences laugh or cry or breathe deeply? We are never told; we only see her making everybody cringe.

Then, after repeated recapture by the authorities, after doses of shock treatment, after hours in a straitjacket, comes the brain operation. The surgeon explains to a hospital audience what he is about to do, how quick and how cheap the process is, but we are not shown the operation in full; we are cheated of the long-awaited climax. Perhaps I should report that, at this juncture, several people left the cinema and your very own intrepid Mr. Steele hid under the seats, but I felt that it was too late for tact; I needed to see the blood flow.

The film ends quietly on the other side of lobotomy. Miss Farmer is redeemed, wears the little black dress and pearls and behaves with decorum. At this point Miss Lange should have looked a little thicker in the middle, but her acting cannot be criticized. She is polite but lifeless; we can tell that the mainspring is gone.

I think that the conclusion we must draw from this movie

is obvious. All actresses should be lobotomized as soon as they are put under contract. It would save such a lot of anguish for them, for their agents and for their directors and, in spite of the surgeon's exorbitant fees, in the end it would save the studios a lot of money.

Throughout the film, the person I understood best was Miss Farmer's mother, superbly played by Miss Stanley. At one moment, she seized hold of her daughter and, in tones of exasperated amazement, cried out, "You had everything; you were a movie star."

I agree. What the hell was it that Miss Farmer wanted?

A few days after our deliciously harrowing visit to the Quad cinema to see *Frances*, I went to see *The Pirates of Penzance*, accompanied by the film editor and the art editor of that other periodical that contributors to *Christopher Street* dare not name. The occasion was jolly and restored my equilibrium. It was like eating vanilla ice cream after a main course of curried nerve endings.

The Pirates of Penzance is pleasant enough but noticeably British in flavor. That is to say, the sets were suitably artificial but never truly elegant and the dancing, though highly energetic, was not real dancing. The movies have raised the level of our sophistication immeasurably; we know that the singing is done on a different day and played back to the actors while they jump about, so we expect them to sing top C while executing double pirouettes. Nay, we have come to demand such miracles, but in *Penzance*, we are not given them. However, dry your tears. Mr. Smith is handsome in all sorts of places of which Messrs. Gilbert and Sullivan never thought, and Miss Ronstadt is charming. She is much too fiercely made up for the close-ups and she has been put into dresses far less appealing than those worn by the other maidens, but she smiles and sings sweetly in spite of these handicaps.

I imagine that before the shooting of her picture began, Miss

Ronstadt wisely asked for the operation that had to be forced upon the more wayward Miss Farmer.

After the movie, we all went to a neighboring café, where I ate quiche. (I know my station in life.) My companions drank coffee. We talked a little about Mr. Gilbert's confection but soon found ourselves discussing *Frances.* It is the taste of curry that keeps coming back.

LAW OF DESIRE

If, in an idle mood, you happen to be wandering up Broadway past the Cinema Studio, you can snatch from just inside the entrance a leaflet advertising their newest release, *Law of Desire.* This sheet of paper tells you that Señor Almodóvar, the maker of this film, is "the last of the great hedonists" and that his current work is a comedy.

I feel impelled to issue a warning.

For all I know, the Señor may himself be as hedonistic as hell, but *Law of Desire* is no such thing, nor is it a comedy, unless Spaniards are like Russians, who, it is said, find humor in circumstances that to other nations would seem tragic. (Dr. Chekhov described *The Seagull* as a comedy, though in it a girl's life is ruined by a brief affair with a heartless philanderer and a young man kills himself.) It is true that almost all the characters in Señor Almodóvar's bizarre tale are seen to be living for pleasure—kinky pleasure at that—but, except for an inexplicable child and the police, no one survives the weird twists of the plot entirely unscathed. I would describe the intention of this picture as heavily moralistic.

The story begins with a young man who looks like the late Mr. Hudson translated into Spanish. He is taking part in a pornographic movie. This sequence is acted with a certain amount of reluctance but with no attempt that I could discern to satirize the fundamental inanity of the antics that he is being asked to perform. When this scene is over, he is rewarded with a wad of quarto-sized bank notes, which he kisses. This leads us to suppose that we are going to behold the history of someone who will do anything for cash. As far as I can recall, money is never mentioned again. What this young man does—and he does plenty—he does for love.

Next, the narrative abruptly turns our attention to a movie director who is engaged in making an absurdly arty film of Monsieur Cocteau's *La Voix Humaine*. At a discotheque, he meets the porno star and takes him home. In spite of an initial lack of enthusiasm for this encounter, the actor is soon allowing himself to become the passive party in a bout of what I can only call frontal anal intercourse. As some of you may have the misfortune to know, this is a pastime about as enjoyable as an operation without anesthetic. Indeed, the victim, of whom at this point we see only his face and the soles of his feet, does evince a certain amount of misgiving but, again, not enough to render the situation comic.

The movie director in this film is a cool character. He has already implored a previous playmate not to fall in love with him, but the new sexual partner pays no heed to any such admission. He immediately becomes an addict of homosexuality to such a depth that he wishes to involve himself in every aspect of his lover's life. He tries to rape the former boyfriend and succeeds in beginning an affair with the sister. The plot of *Law of Desire* is positively labyrinthine. It manages to drag in drugs, sodomy, incest, and transsexuality. It is easy for the audience to lose its way, but I must admit that as soon as the police become involved, momentum does increase to a very exciting pace.

What comedy there is takes the form of hilarious cynicism. For instance, when detectives, searching for murder clues, find in the director's apartment a little cocaine, they do not confiscate it; they use it. As television has recently informed me that the New York police department is now a vast drug ring, I laughed somewhat uneasily.

The acting in this film is acceptable but it is not all of a piece. While all the male characters act dramatically, the movie director's sister (who was once his brother) seems to be in quite another film. She camps madly, looks like Mlle. Moreau, walks like Miss Midler, and packs a punch like Mr. Ali.

In one bewildering respect, *Law of Desire* is like all the other pictures that I have recently seen. In spite of the outrageous sensuality of the events and the crudity of the subtitles, the actual images are almost prudish. Perhaps because I myself have hardly ever worn pajamas, whether sleeping alone or with a companion, I found it ridiculous that the Rock Hudson character wore his underwear against all odds.

The color of the film favors bright red and its general mood is one of uncontrollable passion. It does not have the sorrowful romanticism of *Ernesto* nor the dreamy, steamy beauty of *Querelle* but at least it is much less nasty than *Ménage*. By all means, see it; it is never boring, but do not expect to be either enlightened or elated. Above all, do not hope to find a shred of justification for the wickedness of your ways. The message of this drama is as clear as day—as clear as Judgment Day. Passive sodomy is an addictive habit that leads to the abandonment of all reason and no one who practices this vice can count on living happily ever after, or even long after.

STEAMING

It would be safe to describe the evening of the twenty-seventh of August as a highly original occasion. An audience invited by Mrs. Losey filled the Baronet cinema for a secret showing of *Steaming*—the late Mr. Losey's last film. When it was over, we were all transported in two huge coaches to 40 West Fortieth Street, which turned out to be a palatial ground-floor showroom for bathroom fittings. The champagne did not spurt from the washbasin faucets, nor was it flushed into the various lavatory bowls that were on display, but it certainly flowed. While it was being consumed, people out in the real world pressed their flower-pale faces against the plate-glass windows to watch, amid a gleam of porcelain and a glittering assembly of celebrities (including Joan Bennett) being photographed from all angles and interviewed by a heap of televisionaries. The question most frequently asked was "Did you like the movie?" Basking in such generosity from Mrs. Losey, how could anyone say he had not?

Steaming has several things in its favor. It has a truly unusual setting—a broken-down women's bathhouse in England—and it is consistently well acted by an impressive cast that includes Vanessa Redgrave, Sarah Miles, Diana Dors, and a Patti Love, whose first major role this seems to be. These ladies manage to bring remarkable variety to the occupations of sweating and bewailing the treatment they receive from their husbands and lovers.

Only Miss Dors, who runs the establishment, seems to have enjoyed a satisfactory family life. It is inevitable that she says less than most of the members of her clientele, because there is an unalterable law that ensures the sound of rejoicing shall never be as loud or as prolonged as the voice of complaint. Miss Redgrave has been abandoned by her husband after nearly twenty years of marriage; Miss Miles regrets that, having taken the time to become a lawyer, she is now too old to have children; a young girl, whose mother brings her to the baths to wash her hair and weigh her, sits and dreams of all the lovely food the old lady never allows her to eat; and Miss Love wavers perpetually between rage and despair because she must either live with a man who frequently punches her in the face or else she must work, which she confidently predicts will be borin' borin' borin'.

In the beginning, I thought that all this random misery was going to be intolerable, and your Mr. Steele never quite recovered from the first ten minutes of the film, but, as time went by, I became interested. A theme emerged. News comes to Miss Dors that her kingdom is doomed. The bathhouse is to be demolished to make way for a recreation center and a car park. Immediately, all temperamental differences are resolved, all class distinctions leveled, for nothing unites the English so quickly or so firmly as a disaster. All the customers agree to stage a protest. Their efforts are triumphant and the movie ends with an absurd and rather touching champagne party at midnight in the bathhouse. Even Miss Redgrave casts aside her refinement and her towel. The film might have been called *My Bare Lady*.

Steaming enjoyed a long run on the London stage but did less well here. It will be a pity if the movie suffers a similar fate. It is the first picture to make a justifiable, totally unstrained concession to the modern craze for nudity. However, it cannot be denied that it is very British. The humor is coarse and the outlook grim. It is the work of Nell Dunn and is a shameless feminist and socialist treatise. Whether these qualities rank as vices or virtues is, of course, purely a matter of taste.

The serious weakness of this work is its improbability. When a spokeswoman must be selected to present to the authorities a case for the preservation of the bathhouse, it is not Miss Dors who is chosen, though it is her livelihood that is threatened; it is not Miss Redgrave with her effortlessly upper-class air of command; it is not Miss Miles, the legal expert; it is Miss Love, who has already boasted loudly that she can't speak nicely or even spell. In the theater, the time element of this story may have been mentioned in the program and marked by a division into separate acts. On the screen, it can only be inferred from a lightening of Miss Love's facial bruises. This makes it seem that an illiterate born loser takes no time at all to redeem her accent, learn a speech, and master a lot of facts and figures.

Perhaps a special warning should be issued to readers of this magazine. What goes on in a women's bath house in no way corresponds with the kinky behavior that is rampant in a similar establishment for men. In the entire film, there is not one frame of lesbianism.

Holding, as I do, the opinion that sex is a mistake, I was relieved by this omission. I wish this picture well.

HEARTBURN/
SPECIAL EFFECTS/
PERFECT STRANGERS

What can I say about this film?

It's a bone-dry weepie; it is never boring but it is also never involving; it has been almost universally condemned by the critics and is a huge success.

Now that Mr. Steele has begun to expand his publishing empire at a rate that would have unnerved even Ghenghis Khan, he can only visit a cinema in the middle of the night. We, therefore, attended a showing of *Heartburn* between two thunderstorms at 10:40 P.M. In spite of these arduous circumstances, every seat in Mr. Loew's Paramount Theatre was sold and the line of prospective viewers, which curled round the Gulf & Western building and stretched halfway to Harlem, waited good-humoredly for an hour.

As no one over the age of twenty-five, except me, would stay up so late, the audience was young; it was also enthusiastic and treated the picture as though it were a stage show, greeting Mr. Nicholson's first appearance with loud applause. I half-expected him to look toward us and smile. People also clapped at the end of the film, but with less gusto.

Perhaps this kind of movie about whether I love you more than you love me has acquired some of that old-world charm that once lured audiences to pictures such as *Ivanhoe* and *Robin Hood*. Today, we spend so much time with creatures from outer space that earthlings have begun to seem exotic. Television, which was once so timid, now brings the most extreme forms of violence into our daily lives, affording us the pleasure of being flung from the windows of expensive hotels while munching potato chips, of driving cars over cliffs while sipping martinis, or of giving half our attention to being raped and the other half to our knitting. If the young wish for an occasional evening to refrain from gibbering and twitching in some dim cellar, perhaps they wish to visit a quieter world.

Heartburn is not, however, a bland movie—not by any means a musical without music. Its fault lies in its lack of intention. Its style is minutely naturalistic but it's content highly improbable.

It tells the story of a food journalist who, at somebody else's wedding, sees Mr. Nicholson, a writer with a terrible reputation as a philanderer, and, against all advice, leaps into bed with him at their first meeting and marries him soon afterward. She becomes pregnant with equally indecent haste and later discovers that during her stay in the hospital, he has had an affair with a woman she knows. She leaves him, returns, becomes pregnant a second time, is again deceived by her husband, and leaves for good.

It is simply not possible to like such a woman. She is a journalist and therefore a woman of the world (to put it kindly). She must have known that if she began an affair with anyone at their first encounter, he would be a lecher and, worse, that he would think of her as a tramp. If she married such a man on the grounds that matrimony need not be taken too seriously, she would not have allowed herself to become pregnant. She would know only too well that he would be a dead loss at the "till death do us part" racket.

In its persistent misanthropy, the film reminded me over and over again of *The Women*—especially in the hairdressing sequence, but even here, the fancied treatment of Miss Streep's hair, which would have been out of place if Mr. Hardy were applying it to the head of Mr. Laurel, dissipates the bloodcurdling bitchiness that is so exciting in Claire Boothe's masterpiece.

If anything saves *Heartburn* from disaster, it is the occasional visually comic surprise and a few very funny lines. When Miss Streep tells her father her tale of matrimonial woe, he says, "If you wanted monogamy, you should have married a swan."

Miss Streep is, as ever, superb. Outwardly self-assured; secretly at a loss. As a wife, a disorganized failure; as a mother, totally absorbed in her child. With an infant of one's own, this attitude must be hard enough to maintain, but in the presence of a stage child, it must be well nigh impossible.

Mr. Nicholson is a mystery. Physically, he is totally miscast as a stranger that anyone would notice on some benighted evening across a crowded room. Furthermore, as this is a woman's picture, we see him only in a domestic setting. Here every reaction—the displays of affection, the coy reception of the news that he is about to become a father, the embarrassing sequence in which he sings popular songs about babies—all have about them the chill of dead, feigned enthusiasm. Does Mr. Nicholson know that he is presenting to the camera this almost sinister quality or can he not help himself?

At the very end of the film, at a small dinner party, Miss Streep squashes a carefully made custard pie in her husband's face. This, in view of her reverence for food, is the ultimate measure of her disillusionment.

Were we meant to despise this woman? To forgive her? To pity her? I really couldn't say.

When people concerned with my welfare look gravely at me and shake their heads, I assure them that I can quit going to the Public Theater anytime I want.

I can't.

I'm ashamed to say that I've become a culture addict. My most recent lapse was provoked by television. One evening, when, after watching and partly watching the news, I had decided to go to bed, the words *"It's Alive"* appeared on the screen. They turned out to be the name of a picture made by Larry Cohen. I was at first curious and then hypnotized. It is the best horror movie ever. It is a variation on the *Rosemary's Baby* theme but is free from all that black-magic rubbish. In Mr. Cohen's philosophy, evil does not have to be invoked; it is always with us.

When, a few days later, I was invited to see two of this same director's works in a single afternoon, I couldn't resist the lure. It was just like old times; I was in the cinema three and a half hours and enjoyed every minute of them, but I would not advise a modern moviegoer to indulge in such a celluloid debauch. Because a certain Mr. Rijn is one of the leading characters in both pieces, their plots, in memory, become confused.

The first half of this double bill, *Special Effects*, is about the making of a pornographic movie and it is at times hard to know whether what we are witnessing is Mr. Cohen's or the pornographer's picture. After a while, this duality becomes tiresome, but if at any time you are given the chance to see the second feature, *Perfect Strangers* (sometimes called by the better title *Blind Alley*), abandon everything—even sex—to watch it.

The plot concerns a child who, through the hole in the backyard fence, witnesses a murder. The killer's employers tell him that the little boy must be eliminated. With this in mind, the murderer cultivates the acquaintance of the child's mother, has an affair with her, and, as far as his arid soul will allow, even starts to like her. All the time, however, he knows and we know that he must kill her child or he himself will be executed by the mob. There are a few violent scenes thrown into the story, but its real power lies not in what we are shown but in what we fear may happen. Interest never flags from the grim beginning of this tale to its appalling climax.

THE POPE OF GREENWICH VILLAGE

This is a really good movie.

Above all its other virtues, it is efficient; it contains not one wasted frame. Although the dialogue is full of saturnine humor, it never digresses from the point for the sake of a smart comment on life. The story describes a world governed entirely by greed and vengeful violence, but the camera never lingers indulgently over acts of cruelty. On the other hand, there are no prolonged passages of sexuality or even sentiment. When Miss Hannah (now having unwisely abandoned her fishtail), finds that she is pregnant, we only know of her feelings for her lover when she punches him in the face.

"Did you mean to do that?" he asks.

"I don't know," she replies, giggling. The jokes in this film veer from the brutishly playful to the positively crude. At one moment, Mr. Roberts revenges himself upon a policeman, who has caused his car to be towed away, by lacing the officer's whiskey with a laxative usually reserved for relieving the constipation of horses.

The weakness of this picture, if it has one, is its title. The audience remains entirely unaware that the action is set in New York's phony artistic colony. There is not a glimpse of the dilettantism nor even a breath of the gayness for which this area of Manhattan is so justly famous. We spend our time enclosed in a world inhabited only by corrupt but inefficient policemen and highly organized gangsters.

Trapped in this dark world, a pathetically unprepossessing young man, excellently played by Mr. Roberts, works as a waiter for one of his innumerable relatives. He steals from his employer so ineptly that not only is he himself sacked but his friend, the manager of the restaurant, is also dismissed. Then Mr. Roberts discovers that a huge bribe for the local constabulary is in a safe in a neighboring warehouse. He, his friend, Mr. Rourke, and an impoverished locksmith succeed in stealing the money but accidentally bring about the death of the cop who has come to collect his unjust reward. Inevitable retribution follows. It is quite easy for the mafiosi to find out that it was Mr. Roberts who instigated the robbery and equally obvious that he couldn't have brought off this coup by himself. Consequently, they cut off the thumb of his left hand and put him to work as a coffee boy in their club. Apart from these sundry indignities, they coerce him into betraying the locksmith, and they are on the verge of tracking down Mr. Rourke.

He, however, has the tape found on the body of the dead cop, which will incriminate absolutely everybody in sight. With this, he confronts the Pope, a marvelous character called Bedbug Eddie (Mr. Young), and defies the system.

All the same, this could not be called an optimistic fable. On the contrary, it is an ironic but serious look at the almost inevitable result of being born inadequate and unlovable in perpetual reach of dazzling amounts of success, money, and power.

The entire picture is well acted but it has an unexpected bonus; the corrupt policeman's mother is played by Miss Page. While she is within sight of the cameras, the movie belongs solely to her. Smoking until she almost vomits, swigging alcohol to assuage her bronchitis, she outfaces with appalling but at the same time hilarious cynicism the men who have come to search her home. Mr. Steele and I witnessed this film at the MGM screening room on Fifty-fifth Street, so we were almost certainly surrounded by film critics and worse. The fact that they laughed loudly and even applauded Miss Page proves, I think, what a superb performance she gave.

I was invited to see *The Pope of Greenwich Village* just a week before I was whisked away to England. Mr. Steele realized that this was a lucky coincidence and agreed to accompany me, but this picture is not, on the face of it, what you might term a *Christopher Street* production; it lacks the requisite kinkiness. However, as is well known, your editor never gives up—*never!* On the flimsiest evidence or none, he might, at any moment, suggest that Mr. Holmes and Dr. Watson were involved in a "meaningful" relationship or might hint that the Monster was not, in fact, assembled by Mr. Frankenstein in his laboratory but, rather, was found by him at The Anvil, or might even claim that Mr. Chaplin and the Kid were foundation members of the North American Man/Boy Love Association. During supper after the show, Mr. Steele returned to his perennial theory that to the gay, all things are gay. He pointed out that Mr. Roberts's character had twice made disparaging remarks about homosexuals (a dead giveaway in some people's eyes) and that this had caused Mr. Rourke to remark that he was surprisingly interested in faggots. It is certainly true that the only relationship in the entire woeful tale in which the least vestige of tenderness had been evinced by either parties involved had been the friendship between the two young men. Indeed, when Mr. Roberts had been deprived of his thumb and taken all his painkillers at a single gulp, Mr. Rourke sat beside his bed and fed him with spoonfuls of soup. Considering that the invalid had been the cause of all his helper's troubles, it is impossible to deny that this was a scene of almost saintly compassion. Even so, we must take nothing for granted. Emboldened by having been given a cultural award, I forbid anyone to classify this film as gay—even in the old-fashioned sense of the word. It is exciting but it is grim. Apart from the safecracker's ill-starred wife, there is not one innocent or likable person present.

One terrible day, we shall all have to make up our minds about movies such as this. Their very excellence compounds their insidious iniquity.

I cannot speak with any certitude about the legal system in America, but in England, there are endless court cases whose object is to determine whether or not some obviously filthy film is *art*. If the authorities decide that is has aesthetic value, its nastiness is condoned, if not forgiven, or forgiven, if not openly praised. Nevertheless, it must be obvious to the merest simpleton that the greater the skill which a book is written or a film is directed, the more devastating the harm that it may do.

At the end of Mr. Rosenberg's picture, we are shown two thieves and at least inadvertent murderers emerging into the innocent light of day in a sickly triumph. It is obvious that they are on their way to a life of further lying, cheating, and betrayal elsewhere.

We have come a long way down from the moral certainties of the reign of Mr. Cooper and Mr. Wayne, the midday cowboy. In their halcyon day, anybody who was still standing after the sound of gunfire had wasted its bitterness on the desert air was virtuous to the fringe of idiocy. When these paragons died, they were succeeded by the tarnished heroes, such as Mr. Douglas and Mr.

Sinatra, whose sins were forgiven because they summoned up sufficient goodness to overcome one last challenge. Then the word *antihero* was invented and Mr. Allen ascended the celluloid throne, parading his weaknesses before us for our amusement, surviving chiefly by luck, winning the heroine's love almost by default.

Now we seem to have reached the lowest ring of Hades. In films such as *The Pope of Greenwich Village* and *Against All Odds*, the people who survive the battle are in no way better than those who lost it—lechers and murderers all. Are we to interpret these parables as demanding more of our pity? Are directors reminding us that we ourselves would have sunk equally low in similarly stressful circumstances, or are we being told that even the effort toward integrity is no longer worthwhile?

If this is the message, beware. You may find yourselves among men even more eager to receive this cynical news than you are and even more adept at acting upon its possibilities.

What will become of you then?

SWANN IN LOVE

Its very title warns you that you may be in trouble with this film. You are not allowed to ask why Swann had been spelled with two *n*'s. It is a man's name. You may not ask *who*. The picture has been made strictly for those who have read or at least tried to read *A la Recherche du Temps Perdu* by a certain Mr. Proust, from which massive tome the screenwriters have selected one love affair.

I seem to recollect that a fairly recent issue of *Christopher Street* contained a fascinating article about the lesser work of Mr. Proust. Obviously, your editor takes it for granted that all his readers are extremely sophisticated. I shall not make the same assumption.

Mr. Proust was a weirdo who, although Jewish, was determined to slither like a snake into French society and who, though he suffered acutely from various nervous disorders, insisted on drinking coffee. He died comparatively young in 1922 while struggling to complete his life work, which has been translated into a group of seven books called *Remembrance of Things Past*. This work is now treated with great solemnity by the entire world, but it has its faults. It delves into the social and sexual antics of the author's friends and their servants in such morbid detail that Mr. Connolly said of Mr. Proust, "He has been praised for having had the blind courage to put everything in, but one day he will be blamed for being afraid to leave anything out." Moreover, the entire work is written in a style so convoluted that if you turn the pages too fast, you may miss the principal verb. Worst of all, it airs the author's two abiding fixations. Firstly, he seriously thought that absolutely everybody wanted to enter Parisian society; and secondly, he believed that all men ultimately give way to homosexual impulses. Both these notions are, of course, absurd. However, he did discover one eternal truth. It is not love that inflames jealousy, but jealousy that engenders love.

This theme is deployed twice in *Remembrance of Things Past*. The first time is when Mr. Swann (who is Jewish but is cautiously accepted by Gentile society) becomes interested in a Miss de Crécy, whose past is so shady that his friends will not put up with her. The second relationship that exploits this idea is the one in which Marcel is obsessed with a girl called Albertine.

I think it would have been wiser for Mr. Carrière (one of the writers) to have chosen the latter of these two situations. It is the more compact. At the end of it, Albertine disappears. The affair between Mr. Swann and Miss de Crécy simply deteriorates into marriage and, worse, it produces a child. In the novel, this does not matter. The structure is deliberately labyrinthine; characters disappear for years on end while our attention is taken up with new people. They return later—always in a worse state. The reader is never allowed to forget that time is passing. In the film, the main body of the story all takes place during one day. Then there is an epilogue, which the audience hardly realizes is an epilogue. The viewer is left to work out for himself that ten years have gone by.

The virtues of the film are two. The first is its texture. I have no idea whether or not the costumes are accurate, but they certainly look charming. However, I am not referring only to the furniture and the dresses. There was a subtle parade of relationships that I imagine were taken for granted in the past. The servants of the rich are seen to treat their masters as though they were invalid children. The other strong asset of this movie is the acting, or, possibly, the direction. At the beginning of this century, the upper classes seem to have behaved with extreme formality and complete casualness at the same time. The film captures this strange mixture perfectly.

When I saw *Betrayal*, I did not think that Mr. Irons was sufficiently romantic. Here, as Mr. Swann, he is ideally cast. He looks delicate, neurotic—almost wounded, and in the epilogue, he grows old convincingly. In most movies, the passage of ten years is deemed enough to add a distinct quaver to a man's voice or to curve his spine drastically. In life, this is hardly ever so, but try as we may to resist all change for the worse, as time goes by, we begin to look like airline food—a good imitation of what we used to be but dehydrated. This is the metamorphosis that Mr. Irons presents to us.

Miss Muti, as the girl of Mr. Swann's nightmares, is adequate throughout and excellent when she keeps us guessing whether she is admitting to a lurid past because it is true or in order to silence her lover's incessant questioning.

The part of the Baron de Charlus is played by Mr. Delon. I found him disappointing. In his case, I did not think he had gone to seed visibly enough. I had hoped that at the end of the film, he would look like Mr. Cobb translated into French. I realize, however, that this is a very tricky role. Everyone who had read even a few pages of *Remembrance of Things Past* has his own clear idea of how the Baron should look. The author obviously hated this character and described his deterioration in malicious detail, saying, for instance, that he laughed with his mouth wide open "as though he were alone." Evidently in high society, unbridled mirth was considered to be a breach of decorum.

Although Mr. Proust's work is a funeral oration for dead youth, it is not without humor and *Swann in Love* catches some of it. There is a hilarious scene in which Mr. Irons goes to a brothel in an effort to find out whether Miss de Crécy ever had affairs with any of the girls who worked there. He performs a kinky sex act with one of the inmates without for a moment ceasing to conduct his inquiries and she endures his onslaught upon her person with no other interest than to reply to his questions discreetly. I found it difficult not to laugh, but we were in a screening room and surrounded by an extremely highbrow clientele who evinced no amusement whatsoever. I, therefore, remained silent; so did Mr. Steele.

The dialogue of this picture I cannot judge. It was entirely in French and I understand not one word of any language other than my own. In the print shown to us, Mr. Irons spoke his own lines, and Mr. Steele says that this was the part he understood best, but in France the hero's voice was dubbed into English and subtitled. (You know how tiresome the French are about their language.)

Mr. Proust's work has attracted as much attention from moviemakers as the Bible. It is not quite as long, but it is equally difficult to follow and in it, being Jewish is just as much of a problem. At one time Mr. Visconti thought of making a picture of a volume that occurs later in *Remembrance of Things Past*. It is called *Cities of the Plain* and it deals almost exclusively with the antics of the homosexual characters—a theme that seems to have fascinated that director deeply. At a more recent date, Mr. Pinter prepared a script that in some miraculous way dashed through the entire work in average movie time. On yet another occasion, it was suggested that a version should be made that would feature Miss Garbo as the Queen of Naples. I imagine that the current interpretation is the best we ever shall see.

It is impossible to produce a satisfactory film from a really good book. What renders literature great is at least partly its power to evoke places, faces, objects so that we see them with the eyes of the imagination, which bestow on everything the luminosity of a stained-glass window. Mr. Proust says of the jewelry worn by the Duchess de Guermantes that it looked like tiny glasses of claret. In the movie, even if we had seen actual rubies, we would have beheld them with the eyes in our skulls. We could have praised the thoroughness of the art director, but we would have experienced no wonder.

LUST IN THE DUST/ THE CLINIC

When I was last in San Francisco, preaching to the perverted, on one enchanted evening I found myself with my hosts in front of a cinema where the "world premiere" of *Lust in the Dust* was taking place. Searchlights caressed the facade of the movie house; photographers took innumerable pictures; televisionaries asked countless questions; crowds of fans stood staring or were herded this way and that by amazingly indulgent policemen. The day of the locusts had obviously arrived. As soon as we joined the swarm, the cinema manager darted into the street, crying, "Don't just stand there; come inside." In the lobby, we were introduced to Mr. Divine, disguised as himself. That is to say that he was dressed in a navy blue suit, white shirt, and dark tie. He looked rather like a Catholic priest on his night off. Appropriately, he greeted us with that discreet charm which is remarkable for being in such startling contrast with the bawdy, gaudy glow that he radiates in cabaret and with which, incidentally, we were to be regaled a few nights later at the I-Bar, where, with a blond wig eight inches high and a sequined dress tight from the armpits to the knees, he strutted and shook while cursing or cajoling his ecstatic audience for an hour.

The film premiere ended a few minutes after we had shaken hands with Mr. Divine. We then had the opportunity to meet all the stars—Mr. Hunter, as handsome as ever and still wearing his expression of surprised innocence, Miss Kazan, Miss Gallego (now in *Rituals*) and Mr. Romero, whom only now I remember as co-starring with Miss Dietrich in *The Devil Is a Woman*. In *Lust in the Dust*, he plays the part of a Catholic priest, but to me he will always and unmistakably look like the quintessential, dilettante yachtsman, sunburned, casually elegant, and with hair and mustache so white that they appear as though this were the first time he had ever put them on. I think he is the most effortlessly sophisticated movie star in whose presence I have ever basked.

The actual film in which all these famous names were appearing, I did not see until I returned to New York.

Lust in the Dust was the name mockingly given by highbrow audiences to *Duel in the Sun*—one of Mr. Selznick's later films made at a time when love had just begun to go out of fashion. Mr. Divine's film is a parody of this and all other Westerns. It was produced by Mr. Hunter and Mr. Glaser in New Mexico, where the landscape overplays to such a degree that the actors had difficulty competing. I will not say they failed, but it might have been wiser to build deliberately artificial studio sets such as were used for *Li'l Abner* or Miss Clooney's beautiful film *Red Garters*.

In *Lust in the Dust*, there are frantic searches for hidden gold; there are barroom brawls and long desert shootouts in which no one ever pauses to reload his gun. Brutality, avarice, duplicity, and ravenous sexual appetites devour the screen. Miss Kazan and Mr. Divine, looking remarkably alike, wear garish Lupe Velez dresses that cling to their nipples for dear life and Mr. Hunter is dressed in loving mockery of Mr. Eastwood—the same flat hat shading the eyes, the same dusty poncho, the same half-smoked panatela. He is even photographed in the same back lighting so as to present to us a cloudy but menacing silhouette.

In the program notes, Mr. Hunter is quoted as saying that he "is not making a cult film." He hopes that one day this movie will "take its place with *Cimarron, Stagecoach, True Grit,* and *Duel in the Sun.*"

He's got to be joking.

Mr. Steele and I saw this picture in the very comfortable Sutton cinema and everyone either of us has ever known was present. The show began late and before the lights were dimmed, a babble of conversation such as I have never heard before in these circumstances filled the auditorium. When at last the titles appeared on the screen, almost every name received a round of applause. If the teenagers of New York discover this film, it will become a sort of sun-drenched *Rocky Horror Picture Show*. The same crowd will see it night after raucous night.

There is an unalterable law that if one section of society envies another, given half a chance, it will emulate the worst characteristic of the group that it admires. Most of the men who often put on female attire secretly wish that they were beautiful ladies. Despairing of achieving this aim and fearing to be sent up by their enemies, they mock themselves by becoming more grotesque, more bitchy, more vain than any woman who ever lived, and that is saying plenty. To me there is usually something embarrassing—even wounding —about this ploy, but Mr. Divine succeeds in avoiding this effect. He plunges into the roles that he plays with such good-humored gusto, such happy abandonment that he defies criticism and seems totally free of envy or bitterness of any kind. For this reason, his latest movie could in no sense be termed a drag show. It contains no winks at the camera; no jokes are made that exploit the fact that he is of one sex dressed in the clothes of another. If there are still any unhappy people in the world who have not heard of Mr. Divine, they could accept without hesitation (though not without shock) the notion that the part of Rosie was being played by a real actress.

I saw *Lust in the Dust* during a week of outrage. Only two days previously, I had been invited to a screening of an Australian film called *The Clinic*—meaning a hospital for venereal disease. It really is quite an extraordinary movie, a sort of hilarious medical instruction book on syphilis, gonorrhea and other kindred ailments. Apart from the men and women who are genuinely afflicted with these complaints, other terrified individuals arrive at the clinic with piles, crabs, and various growths on their genitals. All comers are treated with a jovial lack of censure either by a female doctor who is in the process of leaving her husband or by a male who is gay.

The language is the worst I have ever heard from the screen, but the general tone of the film is coarse rather than nasty. It is like "General Hospital" without the sentimentality or *M*A*S*H* without the persistent ugliness. The plot skips from anecdote or, rather, from one case to another with a rapidity that prevents the picture from every becoming boring, but unfortunately, this device also stifles the emergence of any truly comic situations. Comedy demands a recognizable structure.

The Clinic, like *The Summer of the Seventeenth Doll*, could only have been made in Australia. Though there are characters within the movie who evince vehement disapproval, the author of the film treats everything, including the homosexual theme, with a breeziness that may astonish American eyes and ears. They may even find the entire atmosphere difficult to believe, but I can assure them that it is in no way improbable. If that distant continent is the home of the wombat, the emu, the kangaroo and the duck-billed platypus, why should exception be taken to a few faggots? When I was in Sydney, a stranger who could not have been more than seventeen years old asked me why I was so often on television. I smirked, simpered, and admitted that I had no idea.

"So you're homosexual," he said. "Big deal."

THE BOSTONIANS/THE
HEART OF THE STAG

I have now seen *The Bostonians* and I wish to gainsay or, at least, to modify a sentence I wrote last month when reviewing *Swann in Love*. It is *not* impossible to produce a good movie from a good book; it is only impossible to make one from a masterpiece. *A la Recherche du Temps Perdu* is an almost perfect work of art and the film extracted from it inevitably seemed fragmentary. *The Bostonians* by Mr. James, though fine, is a lesser work. Consequently, the picture of that name can and does contain all its virtues.

At the center of this story stands a girl who is pretty enough and has sufficient powers of oratory to be taken up by the women's movement. At first, she is exploited by her father, who is a fake medium. Later, she falls under the spell of Miss Redgrave, the archsuffragette. Then Mr. Reeve, playing a distant cousin of Miss Redgrave's character, comes to visit her and is intrigued by the girl, played by Miss Potter, who is sincere in her social convictions but is irresistibly flirtatious in the presence of men. In the end, after any amount of vacillation, she is prevented by Mr. Reeve from making an important speech to an improbably packed house in a music hall and is furtively taken away by him. By describing the plot in this rather glib manner, I do not wish to imply that Mr. James's novel has been oversimplified: It has not been reduced to a mere battle between good and evil. I saw *The Bostonians* in the luxurious preview theater of the Almi Group where I sat in an armchair as comfortable as a feather bed and was given a glossy brochure containing a most scholarly essay by a certain Ms. Hendin. In this, she points out that the heroine has now been luckily rescued from the clutches of a wicked lesbian, Miss Redgrave, by a noble gentleman, Mr. Reeve. As the film progresses, we cannot escape the realization that his irreproachably good looks, his casual charm, and his muted southern accent are a threadbare cloak for selfishness and a deep contempt for all women. At times, it seems that though he is speaking of love, he is wooing the heroine, Miss Potter, in order to prove a point—to show the world that no woman is capable of a happy life independent of the protection of a male.

The book was apparently one of the least successful of Mr. James's novels, possibly because it does not suggest that virtue will triumph or that love is all. On the contrary, it makes it clear that this bewildered young lady is doomed to a tragic life simply because her devotion was so sincere that she could not bear to hurt either Miss Redgrave or Mr. Reeve. In general terms, to love at all is to be a loser, but I expect that readers of *Christopher Street* magazine know this already.

It is hard, if not impossible, for modern audiences to realize how important moral values were to middle-class women of the last century. No one in this movie appears to do any serious work; everybody had an infinite amount of time to spend on the care of her soul. On the shallowest level, this preoccupation takes the form of preserving decorum, of avoiding the society of "worthless people" such as Miss Potter's parents. At a greater depth, it is concerned with causes—in this case with the emancipation of women. In her morbid fervor for the rights of her sex, Miss Redgrave openly despises men and sinks to the level of becoming Miss Potter's patroness by paying off the latter's father. The lesbian element in her involvement with her protégée is treated by the screenwriter, Mrs. Jhabvala, with the utmost tact, and is acted by Miss Redgrave with a skill that it would be impossible to praise too highly. Corseted by etiquette so tightly that she can hardly breathe, she totters perpetually on the verge of precisely that hysteria for which Mr. Reeve despises her. The principals in this triangle are all excellent. Superman flaunts his romantic good looks with a perfect mixture of grace and insolence. Miss Potter, the prey rather than the prize in this battle of wills, is beautifully cast and made up to look unmade up with quite astonishing deftness.

The look of the film is absolutely right throughout. The colors are harmonious but subdued, as though every person and every thing in Boston were straining toward good taste. The dresses, though elaborate, are never grotesque. Either Americans have more sense of style than Parisians or Mr. Austin, the set designer for *The Bostonians*, is a greater artist than his counterpart who worked on *Swann in Love*.

To my way of thinking, there is only one error in the entire film and this occurs when Miss Potter fails to come back from an assignation with Superman. Miss Redgrave goes to the shore in search of her and, sitting there, imagines the girl has been drowned. We see Miss Potter, looking remarkably like Mr. Millais's Ophelia, lying beneath the water. This cinematic trick offers the audience a spurious moment of drama, which is abruptly snatched away again when it is discovered that she has returned home. Some might say that it unfairly raised our hopes, for truly, the girl's indecision was becoming very annoying.

A week or two before I saw *The Bostonians*, I witnessed *The Heart of the Stag*. Both in time and place, these two pictures could hardly differ more widely. One takes place a hundred years ago in Massachusetts, the other in New Zealand now. All they have in common is their excellence.

The latter production is heavily advertised as being about incest and to make good this boast, almost at once we find ourselves staring down from the ceiling at a young woman's bed, where her father is grunting and twitching while she remains in a trance of terror and disgust. I cannot deny that I am interested in this particular pastime. In many ways, it is like homosexuality. Firstly, it is a sin that is nice; secondly, on the evidence of this movie, it is crude, uncomfortable, and bleak. It does not involve the personality of either party in any way. When not copulating, father and daughter go about their daily chores in such

71

a manner that no one observing them together could guess their guilty secret.

In other respects, incest is vastly different from being gay. The people involved do not claim to have rights; they wear no badges and they never, *never* march. I used to attribute this difference to grammar. Even I, who am fairly careful what I say, occasionally use the word *homosexual* as a substantive (though wild, pink horses could not make me turn the adjective *gay* into a noun). This slipshod use of language makes it possible for gay men to think of themselves as special people rather than as ordinary people with a special way of spending their evenings. The word *incestuous* remains stubbornly an adjective and this prevents men with an inordinate affection for other members of their families from turning their shame into glory. Now that I have seen *The Heart of the Stag*, I think the real trouble with incest is its isolation. There is so little opportunity for cruising, and an orgy would be almost impossible to arrange.

I fear that these observations are a digression. This film is not really about the pleasures of family love; it concerns the sorrows of living in New Zealand. I have been to Auckland and found the experience immensely enjoyable, but I didn't live on a ranch so large that without my parents permission, I could never leave.

The story is slight but very powerful. A girl (Miss Regan) really cannot escape from her situation. Her father, beautifully played by a Mr. Cooper with a stunning voice, is possessive of everything in sight—including his daughter, his guns, and even the stags that wander about his vast estate. (Probably it should be called a sheep farm or even a sheep station.) He is a powerful man and an excellent hunter and marksman. His wife is an invalid who can neither walk nor talk and whom, for pity's sake, the daughter must tend.

Into this virtual prison comes a stranger whose car has broken down on the highway. He decides to stay for sheep shearing because he needs the money. The most admirable quality of this film is its realism. Mr. Lawrence, although playing what in America would once have been the Alan Ladd part, is in no way disguised as a hero. He is a husky, bald man with tragic eyes, but he is also all that Miss Regan will ever get. She decides to escape with him. Their dash for freedom brings about an ending as tragic and as just as act five in an Elizabethan drama. The audience has been prepared for what happens but is nonetheless taken completely by surprise.

Of course, this is one of the eight oldest plots in the world, but the setting is so unusual and is observed with such accuracy and the acting, especially by the two men, is so earthy that I found it impossible to take my eyes from the screen.

I recommend both these films.

MASS APPEAL

This movie is saved from damnation by the originality of its central theme and by the excellence of its acting. The four principal characters, Monsignor Durning, Father Lemmon, Miss Latham, his housekeeper, and Mr. Ivanek, the seminarian, are all very good indeed, but over and above the writing of a film, the directing of it, the photography, and the acting is a factor that has no name—the way the material is prepared for the screen. It is in this respect that *Mass Appeal* is weak, even though the screen adaptation was done by the dramatist who wrote the play on which the film is based.

I realize that even a highbrow audience cannot be expected to endure one—let alone four—complete sermons in a single evening, but something must be done by the screenwriter or the director to imply that a sermon has been going on for sometime before we begin to hear it or that it will continue after we have left the church. Here, all the speeches made from the pulpit seem too short and so confused in intention that they would leave even the most devout congregation completely dazed.

The main theme of this picture is how far a priest should go to entertain and thereafter not lose his parishioners. This is a problem that has to be faced by politicians, teachers, and actors. If your campaign speeches, your lectures, or your stage performances are boring, people will have left your church, your university, your theater before you have had a chance to redeem or educate them. Father Lemmon stands so far to the end of the scale that he is described as expounding "song and dance religion." He admits that to some extent he lies to his flock and he even confesses that he needs his congregation as much as it needs him. At the other extreme is Mr. Ivanek, his pupil in the art of rhetoric. Inspired by all the fatuous zeal of youth, he holds the view that a priest should compel everyone to face the horrible truth about himself and about the world. While Father Lemmon is instructing this wayward young man in the technique of preaching, the movie is absorbing and very funny. If there had been no other issue than thickly to sugar the pill and if, in the course of the argument, we had been able to watch the priest and his student learn something from one another, this film would have been almost perfect. This, unfortunately, is not the case. Into this thesis is woven the topic of celibacy and this subject is further complicated by a discussion of bisexuality. With this secondary thesis, the story never engages fairly.

When the picture begins, we see Mr. Ivanek jogging through the campus. We recognize at once that the age-old problem of abstinence is being given the British public school treatment. (In fact, physical exercise merely aggravates the situation by quickening the circulation of the blood and vitalizing the nervous system unbearably.) Soon, homosexuality rears its lovely head and two seminarians are expelled from the college. If they have been indulging in an illicit liaison with one another in their sleeping quarters, surely their dismissal is justified. In *The Boy Friend*, a woman who runs a pension for girls is asked whether she does not believe in true love. She replies that she would not allow it on the premises. I would say that this was a thoroughly sane attitude. Mr. Ivanek takes a strong line of disapproval, not of his fellow students' behavior but of their expulsion. His protest leads to his being questioned about his own past. He admits that he has had intimate relationships with both sexes. Father Lemmon is not shocked by this revelation but he is worried and his misgivings provoke one of the most absurdly evasive conversations ever heard on the screen. Its elaborate circumlocutions are as inappropriate as those that weaken a similar moment in *A View from the Bridge*. In Mr. Miller's play, acutely realistic elsewhere, there is a dialogue between a docker and his union's lawyer in which a distraught Mr. Vallone squanders hundreds of feet of film in order to say that he fears his niece is likely to marry a faggot. In *Mass Appeal*, when Mr. Ivanek admits his bisexuality, Father Lemmon seems to suggest that the life of a priest will be more difficult for him than it would have been had he merely been heterosexual. I can't see why. In movies made from the works of Mr. Greene, straight priests fall from grace like autumn leaves. However, this is not here the point. The defect in this picture is not its lack of logic but its evasions. Speaking of homosexual seminarians, Mr. Ivanek says, "You mean it would be difficult to keep 'em down on the farm after they've seen Paree"— a farfetched allusion to a musical comedy lyric so old that he would never have heard it. Father Lemmon, obviously relieved to be speaking in riddles, replies, "And, if there are Parisettes to cope with . . ." I ask you. All priests are extremely well educated. The word is Parisiennes and, in any case, why the hell does he not address the subject directly? Could he not have said, "Your sexual urges seem to me much more complicated than those of most of the men who have tried to enter the ministry" or "You will be surrounded by numbers of young men during your training for the priesthood. In these circumstances, will you be able to resist temptation?" To all this interrogation, the young man, in a slightly irritable tone of voice, answers, "I've faced the idea of celibacy," and the subject is not mentioned again. There has not been one word said concerning masturbation, which is the real temptation in a life of abstinence. Why were all these touchy topics dragged into this film at all?

At the end of this extremely muddled picture, we see Mr.

Ivanek walking briskly away from the church in which Father Lemmon has at last brought himself to preach a sermon enlisting the support of his congregation for his turbulent protégé. Presumably, the buoyancy of the young man's receding steps is an expression of his joy at knowing that Father Lemmon's moral courage has finally asserted itself. This in no way resolves the plot. The seminary is ruled by Monsignor Durning, whose concern is with avoiding wasting his time on pupils who will obviously make bad priests. If Mr. Ivanek were applying for the job of a monk, his sin of disobedience would have caused his dismissal long before his bisexuality had ever come to light.

I fear this is where we came in. Should moviemakers toy with sexual topics in the hope of arousing the prurient curiosity of the public and then evade the answers, or should they treat them seriously and risk diminishing the box-office receipts?

The day after Mr. Steele and I witnessed and discussed this picture, Miss Universal telephoned him to ask his opinion of her company's product. He told her that we had greatly enjoyed it but thought the sermons were somewhat improbable. When she asked whether either of us was Catholic, he bowed his head in shame and would forcibly have bowed mine had I been sitting next to him at the time. One of the diatribes in the film was against the sin of having purple hair. I leave you to imagine what I thought of that.

THE COTTON CLUB/A PASSAGE TO INDIA

I think that somewhere there is a dim cellar in which, once a year, all the film critics of America meet. Like Aztec priests convened for the selection of a sacrificial virgin, they huddle together to decide which of the current movies they will totally destroy. Their task is easier than that of the holy men because, though a good movie may be rare, it is not as hard to find as a good woman.

A few years ago, the reviewers fell with all their combined weight upon *Heaven's Gate*. This year they have chosen *The Cotton Club*.

Already their scheme is working. Mr. Steele and I went to Times Square to attend the 8:15 showing of this picture only four days after its opening and the house was half-full. Nevertheless, I am happy to report that the audience applauded every step that was tapped and almost every word that was uttered. They were right; it is the dialogue and the dancing that are the best features of this exciting film. The script expresses with piercing clarity the condescension of those whom Mr. Porter despised for "going to Harlem in diamonds and pearls" and it gives us the opinion that —sometimes wistfully, sometimes violently—black artists held concerning this situation. "There's only two things I gotta do in this life: I gotta stay black and I gotta die," one man says, and when a girl remarks that she wishes to appear on Broadway, her boy-friend, with an expression of doleful amazement, says, "That's white show business."

When even I was young and living in London, an entertainer called Miss Mills (oh, I forgot my promise—Florence Mills) ap-peared in a revue called *Blackbirds*. Her most famous song began "I'm a little black bird looking for a blue bird just like the white folk do." She felt the need to explain to her audience that a black girl might want happiness almost as though she were white. I belabor this point because it parallels the view that the world held of gay performers before the dawn of Mr. Fierstein. Their art was admired but the joys and sorrows it expressed were considered quaint—not quite as serious as the passions of real people.

The other great asset of *The Cotton Club* is the high standard of its dancing. There is a scene in the Hoofer's Club where several middle-aged—nay, older—gentlemen demonstrate to one another their skill with taps, like machine gunfire combined with a gliding motion that is miraculous to behold.

The singing is not bad either, but unfortunately, only two

songs are free from interruption by bullets or other lethal hazards. One of these more fortunate numbers is the famous "Am I Blue?" sung by the heroine to a cornet accompaniment from the hero; the other is called "Ill Wind," a beautiful lyric presumably composed by Mr. Ellington.

I must not, however, give the impression that *The Cotton Club* is a musical. If it was judged by that standard, it would not be the equal of *Love Me or Leave Me*, in which the flawless Miss Day sang and sang and sang while only a few of her best friends were shot. What we have now is a gangster movie with songs and dances. Chiefly, it is the story of Dutch Schultz, a mobster very strongly played in loving memory of Edward G. Robinson, but, to confuse you still further, he is not the hero, who is a white musician in a black band and who becomes involved in sundry underworld activities because he is employed as the escort of Mr. Schultz's girl friend. Rather improbably given an introduction to the movie industry by Miss Swanson, this young man leaves for Hollywood, returning when Mr. Schultz is dead to take the heroine away from all this to a life less violent but not necessarily less immoral. In the meantime, every member of a cast of thousands has been betrayed by somebody and almost everyone has been murdered.

Finally, this film achieves an effect that could not be produced in any medium other than the movies. For this Mr. Coppola deserves extra marks. As the lovers leave the city, their departure is intercut with—nay, becomes the same thing as—a cabaret act in the club, performed by dancers dressed as railway porters and carrying suitcases. It is impossible to discern whether Grand Central Station is a building or a backdrop—whether the participants in the scene are acting living or acting acting. This catches the very essence of Manhattan. It may not be the "gayest" city in the world but it is certainly the campiest. In a hilarious *Vanity Fair* article about "Dynasty," a Mr. Schiff suggests that to try to define the word *camp* would be in appallingly bad taste. As my reputation has never been based upon refinement or discretion, I will make the attempt. The verb *to camp*, as soon as it stopped merely meaning to sleep with a lot of soldiers in a field, came to signify the performance of an action not for its intrinsic value to you or anyone else but, rather, to display and to relish your talent in doing it, or, if talent is lacking, your style, or, failing style, your sheer nerve. In New York, we are all actors.

I am glad that I saw *The Cotton Club* at a regular cinema because the audience reaction was so reassuring, but it does mean that I am unable to apportion praise or blame. I was not given one of those huge synopses behind which, at previews, I can hide my ignorance as to which actor is playing which part. The only person in the film that I recognized was Mr. Gere because he always looks like Mr. Flynn with the edges beveled.

In the same week that I saw the film about Harlem, I was invited to another picture that concerns the unbridgeable gap between races. *A Passage to India* is a more serious film and that is its trouble. It is adapted from a novel by Mr. Forster and from a play by Santha Rama Rau. In England, Mr. Forster, silently forgiven for a dreadful book called *Maurice*, is more or less sacred. Mr. Lean, who wrote as well as directed the film, has not dared to leave anything out of his script. The story describes how an English girl accuses an Indian of trying to rape her, withdraws the charge, and thereby nearly causes a riot. Once Dr. Aziz, the Indian in question, is exonerated, the film should end, but it staggers on with a lot of needless tidying up; a totally new character, who never utters a word, is introduced and we are regaled with a prolonged stare at the Himalayas—a banality, to say the least.

By the time these words are in print, Christmas will mercifully have come and gone. They were written while Mr. Claus was up to his old tricks. In order to keep pace with him, I not only witnessed two movies in one week but also went to several discotheques where, as Mr. Schultz would have said, there was as much food and drink and pussy as anyone could want. Without attempting to sample the last of these three ingredients, I managed to enjoy myself, but no one was shot; nobody's blood dripped from a chandelier. New York nightlife is not what it used to be.

MASK

If this review seems somewhat skimpy, I apologize. My impressions of *Mask* are now slightly dimmer than they were originally. Since seeing the film, I have been compelled, like Ghenghis Khan, to travel to the uttermost borders of my kingdom to make sure that all is well. In this spirit, I have recently visited Los Angeles (rainy), San Diego (sunny), Chicago (snowy), and Boston (neutral). The experience has left me rather dazed, but certain ideas about the movie have remained in view.

The title is misleading. A mask is a device deliberately adopted for purpose of deception or, at least, as a form of coquetry. The appearance worn by the hero is something he longs to shed but cannot. *Mask* is really *Son of Elephant Man*; it concerns a youth of sixteen who, almost from birth, has suffered from a rare disease that has caused the bones of his skull to thicken until his face has become completely disfigured. Unlike the elephant man, whose entire skeleton was distorted, it seems that only the head of this young man is affected. Perhaps because the time is now and the place is America, he is less badly treated than his predecessor. When, for instance, he goes to school, the other boys hardly tease him at all. I found the mildness of their attitude unbelievable. Adolescent males are, by and large, a horrible species and in herds they are downright savage. Even the schoolmates who could refrain from openly jeering at him would have been quite unable to restrain their curiosity, but there was not one scene in which crowds stood round the wretched creature and asked how long he had been afflicted and if whether his condition hurt.

Such improbabilities do not, however, seriously detract from the merits of the film because it is largely about the child's mother, played by Cher. The part is a difficult one because it is not clearly defined. We learn that this woman was married to her son's father and that he disappeared long ago, but we do not know whether he left her because of their infant's disease. What we see is that she is now struggling heroically with a gypsified existence among a bunch of motorcycle freaks. These men are as affectionate to the benighted boy as they know how to be. They treat him as an Englishman treats his dog. (There can be no greater love.) It is not plain whether Cher has fallen in with these cozy and handsome hooligans because they are so nice to her child or whether she is pursuing the life she would have chosen in any case. The same can be said of the fact that she is a drug addict, though it is evident that her son feels acutely that, for this, he is to blame.

With this rather hazy material, Cher works wonders. Around the vagueness of the story, she weaves her own personal mystery. In this, she is lovingly abetted by her photographer. He gives almost as much time to close-ups of her face as Mr. Daniels used to bestow on the features of Miss Garbo. Cher is as beautiful as a drawing by Mr. Botticelli; her huge eyes are partly veiled by paper-thin eyelids, which leave the formation of the eyes completely visible within their sockets. Her hair, on the other hand, is wild and harsh like that of the girls in Pre-Raphaelite paintings. Only her body is completely—nay, startlingly—modern. She is tall and rangy and so lean that you fear that her collarbone will saw its way through her hazardously thin shoulder straps. The ultimate effect of her appearance is fascinating but totally unfeminine. Her movements are slapdash—almost brutish. Even her unswerving love for her offspring is flung at him and at the world like an insult. This is most noticeable in a very powerful scene when she enrolls the boy in school. Cher, who seems to be perpetually at war with authority, nags the principal into accepting her son. At the end of the term, he has done well and she is gleefully triumphant. Even his cycling buddies are impressed, and the one who has never spoken manages to utter the words "I'm ... proud ... of ... you."

When school gets out for the summer, it is suggested by the staff that the boy might like to work in a recreation facility for blind teenagers. In no way unaware why this idea has been put forward, he agrees. In this way, he meets a young blind woman who, of all things, is grooming a horse. I thought this an improbable situation, to say the least. Horses are extremely vicious animals and you need all your wits about you even to approach the beasts—let alone to touch one of them. However, these circumstances do provide the setting for a romantic passage in which the young couple take to one another. Needless to say, when the girl introduces her boy friend to her parents, they become determined to keep the teenagers apart.

Mask is a weepie but, with her no-nonsense manner, Cher manages to offset the sentimentality of the film. The only sequence she cannot succeed in redeeming is the death scene. In this, she enters her son's bedroom one sunny morning and, raising the blinds, talks to him with cheerful brusqueness to wake him. When he does not stir, she places her hand on his brow. "Cold," she says, and touches his arm. We see that she realizes he is dead, but at that moment there should have been a longer pause—a slower, stronger reaction. Though she had been warned he would not have a long life, she would have evinced some disbelief—even some horror in the presence of death. This whole incident passes too unemphatically and almost at once we are being fobbed off with the cliché of objects being flung about the room. Then we are shown the map on the bedroom wall.

In a previous scene, we saw the young man sticking pins into various European cities that he planned to visit with a friend when he left school. Later, this companion decided not to make the trip and the pins were angrily removed. Now, Cher replaces them and murmurs, "You can go anywhere you want now ..." A woman whose movements are brutish and whose language is full of obscenities is hardly likely to give way to a poetic flight of fancy such as this.

The bid made by *Mask* for our sympathy is justified. This woman has fought a desperate battle for sixteen years and has finally lost her only child. He has been deprived of his hope of touring Europe, of his girl friend, and of his life. Unfortunately, this very real message is, at times, delivered in a slightly mawkish tone of voice.

Though *Mask* is hopeless, it is not like *1984*, loveless. You may not be able to enjoy it but you can gain something from it. After all, we are constantly being asked by the movie industry to extend to formerly unimagined limits our capacity for fear and disgust. It is only right that we should also put to the utmost test our compassion and our pity.

I do not think the fact that this film follows with shameless haste upon the paws of *Elephant Man* is merely a relic of Hollywood's old practice of working a profitable theme for all—and more than all—it's worth. I regard it as a grim warning about our common future. The bomb will fall; radiation will seep into the bloodstreams of even the remotest inhabitants of the globe; their children will be far more misshapen than Cher's son or even poor Mr. Hurt. How, if any one of us is there to greet them, will we welcome these strange looking people? So far, we have shown a lamentably parochial attitude toward mutations. Are we now being prepared for a race of beings who will thrive on radioactive food and will possibly pity us for having had only one head each?

1918

In 1918, I was nine or ten. I remember it all horribly well. Death was everywhere. It did not arrive only in telegrams sent by the War Office to the wives and mothers of men in France; it also floated on the leaden air in the form of Spanish influenza. Even I, in my tinsel tower, became aware of it. A son of one of my mother's friends died of this sickness a few days after becoming ill. In that year, I was reluctantly but rapidly leaving the state of childhood in which, if there was a crisis, I could always become effectively ill. Time and my father (both grim) were relentlessly pushing me toward boyhood, for which I had no aptitude whatsoever. Every day was miserable. For these very personal reasons, I did not expect to enjoy greatly Mr. Foote's film.

I also had more general misgivings.

The past is a mistake. I have always hated the long ago and the far away. I never go to museums, but, upon reflection, I must admit that the really distant past is not particularly distasteful. When I see a movie about ancient Greece or Rome, it passes before my eyes like a pageant. I do not feel that I am identified with the events depicted or the people who took part in them. I do not really believe in them. History is a sort of science fiction in reverse. It is the irrevocable time through which I have lived that fills me with despair, just as it is the places that I could but will not ever see that make me restless. It is not that I have had a particularly tragic life or that I wince with remorse every time I recall the mean things that I have done. What makes my heart so heavy is the realization that issues that were once all-important are now so trivial. Looking back at our youth is like surveying a landscape from the window of a train. We see two people walking through a field and we fancy their journey may be one that neither of them will ever forget, but even as we watch them, they become specks in the distance. All long stretches of time and space induce melancholy. For this reason, I prefer to live in large, crowded cities where vision is usually limited.

The film *1918*, is drenched in precisely this long littleness of life.

In the early autumn of that dreadful year, the inhabitants of a small town in Texas are taking the First World War as seriously as their limited imaginations will allow. Someone is drilling a few misfits too hopeless to be drafted or shamed into joining the armed forces; some ladies are rolling bandages. (The only detail that I missed here was the endless mileage of khaki wool being knitted into scarves, gloves, and Balaclava helmets.)

Within this parochial framework, the narrative concentrates on one ordinary family. It consists of an irascible but well-meaning father, his apologetic wife, their daughter, played by Miss Foote, her husband, of whom her parents did not originally approve, acted by Mr. Converse-Roberts, her younger brother, and her tiny baby. If this family portrait has a central figure, it is Miss Foote. She is frequently photographed in close-up, looking beautiful but, quite rightly, totally without glamour. When the baby dies of influenza, Miss Foote discovers that she is again pregnant and we are drawn into her feelings about this forthcoming event. Her pale emotions change from hour to hour—occasionally from moment to moment. Sometimes she is glad, though hardly overjoyed; at other times, she feels that she is being disloyal to her dead child by concentrating all her thoughts upon the new infant in her womb. I am sure that these strange shifts of mood are commonplace among pregnant women, but to a cinema audience, they are mystifying without being really exciting.

The script compounds the remoteness of these scenes by requiring Miss Foote to deliver her lines in an entirely unnatural way, as though she was reading from a slightly old-fashioned novel. Subsidiary clauses are woven into her sentences with such grace as to be almost absurd. Furthermore, she moves as though she were sleepwalking and must speak, as must the entire cast, with a pronounced Texan drawl.

The First World War was a horrible affair. It was organized by a Mr. Haig, whose idea of military strategy was to herd more and more troops toward the banks of a river called the Somme until the brave and the beautiful died like stampeding cattle. The desperate folly of that confrontation is everywhere apparent or is hinted at in the background of this film—the finest sequence being a humiliatingly cheerful welcome offered by the townsfolk to a handful of returning soldiers, one blind, one crippled, others almost embarrassed to find themselves unscathed.

The fatality of the era and the remoteness, the smallness and the ordinariness of the place, are presented with marvelous deftness and accuracy. Every detail is right, but some of the situations are not. When her sixteen-year-old brother tells Miss Foote that he may have gotten a local girl pregnant, she hardly seems shocked or even surprised. When he adds that there is to be no wedding but, instead, an abortion, her expression never changes from one of weary acceptance. Without a murmur, she abets his crime by handing him her only two hundred dollars (which, for all I know, might equal a modern two thousand). Texas is a state where, even today, except at South Fork, sex is almost unknown. In view of this fact, I thought her lethargic response highly improbable.

The acting of this film is excellent except for that of the young brother, played by Mr. Broderick. When, in order to borrow money from his sister, he is compelled to confess to the sins of gambling and fornication, he seemed to me not only unashamed but even unembarrassed. Mr. Steele forgave him, but Mr. Steele is not to be trusted. His judgment may have been clouded by the young man's blazing dark eyes and general good looks.

Watching this movie is like looking at a photograph album belonging to a very old lady and turning the pages slowly. The furnishings are quaint; the costumes are dowdy. (Women in those days were even a different shape.) Each tableau is rich in detail; each person has a tiny history. In real life, this would be a pleasant way to spend a couple of hours. When we are told that a certain building was the parents' home, we gaze at it blandly for a moment; when we are informed that a lady in a white dress was a kindly neighbor, we smile at the smiling face; if told that she died, we do not ask why. We merely turn the page. No pattern is sought, but that was life. This is a movie. We have the right to be edified, shocked, frightened, or amused. The trouble with 1918 is not only that it packs no punch; it has no point of view—or none that either I or Mr. Steele could discern. Toward the end, we are shown a vase of flowers—which has been placed by a strange woman on the child's grave—blown over by the wind. What does this shot mean? We have spent a hell of a lot of time in the cemetery in this film. Are we now being told that to mourn is futile—is wrong?

When the lights went up in the nearly empty auditorium of the Coronet cinema and we realized that what we had seen was all we were going to get, some booed. This was naughty. The picture must be praised for the virtues of consistent texture and absolute sincerity. Indeed, it might be called a work of art, but that, of course, is not enough.

We want movies—movies—movies. . . .

THE SHOOTING PARTY

In the last issue of this illustrious magazine, I said that the past is a mistake. I was then speaking my mind about a film entitled *1918*. I have now seen *The Shooting Party*, which might just as well have been called *1913*. In the new picture, five years have been added to the remoteness in time and two thousand miles to the distance in space. It takes place in England in the autumn not only of the year but also of its civilization.

Everything compounds the melancholy of the period and of the location. The exterior shots are of misty mornings and forlorn dusks in the dreary English countryside; all color has become a greenish brown. The interiors show us ill-lit rooms crowded with heavy, dark furniture. Even when there is a fancy dress party, it looks dim and the intended gaiety of the participants is chilled by embarrassment. In a sense, the art direction of the film is its greatest virtue. Not only are we shown in accurate detail a way of life that will never return but we see it as though it were a painting executed long ago; the varnish on the movie has become clouded.

The entire story, such as it is, is a series of anticlimaxes mounting—nay, sinking—to disaster.

To a large country house, where Mr. Mason lives with Miss Tutin, their children and even their grandchildren, come assorted guests, including a very rich German gentleman—to add a note of foreboding, because they are within a year of the Great War. The day after they arrive, the men set out at dawn to shoot pheasant. They are followed later in the day by the women, for a picnic. Do not imagine that they all flop about on raincoats and swig Coca-Cola. A vast tent is erected, seating accommodation is arranged, and champagne is served.

To two of the guests, the occasion has become a grim contest of marksmanship and this provokes Mr. Fox to fire at a bird that has almost reached cover. The result of this "ungentlemanly" action is that he hits Mr. Jackson, a poacher who was only doing duty as a beater because someone else was ill. A doctor is summoned, but Mr. Jackson dies uttering the words "God bless the British Empire." The party is over; the suns sets mournfully behind the silent landscape—a symbol of the dissolution of life as the English upper class had known it.

As the shooting party goes slowly home across the darkling fields, carrying the body of the poacher, a voice on the sound track tells us that while we can, we should believe—presumably in the old values. If this message comes to us from the romantic young woman, it is acceptable; if it is the voice of the movie itself, it is intolerable. It was precisely this naïve and isolated optimism on the part of the British aristocracy that caused the fall of its civilization.

Miss Colegate's book, which I have not read, may be written entirely from the point of view of the young female guest who, though married to Sir Robert Hardy, falls in love with another member of the house party. This may give the book a unity that is lacking from the movie. She is not enjoying the occasion; she cries when the birds fall from the air, their breasts covered with blood; she hates the world ruled by men who, as Mr. Mason points out, have bred and reared the pheasants solely in order to kill them, but she cannot help loving men. The way the film tells the story, it contains too many plots, all of equal importance and woven together in short, confusing sequences. There is a sordid intrigue between the German gentleman and an outrageous vamp; an attempted wooing of a housemaid by a valet who copies the discarded love letters of one of the guests; and the possibility that a domesticated duck belonging to the grandson may accidentally be shot. We are given a catalogue of unfulfilled expectations. Anything called *The Shooting Party* must end with the planned or accidental death of somebody, but here the tragedy of Mr. Jackson is totally unsatisfactory, for neither the audience nor anyone in the picture has learned to care about him. We neither mourn nor rejoice at his death.

This will not do.

The value of this film, apart from its beautiful, lugubrious photography and its consistently good acting, lies in the fact that it provides us with one last glimpse of Mr. Mason. This is not quite as affecting as the final appearance of Mr. Tracy in *Guess Who's Coming to Dinner* because everyone involved in that picture knew that its star would soon die. This gave his protestation of love for Miss Hepburn a special poignancy. He was a lovable man who, except when he was Mr. Hyde, never played an unlikable character. Mr. Mason, on the other hand, spent most of his early life hitting a certain Miss Lockwood or rapping the knuckles of Miss Todd with his walking stick. His public grew to respect rather than to love him. Nevertheless, he survived the difficult transplantation from Elstree to Hollywood, which extinguished so many other British actors.

Moviemaking is not an art that flourishes on English soil. The great silent films were German, and when talkies were invented, the United States took control, firstly because more people with money speak American than any other language, and secondly because film is the medium that can most vividly express physical personality. It is this obsession with individuality that is the driving force of American life and has made California the land where stars grow on trees. For this reason, even now, most actors and actresses want to make at least one first feature on the West Coast. Many succeed but few are able to cling to their status, and it is by watching the careers of those who have migrated from other countries that we realize how much more exacting the standard of stardom is in American than elsewhere.

When Miss Kerr went to Los Angeles, she was put into *The Hucksters*. She seemed so tame that it might have been the end of her career. Miss Simmons's first American movies were so weak that I cannot remember their names; she didn't even look beautiful until she became the star of *The Robe* (after which for years she never took off her toga). Mr. Mason's first venture in this country was ominously entitled *Caught*, but he managed to survive his mistake by parading his cruelty. He tore a perfectly good dress off some poor creature in one film, insulted Miss Gardner in another, and so on. Only much later, when he had deeply etched his mannerisms into the consciousness of his audiences, did he risk being benign or displaying that grandeur that is essential to American stardom.

He once said, "I am only allowed to stay in the film business because of the funny way the words come out of my mouth." He knew what he was doing. His method of speaking was the opposite of that adopted by another recently dead British actor. When Mr. Burton spoke, his lips strode forward like medieval pages trumpeting his words. Mr. Mason did the opposite. His lips huddled against his teeth keeping his tongue prisoner inside his mouth, where it strove against all odds to communicate with the world. His voice was discreet and at the same time oracular. For this reason, the part of the host in *The Shooting Party* suited him well. I was pleased that though his final appearance was not in a memorable picture, his part in it was honorable and that he played it to perfection.

THE WALL / ELÉNA AND THE MEN

Arriving back in New York from Baltimore, I found the world of entertainment had become an arid waste. In desperation, I nagged Mr. Steele into accompanying me to a secret screening of *The Wall* at the Public Theater. This film had been heralded as the greatest story about prison life ever to come out of Turkey. To

Mr. Steele, it seemed the greatest turkey ever to come out of prison life.

Nevertheless, it is a work that must be taken seriously.

The Wall was made by Mr. Yilmaz Guney, who has been in jail on and off for a total of nearly twelve years. He knows his subject and is determined that we shall understand him. For almost two hours, we are confined to a prison where no day passes without appalling suffering being inflicted not only by the warders and guards on the criminals but also by the bigger and stronger boys on their weaker cell mates.

If the film has a story, it is of a boy of twelve (masquerading as a fourteen-year-old) who is sodomized by a guard and then urged by his companions to report this fact to the doctors. When he cannot summon up the nerve to do this, he is shunned by the other boys. This is more than he can bear: He tries to escape and is shot.

The scenes of violence are marvelously put together. It is hard to realize that we are watching fiction—that, in fact, every few minutes someone must have stopped the action to smear more artificial blood on the faces of the actors. However, although *The Wall* is horrifying, it is not lurid; we are never allowed to derive from this film any satisfaction for our kinkiness. When a warder rapes one of the boys, we do not watch this happen; we only see the small victim return from another room to sit, broken and ashamed, in his dormitory. When all the boys are ordered to strip, they cover their genitals and, even with their faces to the wall, they hide their buttocks by clasping their hands behind them. The only moment at which you know what emerges is when some jeering screws demand that a boy, whom they consider effeminate, show them that he is male. As he exposes a terrified penis, he is cursed for not being a Moslem, because it is not circumcised. I was vividly reminded here of the situation in Northern Ireland, where instant death can result from not being a Protestant.

The Wall occupies the bleak no-man's-land between the documentary exposé and the drama. It is monotonous and repetitious but I think that these are intentional effects; we are not meant to hope that in prison one day will be much different from another. Almost every shot is photographed between bars or from behind wire netting, but this is because the director feels the whole of Turkey is only one vast jail. The film is not intended to be entertainment.

Judged by its own standards, it has very few faults. The subtitles are appallingly spelled and the American slang in which they are phrased is slightly phony. Furthermore, the device of putting radio advertisements for various luxuries on the sound track does not work. Either they should be omitted altogether or they should be more frequent; it should be made clearer that they come from the radio in the warders' office and they should be placed at moments where they would have greater ironic effect.

Almost all films about incarceration show us not only the ruthlessness with which punishment is administered but also instances of elaborate cruelty. In *The Wall*, two prisoners—a man and a woman (who have a child born to them in jail)—are led to believe that they have permission from the authorities to marry. They dress in their best and, amid the cheers of their companions, proceed to the room in which they imagine the wedding ceremony will be enacted. On arrival, they realize that they are not to be wed but to be hanged.

This incident seems so monstrous that at first it makes the victims of it appear innocent, but, in fact, they have committed a murder for the least worthy reasons—so as to be free to indulge their lust for one another. The message seems to coincide with that of a famous French film called *Nous Sommes Tous des Assassins*.

The problem of how to curb the vileness of human nature cannot, I fear, be solved as Mr. Yilmaz Guney hopes—by democratic government. Politics are not a moral science and do not solve moral problems. Society has only one object and that is to preserve itself. This it does by eliminating diversive elements. To determine who or what these are, it invents laws. Someone has then to be found who will undertake to enforce these rules; it is a profession that attracts bullies and sadists. If they are not cruel to begin with, they rapidly become so. This is a state of affairs from which there is no way out. The bomb is now our only friend.

The very next day after seeing *The Wall*, I went to the very same cinema to watch *Eléna and the Men*, a film featuring Miss Bergman, made in 1956 by Monsieur Renoir. No one can say that the Public Theater lacks catholicity. On Thursday, it showed one of the grimmest pictures I have ever witnessed; on Friday, one of the most frivolous.

Eléna is set at the beginning of this century; the women wear frilly clothes and the men are dressed in uniforms encrusted with gold braid. The prettiness of the picture is unremittingly like a meal of marzipan, whether we are looking at close-ups of Miss Bergman or crowd scenes in which the French seem to be a nation of barbers. There is a complex political plot but unfortunately neither the audience nor the participants are expected to take it seriously. The cast includes Mr. Marais, Mr. Ferrer (Mel, not José), and Mlle. Greco. All set perfectly within the limits of the film's style and the star even succeeds in being excruciatingly feminine without becoming nauseating. As with *The Wall*, the weakness of this film is its subtitles. Such a picture should have been dubbed. By the time you have read the words printed at the bottom of the screen, you have forgotten whether the phrases they translate were uttered sincerely or with irony. This makes the dialogue sound pedestrian.

Monsieur Godard has compared this work with *The Magic Flute*; to me, who does not hold with music, it seemed like *The Merry Widow*. I have no objection to frivolity, but there is something slightly annoying about this kind of film—especially when it is made by a Frenchman. I know that we are all forbidden to make racial judgments, but after my two evenings at the Public Theater, I am left with the impressions that Turkish men have had a consistently bad reputation ever since Lord Byron took against them for trying to conquer Greece. The Turks seem to be a nation given to excessive cruelty and the growing of the most handsome mustaches in the world. On the other hand, the French appear to think that they invented flirtation. Their films on this subject are almost always pervaded by a cloying quality of self-congratulation.

I found much to recommend in both these movies, but if my praise is guarded, what do I really want?

I suppose I require variety with consistency and narrative that is totally engaging without being oppressive.

TURTLE DIARY/ORNETTE COLEMAN

Our visits to the movies now have definitely become group therapy. Four of us went to Cinema 1 to view *Turtle Diary*. We were very nearly five. Driven by my anxiety neurosis, I was a little early for our rendezvous. While I waited for Mr. Steele and his merry men, I was accosted by a kind stranger who told me how wonderful I was and engaged me in conversation. As the other members of our party arrived, he told them how wonderful they were. Mr. Steele might have guessed from all this praise that we didn't know one another very well, but, being a romantic, he did not make this assumption. Instead, he imagined that we were all lifelong friends and gave the stranger, who had not an ounce of kinkiness in his entire body, a copy of *Christopher Street* magazine. (At all gatherings of any kind, Mr. Steele does this, as other people offer cigarettes.) If, before the next issue of this periodical appears, its offices are bombed, we shall all know whom to blame.

We had chosen to see *Turtle Diary* because the script was by Mr. Pinter. I owe him undying loyalty because, while I was only English, he made heroic efforts to secure me a grant from the Arts Council. To some extent, our faith was justified. The film does contain many delightful instances of what may be called the Pinter effect—the placing of short, idiomatic, inconsequential remarks between two pauses that give them a comic gravity. In fact, it is possible to praise everything about this film except the details of the story.

The basic idea is good. It concerns the well-intentioned theft of three sea turtles from the London Zoo and the returning of them to the sea.

The photography is apt; it is all in what Miss Goldberg might call "the color turtle"—a brownish green, very English. The acting is good. Mr. Kingsley mastered the Pinter method in *Betrayal* and here uses it to great effect. Furthermore, the dark fire that flashed fiercely from his countenance when, as Mr. Gandhi, he set India free still glows dimly in his eyes as he dreams of home rule for turtles. His costar, Miss Jackson, has to work harder than he. She was born to play Elizabeth Tudor and, indeed, might easily take over England if Mrs. Thatcher ever gives it up. Miss Jackson permanently wears the expression of a woman by no means pleased at having been disobeyed. This slightly threatening impression is reinforced in this picture by her no-nonsense hairdo. Nevertheless, she overcomes these physical disadvantages and even gives credibility to asking an attendant whether the turtles in his aquarium are happy. The reply is stunning. "I doubt it, madam; they are in prison." (They have, it seems, been in captivity for thirty years.) The gentleman who utters these words and who is a Mr. Gambon is superb.

The trouble with this film is that there is no trouble. As soon as Miss Jackson and Mr. Kingsley take up the cause of turtle lib, they find they have absolutely no difficulty in enlisting the help of the keeper and he, in turn, is able to transfer the three hideous creatures in question to a van with positively annoying ease. All the apparent hazards of the journey to the Devonshire coast turn out to be false. A garage proprietor watches with keen interest while Mr. Kingsley and Miss Jackson pour buckets of water into the back of their van, but he does not act upon his suspicions.

I longed by the end of the story to learn that the turtles had died or walked back to the zoo or that their liberators had been imprisoned or *something*.

When this mission impossible has been accomplished, the story is not ended. Each of the main participants returns to the dreary bed-sitting-room life, where Mr. Kingsley discovers that a fellow lodger (played by Miss Bron) has committed suicide. She is found with one hand on a book open at the words *Burial at Sea*. What does it all mean? Is life intolerable if one has no caged animal to release?

If the freeing of the turtles is a symbol for the liberation of Mr. Kingsley and/or Miss Jackson, we are in trouble. Back in his room, Mr. Kingsley becomes involved in a brutish fight with another inmate twice his size over the trivial matter of the latter's failure to clean the communal bath (who cares?), while Miss Jackson begins an illicit liaison with the zoo keeper. She can't be blamed for that. He is an adorable gentleman with the frame of an ox and the heart of a lamb but this is, to say the least, an unlikely union. In Britian, except among homosexual men, not even sex can transcend the barriers of class.

If freedom only produces violence and fornication, surely we all would be better off spending thirty years in a dimly lit tank full of dirty water.

I also visited the Public Theater at the invitation of Ms. Clarke, who, you may remember, became famous some years ago for making a movie called *The Connection*.

This was my second visit to this excruciatingly cultural establishment; I had witnessed *Queen Kelly* there a month or so previously. If I go there again, I think I shall have the right to consider myself an honorary highbrow. In England, a highbrow is anyone who is willing to sit in tiny cinemas watching French films. He usually wears dark glasses and talks throughout the performance. Here, the preoccupation of the intellegentsia is largely with American silent films and they are viewed with reverence even though at the time of their first release, the same audience considered them vulgar and trashy.

Miss Clarke's film is none of those things; it is touching and funny but it is obscure and this may prevent it from being shown to ordinary mortals.

The director says that she next wishes to devote herself to a fictional subject, "so that I can lie" she explained. However, *Ornette Coleman* is not quite a straight documentary. A child plays the part of the composer when he runs away from home, and a young man acts his adolescence. I most enjoyed seeing Mr. Coleman himself either sitting with friends or playing his saxophone before a symphony orchestra or in open spaces in distant parts of the world.

The trouble with a picture of this nature is never with the star; it is with the music itself. People who like the wretched stuff claim that its appeal is universal because, unlike poetry, it requires no translation from one language to another. What no one ever mentions is that it is universally difficult to understand. If shown a painting, even an ignoramus can say, "It's nice but I never really liked blue." Such a comment may provoke scorn but, at least, it can be understood. If, after being forced to listen to a symphony, someone was to remark, "It's nice but I never really like the key of C major," he, too, might be ridiculed, but to me it would show he was a genius. Though nowadays, the hills are numb with the sound of music, I doubt that there are many genuine music lovers.

When the movie ended, Miss Clarke and Mr. Coleman appeared—so that they might answer questions from the audience—before us in a blinding light cast upon them from the projectionist's booth. This part of the program, which might have been its crowning glory, was not well staged by the Public Theater. Though Miss Clarke was walking with a stick, having fallen down on various continents, she and her star were compelled to stand in the cramped space between the front row of seats and the screen and I think the audience felt reluctant to prolong this uncomfortable situation. However, the victims went into their act very courageously and the ensuing dialogue was lively. Mr. Coleman wished (I think) to tell us that the playing of music was liberating—even a mystical experience—but he speaks in the same way that Miss Stein wrote, using the same word several times in different capacities. When his lips stopped moving, Miss Clarke confessed that she had not understood a word that he had said and she added, ". . . but then I never do. That is why working with him was such a satisfactory collaboration."

To me, this was the high spot of a very stimulating evening.

DOWN AND OUT IN BEVERLY HILLS

Mr. Steele prophesied almost gleefully that we would hate this film. I am not among those moviegoers who recommend pictures with the words "It's terrible; you'll love it." I therefore went to the Ziegfeld Theatre with misgivings. I left it positively elated.

Down and Out was made as though Dr. Westheimer had written the script for a Frank Capra production. It is the delinquent offspring of the bedroom farce; almost all the traditional ingredients of that kind of entertainment are present. The housemaid is seduced first by her employer and then by the guest, who also has go at the lady of the house and the daughter, after which he is chased hither and thither by the irate father. Of course, none of these events is presented as shocking because the time is now and the place is California.

The plot of this saga of licentiousness hangs on a chain of improbabilities. Mr. Nolte plays the part of what we might call a "bag gentleman," though, in reality, there is no such person in Beverly Hills. While he is asleep in the street, his dog runs away with a jogger and is never seen again. Searching for this perfidious quadruped, its owner strays into the garden of a rich married couple, played by Mr. Dreyfuss and Miss Midler. Here, he fills his pockets with stones and jumps into their swimming pool. He is rescued by Mr. Dreyfuss, who administers mouth-to-mouth resuscitation (we should be so lucky) and makes him a permanent guest in his home. In return for this hospitality, Mr. Nolte brings havoc and redemption in more or less equal measures to almost everyone within range.

This unlikely situation provides Mr. Mazursky, the director, with endless opportunities for satirizing the foibles of rich Californians—their reliance on psychoanalysis, their childish belief in Western mysticism on the one hand and on the other, their enslavement to the acquisition of wealth and the Sybaritic life. The consequences of these follies are also catalogued. The Dreyfuss marriage has stagnated; their daughter suffers from anorexia; their son is homosexual in a most uneasy fashion. Even their dog is a nervous wreck.

What makes this picture so enjoyable is not the exaggerations of its narrative but the richness of its texture. Every inch of every frame is utilized. While, in the foreground, the actors are doing or saying one thing, behind them a television screen is telling us something else. The audience is completely embroiled in every incident. When, for instance, the vagrant attempts suicide, it would be sufficient in most movies for the camera to watch his rescue from the edge of the pool, but here, when Mr. Dreyfuss dives, we dive with him and float about in cloudy water, where the fully clothed form of Mr. Nolte lunges toward us like a giant ray fish. There is even icing on this delicious celluloid cake. Though it is largely a visual comedy, the lines are funny, frequently very funny, and when they are banal, they are knowingly so.

All the major roles are well cast and acted with great gusto. Little Richard, as a paranoid neighbor, angry that the tone of the district has been lowered by an influx of Arabs, positively flings himself into his part and Miss Midler is by no means content merely to slap us in the face with her hilarious vulgarity; she delivers her lines with acute comic artistry. Mr. Dreyfuss has a more difficult part than either of these because though he is gargoyle of materialism, he is dimly aware of this—alternately boastful and ashamed. He is particularly good in a scene where he tries to ingratiate himself with his guest's vagrant companions.

There is also in this already formidable cast a dog called Matisse.

A dog is a horrible thing to happen to anybody—especially on the screen. In real life, the nicest compliment that can be paid to a domestic animal is to say that no one would know it was there and the nastiest fate that can befall a guest is to be coerced into paying attention to an animal as though it were human. Needless to say the Dreyfusses indulge their pet to the point where they have little time for their children; they even have the wretched thing psychoanalyzed. I seldom laugh "ha ha" at a movie, but there is a moment in *Down and Out* when I was provoked to audible merriment. It came when the dog's analyst is trying to coax his patient into eating something. The animal's response is to pick up its plate and throw it over its shoulder so that the food flies all over the floor. If Rin Tin Tin was the Gary Cooper of the canine world and Lassie was its Greer Garson, then this dog is the reincarnation of the silent comedian Ben Turpin. It is the most hideous living thing I have ever seen and it makes full use of its defects, surveying the ludicrous antics of its owners with a baleful gaze from one pale and one dark eye.

It would be hard for a mere human being to upstage or upscreen this creature but no one can deny that the star of this picture succeeds.

Mr. Nolte is like the sun, both in radiance and magnitude. I advise you not to sit too near the screen.

Just as the preview of *Out of Africa*, admittance to *Down and Out* was by invitation only and, once again, though on this occasion the auditorium was vast, it was crowded. Miss Miles, who is never absent from any important event in the world of entertainment, very kindly offered to seat one or two of us beside her in the royal enclosure, but we were a party of four. Mr. Steele had invited two professional "foodists," who left us later in the evening to spread alarm and despondency among some of the more expensive chefs of Manhattan. Because of our number, we were obliged to sit almost in the front row of the house. I suffered severe sunstroke when Mr. Nolte's completely naked body, the color of a roasted chicken, loomed up but a few feet from me and eighty times its considerable life size.

Every frame of this movie is enjoyable and if we are content to regard it purely as a glorious farce, it cannot be faulted. If, however, we try to see it as a satire, a smog of confusion immediately arises. As a cure for their ills, Mr. Nolte offers his own brand of Saroyanism to the men of the Dreyfuss household and to the women, his you know what. To the son (who might be considered a borderline case)—though he somewhat heartlessly undresses in front of this confused young man—he only offers sympathy. If this film had been called *Down and Out in Oklahoma City*, where I am told sex is unknown, this might be an efficacious remedy, but in Beverly Hills, sex grows on trees. Nay, we can say more. When the movie industry finally dies of self-indulgence, when the imported palms wither by the roadsides, when the last swimming pool runs dry and the sands of the Californian desert flow silently across the cities of the plain like a sheet being drawn over the face of a corpse, it will be precisely because the inhabitants of this doomed terrain succumbed to the belief that the best that money could buy was pleasure and that the only worthwhile pleasure was sexual excess.

Moreover, if carefree vagrancy is so wonderful that the notion of it bursts like a glimpse of paradise upon the imagination of a rich coat-hanger manufacturer, why did Mr. Nolte, who is its embodiment, sink so low that he became distraught at the loss of a mere dog—and a mongrel at that. And why did he attempt suicide?

During the last few moments of this film, Mr. Nolte, having brought them his gift of disturbing enlightenment, leaves the members of the Dreyfuss household. The entire family watches him depart. Seeing them almost smile at him, he retraces his steps and backs into the house. What does this mean? Are we meant to see that, after all, wealth, sex, and psychoanalysis really are the best we can get in the worst of all possible worlds? Is *Down and Out in Beverly Hills* a satire on a satire?

OUT OF AFRICA

Miss Streep is doing it again—playing the part of yet another extremely annoying woman. On this occasion, she is a real-life aristocrat from Denmark.

Four of us went to watch her do this at Mr. Loew's Tower East on Third Avenue. Apart from Mr. Steele and me, there was one of his slaves, who, at midnight after the movie was over, was sent home to write the whole of the next issue of the *New York Native* before morning. We were also accompanied by a handsome doctor, recruited either because of his looks or in case any of us fainted. The film was almost three hours long and we felt every moment of it.

At the outset, a caption appeared telling us that the movie was based on a true story. What a terrible warning! As always, it meant, "If you find parts of this narrative dreary and lacking in a cohesive plot, we are not to blame. You Know Who wrote the script." A picture is never better and is often worse because it is true.

In real life, Miss—I beg your pardon—Baroness von Blixen must have been a remarkable woman, a sort of trailer for the suffragette movement. She was physically braver than most men and socially she was without fear of any kind. She was an indefatigable worker, exceptionally free from the languor and the hysteria that afflicted most of the well-born women of her day. She was also fiercely loyal to her inferiors. The best sequence in the entire film is the one in which she kneels before the new high commissioner, begging him to give back to the Africans who had worked for her the land that the British had stolen from them. It follows inevitably that with this sort of behavior, she was an embarrassment to her equals. The movie audience shares this reaction. She is only less irritating than the heroine of *Plenty* because the appalling misfortunes that overtook her are real, though most of them could have been avoided by sitting in a Danish palace and doing embroidery.

The part of her life story dealt with in *Out of Africa* can be summarized thusly. Having no intention of living a pampered or even a sheltered life, when Miss Blixen meets a man who is going to Kenya to become a dairy farmer, she asks him to marry her, offering him her title and her wealth. With some amusement, he accepts her proposal and she arrives in Nairobi an hour before the wedding. She is soon annoyed to find that they will not start a dairy farm. Instead, they will grow coffee or, rather, she will grow it, because, almost at once, her husband loses interest in work and takes to women, which, to my amazement, he finds less of a strain. Needless to say, the marriage falls apart but not before an exchange of love tokens has taken place; she has given him most of her money and he has given her syphilis.

After some time spent in Europe undergoing a cure, the Baroness returns to Africa, where she begins an affair with a safari guide, or big-game hunter or whatever. They make love in various tents and talk incessantly about their relationship with one another. This is something that I have never known a man willing to do, and, indeed, Mr. Redford does evince a certain impatience with this pastime.

The main theme of their perpetual quarrel is his refusal to ask her to marry him, although, because of treatment by the European doctors, she cannot have children and does not really need to be married. She is also irked by his habit of leaving her every few days to go on safari, or sometimes merely to go. She never seems to realize that it is her incessant nagging that is, at least in part, the cause of his frequent departures.

The makers of this movie have done everything possible to bring its period and its setting close to us. We really live the life of a colonial planter; we experience to the full the hardships of growing and harvesting coffee. The ceremonials of the British ruling class are presented to us in all their starched absurdity. The dangers of Africa threaten us with genuine immediacy. The moment when a lioness approaches to within twenty yards of Miss Streep is truly involving, but when you have left the cinema, you cannot help thinking that if this tale had been called *Out of New Jersey*, it would merely have been yet another story about whether I love you more than you love me, which I imagine we are all agreed is a subject beneath our contempt.

To some extent, Mr. Pollack, the director, seems to be aware of this dilemma, but he does not always deal with it well. He occasionally shows us unnecessary travelogue views of the region at various seasons and different times of day; he give us glimpses of native warriors running but not to or from anything in particular and the cutting is so arty that at times it is confusing. Furthermore, for fear of seeming prosaic, the dialogue is sometimes slick. For instance, when Miss Streep has crossed half the continent to bring supplies to her husband and his soldiers during the Great War and has arrived in a thoroughly bedraggled state, all he has to say to her is, "You've changed your hair." He has not been shown to be an entirely heartless man and this is a serious situation. He could have been relieved that she had arrived safely and/or furious that she undertook the journey herself instead of sending another on such a hazardous mission, but flippancy seems to be out of place.

In spite of all this, *Out of Africa* has considerable assets. As the husband, Mr. Brandauer is excellent, handsome and sly but not altogether unlovable. Mr. Redford, as Mr. Cunningham points out, makes no attempt to be like an Englishman, but he is good as the untamed lover. In all his films, he wears an expression of suppressed rage and here it suits the part perfectly. Moreover, he spares himself nothing. The dried-out skin texture that comes to all blue-eyed people who live for long in Africa is never concealed from the cameras, but though his name is billed before hers, it is to Miss Streep that the picture belongs. She is amazing. Once again, she plays the part of a woman who wants love on her own terms, but she is by no means repeating previous performances. Now she speaks with a slight Danish accent and her face is flatter—perhaps like a Danish pastry. Her stoicism in the face of dreadful misfortune must not be mistaken for underacting.

The film is part of what the French might call another "new wave," all concerned with the sins of the British Empire or, at least, the colonial system. First, in *A Passage to India*, we shared Mr. Forster's sad view of that country under foreign rule. Then we saw much the same thing in *The Jewel in the Crown*. The English now seem anxious, if not to atone for their despotism, at least to admit it. In America, this theme is even more popular. Its lure may be a fiendish glee at watching an erstwhile landlord totally dispossessed.

On the night we saw *Out of Africa*, though admittance was by invitation only, the cinema was full, chiefly of young people. They squeaked with delight at every glimpse of a monkey or a water buffalo and found the singing of the national anthem on New Year's Eve in Nairobi hilarious. At the end of the film, they applauded loudly, yet they had no memory of life in the colonies at the beginning of this century. Worse, it is unlikely that they had read any of the *Seven Gothic Tales* that, under the pen name of Isak Dinesen, the Baroness was later to write. As Mr. Steele remarked, it was a pity that when Miss Streep begins to tell a story to Mr. Redford, there is no inkling of the twilit, bewitched, and bewitching genius of this remarkable woman.

THE DRESSER

To anyone who is kind enough to have made a habit of reading this page, I apologize for having deserted my post last month. I was sent to Austin (very beautiful), to Dallas (very American), and to Chicago (very kinky; three times in four weeks, while onstage there, I was asked why I was wearing no underclothes). In all that time, I only saw one film. It was entitled *My Dinner with Andre*. I could not bring myself to make a report on it because it was as boring as being alive.

Now I am back in New York and have been with your Mr. Steele to see *The Dresser*, which is quite another matter.

If I say that this is a backstage movie, I must immediately rush on to qualify this description. It is not an American picture; it is not like *42nd Street*. It is British and therefore tells a tale not of effortless overnight success but of day by day humiliation and defeat. Everybody in the film is utterly ignoble. The stage manager steals; the leading lady is unfeeling; the actor-manager is a capricious tyrant and his dresser drinks. If you ever thought of taking up residence in the British Isles, let this picture be a warning to you. In that benighted region, you may discover eccentricity—even talent, stoicism—even courage, but you will find no happiness.

Outside of documentaries made at the time, I have never seen a picture that creates in such detail the bleakness of England during the Second World War. In the railway scene, all the station staff is rude; in the street scenes, half the houses are burned or burning, with their former occupants sitting dazed on the pavement; in the provincial theaters, there is an orchestra of one pathetic violinist; and everywhere everyone who comes within sight of the concern is as unattractive as a human being can be except for one girl, and she tries by illicit means to steal the part of Cordelia away from the leading lady.

Usually, when a critic praises the art direction of a movie, it is a sure sign it is a damned bad film—that a slow narrative has been tricked out with arty glimpses of two ears of wheat posing against a cloud. In *The Dresser*, this is not the case. Whoever chose the locations and built or decorated the sets possessed total recall of the 1940s.

This picture is the story of the final days of one of the actor-managers who, in the beginning of this century, forever used to drag his own company round the larger towns of Britain. They only performed Shakespearean plays or other works that they considered to be classics. Quite unashamedly, they were in the culture racket. In their opinion, it was less their function to entertain than it was their duty to uplift. The weakness of this setup, as with any monopoly, was that all the power was in the hands of one person and it went to his head. The central performance often became self-indulgent. Overtly, this film is an enactment of this general arrangement, but secretly it is a savage caricature of a certain Sir Donald Wolfit. Even during his lifetime, the entire profession made fun of him. When told that Sir Robert Helpmann was about to dance a ballet called *Hamlet*, Miss Gingold asked, "Why not? Wolfit has been singing it for years." When Mr. Wolfit died, a program was shown on television that quite shamelessly ridiculed him. Among the celebrities taking part in this documentary was Mr. Harwood, who wrote *The Dresser* and who obviously knew the actor and the whole backstage ritual very well indeed. Viewed from the wings, the sound effects for the storm scene in *King Lear* are hilarious and the histrionics of the nightly curtain speech are absolutely true to life. However, Mr. Wolfit was the only man within living memory with the vocal stamina to attempt such marathons as *Tamburlaine the Great*, and in the glimpses that we are shown of the final moment of *King Lear*, it is greatly to Mr. Finney's credit that although he acts them grandiloquently, he does not act them badly.

Throughout the film, Mr. Finney is quite remarkable. You have only to cast your mind back to what he was like as the police chief in *Murder on the Orient Express* to become aware of his amazing versatility. There, he was neat, oily, sly; here, he is bombastic, ruined with flashes of leonine majesty.

He shares the audience's attention with Mr. Courtenay, who plays his dresser—part bossy nanny, part abject slave, and at all times, an incomplete human being who can no longer live in the real world. In his own eyes as well as everybody else's, the only justification for his existence is that with the passage of time, he has come so completely to understand his master. Mr. Courtenay comprehends his part perfectly and, with deadly accuracy, plays it as what his employer calls a "nancy-boy"—speaking through his teeth, arching his back, walking with tiny, hurried steps and holding his hands before him like the paws of a begging Pekinese dog. Even while I praise this actor's skill, I know that I must issue a warning. There are many homosexuals who will be annoyed by this performance. These people often endure—nay, enjoy—any amount of transvestite camp in the theater but will fly into indignant rage when an effeminate man minces across the stage or screen, although we all know that the former antics are an obsolete parody of femininity, while the latter are simply portrayals of human beings who still exist among us. Because I am aware that this condemnatory view is commonly held, I would say that no gay man who habitually wears a mustache should see this film. I would have scrawled these words on the facade of Cinema 2 but I didn't have my spray can with me.

Mr. Steele and I were agreed that this film is too long and that the dresser's final speech is confusing. In it, he declares his love for Mr. Finney. He does this immediately after words have been uttered by the stage manager, a woman who was secretly in love with the actor. This makes it seem that Mr. Courtenay was also in love with him. Nothing else in the movie corroborates this notion. Much more plausible is the idea that, in spite of themselves, these two utterly different men became mutually dependent and fell prey to all the irritation that such a relationship inevitably provokes. We never dislike anybody so much as when we realize that he is all we've got. Another weakness in the final scene is that the dresser expresses no remorse, although by forcing his employer to go onstage, he has at least hastened his death, if he has not actually caused it.

This slight weakness aside, *The Dresser* is a powerful film. I cannot quite bring myself to say that you will enjoy it. It is utterly joyless. I can only claim that it tells its grim tale with sparks of humor and in merciless detail.

PSYCHO 2

The film that used to be named *Psycho* must now be retitled *Psycho 1*, just as the conflict that was at first grandiloquently called the Great War had later to be renamed World War I. I saw Mr. Hitchcock's movie twenty years ago with old-fashioned eyes. Even then, I thought the great director was on the way down.

A nation can be said to have become decadent when it starts to set more store by its differences from other nations than by that which it holds in common with them. The same is true of individuals—especially artists. In other words, if style has become separate from and more important than content, things are going badly. This was what gradually happened to Mr. Hitchcock. In the beginning of his career, he was without effort a highly idiosyncratic director; like the Surrealists, he trafficked in terror by day. In his earliest films, he felt no compulsion to drag us down dimly lit alleys or leave us alone in dark houses. His heroes were placed in terrible danger in Arab market places, in the lobbies of grand hotels, in the stalls of crowded theaters. At that time, the message was clear and universal. We are never safe.

As years passed, Mr. Hitchcock grew accustomed to his power to frighten us. He became like a woman who, always wearing the same perfume, increases the quantity until strangers start to choke when she enters an elevator. In *Psycho 1*, one of his later works, we see the director quite obviously casting about for something bizarre with which to scare us. On this occasion, what he found was the blood of Mrs. Curtis. As this sacred fluid gurgled down the bath waste, the audience gurgled with it. That was nice, but merely to be frightened by a film is not enough; we must also be encouraged to care. It is precisely in this respect that a picture can be so much more powerful than real life. In our daily lives, we seldom find the time or the strength to lay aside our own burdens and concern ourselves with the sorrows of our neighbors, and when we do, we rarely understand them well enough to offer useful sympathy. In the cinema, the opposite is true. There we deliberately set apart a few hours in which to forget our own miseries and there we are presented with someone we immediately know more intimately than we shall ever know anyone we have not paid to see. We eavesdrop on his very sighs and whispers; we gaze at the moisture on his brow—at the tears on his lashes. Moreover we do all this without our presence being known to him and therefore without embarrassment. Our scrutiny does not provoke its object to put up barriers, to cover his nakedness or, on the other hand, deliberately to exhibit himself.

I could not truly say that I cared deeply about anyone in *Psycho 1* and the character I did like was killed halfway through the picture. It was therefore in a spirit of desperate optimism that, at the invitation of Mr. Steele, I set out for the preview of *Psycho 2.*

Outside the Rivoli, there was sound of revelry by night and bright the flashbulbs shone on fair women and brave men. By seven o'clock in the evening, the crowd was big enough to enrage the police. Ten minutes later, when Mr. Steele arrived, the crowd was large enough to annoy itself. Like lost dogs, your editor and I darted this way and that, whimpering in search of one another, meeting only when it was almost time for the movie to begin. I fear that the premiere of Mr. Perkin's film will go down in the history of American entertainment as one of the worst organized events. Although we had numbered seats, we were never allowed into the theater.

Broken and disillusioned, we tottered into an Indian restaurant, where we pooled our curried tears. Between sobs, Mr. Steele remarked that we were the victims of America's national weakness—its misplaced passion for immediacy. People had almost trodden their fellowmen under foot to see a movie that would be shown to all the world three days later. That apparently was not soon enough. Everything in Manhattan has to be here and now.

Forced by our misfortune to be less feverish than the rest of New York, Mr. Steele and I crept into the Rivoli the following week, for all the world as though we were ordinary mortals. In spite of all the advertising furor, we found the picture was not doing well. On an evening when the weather was so hot that one would have thought that it would be a pleasure to sit in any air-conditioned cinema whatever the movie, we were almost the only people present.

Psycho 2 is a much better film than rumor had led us to expect. The murders are grisly but convincing and the acting is good, especially that of Miss Miles, who refuses to camp however out-rageous the plot becomes. The picture is especially successful as a parody of a Hitchcock movie. It contains but does not exaggerate all the master's mannerisms—the stagy scenery, as in *Marnie*, the frequent turns of plot, as in *Spellbound*, which, like the present film, had a surprise ending beyond the expected ending.

What was wrong with the evening was not the film but the audience. They refused to be engaged.

The British refuse to be involved in sex and apparently Amer-icans shield themselves from being scared. No wonder they only like plays about plays; they have lost their capacity for experiencing real life. *Psycho 2* was hardly any more bizarre than the Manson case and certainly contained no more murders than the six o'clock news. Our lives are full of terror and degradation because we are a violent and depraved species. Why do we not admit this fact and, by taking the movies seriously, prepare ourselves for our probable fate?

But no. Mr. Perkins had only to turn his gaze apprehensively toward a half-open door for everyone in the auditorium of the Rivoli to burst into entirely artificial squeals of mirth. It would seem that it is not merely certain directors who have become decadent but their audiences as well.

There was a time when homosexuals used to imitate the worst characteristics of the rest of the world. Shall we feel flattered or disappointed when heterosexuals start adopting the more annoying traits of gay men and begin to recommend films with the words "You'll love it; it's so *bad*."?

THE HUNGER

Fifty years ago, if you had told any girl—any nice girl—that she looked sexy, she would have slapped your face. Life was pleasant then. There was a lot of flirtation and very little fornication or, if your interests lay elsewhere, there were a great many mysterious threats and very little murder. People lived largely in the mind and always seemed to have some adventure to which they could look forward.

Now all that has changed. Nay, everything has been reversed.

In the 1980s, fulfillment precedes desire. This nasty state of affairs is reflected in many of our contemporary movies or, possibly, it is caused by them.

Just such a film is *The Hunger*; it should have been called *The Glut*. It drips with blood and oozes sex.

I myself belong to Vampires Anonymous and I can assure you that a vampire's life is not easy. After a while, you need a fix every few hours. It is a little like being a diabetic but much more like being a drug addict; you can expect no sympathy from anybody—especially not from the police. On the credit side of this lifestyle is the fact that you become very rich. In this film, Miss Deneuve lives in a town house big enough to justify the installation of an elevator and all the rooms are decorated in muted but perfect taste, with priceless works of art dotted about them. Presumably even fifty cents put into the capable hands of Mr. E. F. Hutton in the time of the Pharaohs would yield a considerable yearly income by 1983. Apparently, you also become strong. When Mr. Bowie grows too old to walk or even crawl, his hostess is able with no obvious effort to carry him to the attic and place him in his coffin beside a few of his precursors. She looks like a tired housekeeper taking an extra blanket to one of the guest rooms. The disadvantages of vampirehood are that, while remaining a prey to hideous appetites, you cease to feel any emotion and are incapable, except when slitting somebody's throat, of making any swift movement. Miss Deneuve drifts about her house like an underwater swimmer. Indeed, *The Hunger* is like a vehicle for an unhealthy Esther Williams, photographed not in her habitual bright blue swimming pool but in a badly kept canal.

The plot of *The Hunger*, if such there be, concerns a rich woman who spends her life giving strangely lethargic music lessons or bickering wanly with Mr. Bowie as though they were two touring actors filling in a Sunday afternoon in a provincial town. In flagrant defiance of the Trade Descriptions Act, she offers her victims everlasting life. They learn later that they have only been given three or four hundred years, at the end of which niggardly span they start to age at the rate of several years a day. When we first meet Mr. Bowie, this process of disintegration has already begun.

Meanwhile, in another part of town, Miss Sarandon is having a jolly time watching a small monkey turning into a skeleton. She is working on a cure for premature senility. Mr. Bowie hears of her research and pays a visit to the hospital where she is employed. Here, we encounter the film's only glimpse of reality. He sits all day in the waiting room growing older by the minute. No one comes to his aid. In the very next sequence, we are right back in our world of fantasy. Miss Sarandon calls on him without mentioning money. A likely story! She meets Miss Deneuve and they become lovers. How much time passes, it would be hard to guess, but one fine day there is an earthquake. The house rocks, the coffins in the attic burst open, and the living dead arise from their crumbling inertia to revenge themselves upon their hostess, who then also lapses into instant decay.

Why? How? What does it all mean?

I have demanded an explanation for these events from several people, including the kind gentleman who procured complimentary tickets for your editor and me at the 8th Street Playhouse (where incidentally the patrons are treated as though they were royalty). So far, no satisfactory exegesis has been forthcoming. In fairness to the film, I ought perhaps to admit that I am by nature feebleminded and that toward the end of the picture, Mr. Steele's attention was diverted from the screen by an unusual incident that occurred in the auditorium. A gentleman who had arrived conspicuously late and seated himself near to us left surreptitiously earlier, taking Mr. Steele's briefcase with him. Your dauntless editor pursued the thief out of the theater into the lobby, and up the stairs to the gent's. There, the culprit vanished, but the case was found on the floor of a locked cubicle. That you are at this moment reading your current issue of *Christopher Street* is due to a miracle. Nothing was stolen. Needless to say, the management was abjectly apologetic and called the police immediately. They arrived but arrested nobody.

Somewhat shaken by the film we had just witnessed and the disaster we had so narrowly escaped, Mr. Steele and I went to a charming café nearby to steady our nerves. There, he was kissed over by a delightful lady who knows more about the future than most people remember about the past. She was in a state of high excitement. She had just received from a customer, to whom she had promised a *free* glimpse of things to come, a check for a sum of money that would have ransomed a king. I mentioned these events in order to make a comparison. Life is under no obligation to obey the laws of probability, but the movies are another matter.

However fantastic the premise upon which a movie is based, nothing excuses illogicality. A good picture is a series of gloriously foregone conclusions—a moral crossword puzzle. A scenarist has only two weapons with which to conquer his public. These are suspense and surprise. A truly great screenwriter uses both. He warns his audience of impending danger, but when disaster strikes, he makes it worse than anyone could have foreseen, though no more than his villains deserve. This will one day be known as the Hitchcock principle. I cannot say that *The Hunger* obeys this precept.

This, however, does not mean that the movie is not worth

seeing. The photographic tricks—the aging processes—are a wonder to behold. The photography is excellent throughout, but its very consistency tends to make its subject matter like the Sahara desert—impressive but boring.

The two leading ladies quite rightly do not act. They present their glorious bodies to the cameras, drift about the screen like sleepwalkers, and glow. They are incandescent with moral decay. The acting is done by the music student of Mr. Bowie. The former brings to the bizarre story its few moments of innocent common sense. It is through her alone that we receive any idea of a bunch of weirdos living in secret isolation in the midst of the normal world. Mr. Bowie's performance is even more remarkable. While seeming to doze in a hypnotic trance, he manages to make us aware that beneath his mask, he is sick, terrified, and consumed by an irreversible anguish. I confess that I was amazed by the high standard of his acting. I had thought of him as a pop star—a profession nothing can justify except the wages.

Finally, for outshining any other asset this film may have, is the charisma of its star. She is a very cool, up-market vampire, scorning to sleep in her coffin or wear joke-shop teeth. When I last saw her in Mr. Polanski's *Repulsion*, she was a pretty French girl. Now, she is a sophisticated, superbly elegant American woman. The one thing that I would not wish on my worst enemy is eternal life, but if anything could compensate anyone for having this appalling burden laid upon him, it would be the delight of being bitten by Miss Deneuve.

BURROUGHS

Miss Havoc once said, "Men are on the way out." As always, she was right but, on this occasion, she did not say enough. It is the entire human race that is becoming redundant not only at work—because of widespread automation—but also at play. In happier times, during their leisure hours people took an interest in one another. They gathered together in opulent or elegant surroundings to enjoy each other's company. Now, in all places of urban entertainment, the noise has become so loud and the darkness so deep that each reveler is virtually alone. Apparently he no longer requires that his identity shall be affirmed by his friends. He prefers to assure himself of his existence by constantly being photographed by strangers in the fitful gleam of flashbulbs that shoots like lightning through the feverish gloom of American night-life, and rather than conversing with companions, he likes to be interviewed by journalists who are now only people who will listen (even if they do not always believe).

This universal desolation is in no way diminished by the promiscuity that rages like a fire through the life of modern cities. In fact, with every smash-and-grab raid perpetrated upon the sexual organs of a stranger, contempt for the soul increases, but although we no longer wish to converse with our neighbors and our lovers, the desire to understand personality never quite dies. It is transformed into the craving for details about the lives of celebrities. When I was young, the public had to be content with "profiles" of famous people that appeared in newspapers and magazines, but profiles were precisely what these articles were—recognizable outlines and nothing more. When radio arrived, the sound of a well-known voice colored the dry biographical facts, but this was still not enough. Someone had to invent television so that images and facial mannerisms could be added. Television, however, is a medium perpetually on the move. Very few of its programs last for more than an hour. Therefore, finally, the cult of personality—the opportunity to get to know someone who has vanished forever from our daily lives—has moved into the cinema.

As far as I know, this kind of program began with *A Bigger Splash*. This was an evening spent in the presence of Mr. Hockney, a ramble through his home, an introduction to some of his friends, and even a moment or two spent standing with him in the shower.

After a long lapse of time, this fascinating experience was

followed by *My Dinner with Andre*, which, alas, was as boring as being alive. It told us where Andre went and what he did but not who he was. The only gentleman of my acquaintance who believes in money assured me that this venture grossed 18 million dollars. This rumor, however unfounded, would by itself inspire other moviemakers to attempt further personality films.

The newest of such programs is now showing at the Bleecker Street Cinema; it provides us with a daunting glimpse into the soul of Mr. Burroughs.

The Bleecker Street Cinema is as deliberately an "art" house as you are ever likely to frequent. The lobby is as barren as an abortionist's waiting room of old, the ushers are dressed like subversive art students, and the auditorium is the size of a preview screening room. Even so, it was not full. I was surprised, because this is an interesting movie.

Originally, I was invited by Mr. Steele to witness this film in the company of the most handsome man in the world. This offer was later withdrawn because your editor prophesied that the weather was so bad that by the time we left the cinema, whole horses and carts would be floating by in the street. (A likely story!)

I cannot, therefore, tell you what the most handsome man in the world looks like but I can say a little about the author of *Naked Lunch*.

To some extent, I knew what to expect from this movie about Mr. Burrough's because I have met him in real life. Our confrontation did not take place after midnight in a dim room behind a notorious bar but at five o'clock in the afternoon at a tea party (with cucumber sandwiches yet) presided over by Mrs. Mason. This fabulous lady is famous for having written *The Love Habit*— a how-to book telling middle-aged women the way to win and keep the love of schoolboys. It may have been because of this work that the two writers came to know one another. The polite setting that our hostess provided for my meeting with Mr. Burroughs was appropriate. He is one of the aristocrats of pornography, in the noble tradition of the Marquis de Sade. The sex lives of the proletariat are by the very nature of their surroundings rendered so deliciously sordid that no artificial degradation is required. It is the well-born and the well-heeled who must forever twist and turn between the stained sheets in search of the grit of depravity without which they might lapse into elegance or spirituality.

Within minutes of our being introduced, Mr. Burroughs made the statement that what was worth having was worth fighting for and I had said that what we can only retain by force we should try to do without. Our conversation was brief.

After my hour-and-a-half visit to the Bleecker Street Cinema, I feel that I know Mr. Burroughs a little better.

The film has its faults. The sound track is occasionally almost inaudible; the color is thin and often the screen has the Cassavetes look. People leave the middle of the picture before they have left the center of our attention, but these are purely superficial defects. The subject matter is enthralling. Mr. Burroughs looks like that quintessentially English actor Mr. Hyde-White, and he speaks with the voice of an exhausted George Sanders, but, with this minimal equipment, he tells a tale so horrifying that members of the audience sitting near us gasped.

There is one fictional episode. This is an operation performed by Mr. Burroughs on an unspecified patient with the aid of one of those plungers customarily used for unstopping drains. Blood be-spatters everything and almost engulfs Mr. Curtis, disguised as a nurse. Though less visually shocking, the factual parts of the story are far more bizarre. At times, it seems that the central character and almost everyone connected with him were in love with death. His companions on car rides urged him to drive more recklessly; his wife invited him to shoot a glass from the top of her head (he missed and killed her); his son died in early manhood.

Costarring with the hero are various famous people—Mr. Southern; Mr. Bacon, the British painter; and Mr. Ginsberg, the only person who seems to have been really fond of Mr. Burroughs. All these men are in marked physical contrast with the central character. They are big and round, whereas Mr. Burroughs has length but no breadth.

Because he recently celebrated his seventieth birthday at the profane church on Sixth Avenue, we know how old he is and we cannot but marvel that he has for so long survived so much self-inflicted punishment, injecting into his pale veins in a spirit of hilarious research almost any chemical that came to hand.

At the beginning of this documentary, he is described as the most influential writer of our time. I was surprised at this estimate of his work, but, as a person—as a member of the profession of being—Mr. Burroughs has no equal.

See this film.

QUERELLE

In an earlier number of *Christopher Street*, I wrote that what is required of a movie is a saga of human depravity. In *Querelle*, you have it.

Pornography is the selling of sex without mentioning the price. The guardians of our morals are forever complaining that the sex and violence that enliven our television entertainment are too explicit. In truth, the harm done is the result of a lack of realism. If, for instance, you push someone out of a high window and then look down on your handiwork, in real life your victim will not look as though he were taking a nap in the garden. Two ambulance men will soon arrive with plastic bags, and while gathering the scattered limbs, they will discreetly say to one another, "Do you think we've got it all?" Similarly, when you shoot someone, he cannot be relied upon to die either at once or in silence. He is quite likely to writhe about at your feet, screaming, crying, praying, or in some other way behaving badly. If viewers were shown their unpleasant responses to cruelty, they might be less inclined to commit murder. The same is true of fictional treatment of sexual encounters. In real life, they are seldom accompanied by violin music. The air about you does not turn pink and the nastiness of your opponent's body is not redeemed by being seen in soft focus. More important is the fact that even those who are willing to face sex without the benefit of these ameliorating agents seldom emerge unscathed. The results of a life of carnal pleasure were various forms of venereal disease, unwanted or, worse, partly unwanted pregnancy, nervous exhaustion, financial expense, and, unless you are careful to chose thoroughly unlikable partners, emotional involvement, but few of these consequences of promiscuity are ever brought home to love stories.

In its violence, *Querelle* is a deeply immoral film: It contains two murders, both of which are pointless and as slick as a Bond movie at its worst. The same harsh judgment cannot be passed on the sexual scenes. The appalling discomforts of passive sodomy are made abundantly clear and even the milder relationships are swathed in turgid psychological reactions.

Technically speaking, this film is not hard porn; you know what is never seen either in action or at rest. I do not think that this omission is an example of the director's good taste. It seems more likely that Mr. Fassbinder hoped that his work would be shown in other areas than that no-woman's-land that lies where Eighth Avenue meets Forty-second Street. Mr. Steele and I saw this picture in the Gulf & Western skyscraper that looks down with mercy onto Columbus Circle, which must be the most august filthy cinema in the world, but, in spite of this impressive launching, I doubt that this film will ever be generally released.

In an eighteen-page synopsis generously presented to us by the management, Mr. Davis, who plays the name part (one can hardly say "the hero") and whom you may have witnessed as the friendly sharecropper in "Roots," says that he does not consider *Querelle* to be about homosexuality and crime. I cannot think why he made this statement; the movie is about nothing else. Almost all the characters are whores or sailors, and the camera seldom leaves the brothel in which they meet to fight and fornicate.

The plot starts by being about the smuggling of opium into the French seaport of Brest, but this theme is speedily and glibly abandoned for an "A desires B who wants C who fancies D" mix-up as complicated as the story line of an eighteenth-century opera. Matters are made more confusing by the fact that (or so Mr. Steele claims) the sound track was originally in English but was later translated into a foreign tongue and now carries subtitles that occasionally give place to quotations from the classics flashed onto a white screen. A final touch of mystification is added by giving two parts to one actor for no reason whatsoever. Unlikelihoods are piled one upon another until, toward the end of the film, a naval officer is seen walking around with his arm across the shoulders of an ordinary seaman. At that point, credulity dies.

Beneath these superficial improbabilities lies an even greater confusion.

Presumably, Monsieur Genet endured a Catholic childhood. From this, he never seems to have recovered. Just as some people spend money as fast as they earn it so as to escape the tortures of having to do something sensible with it, so Monsieur Genet keeps attempting to fling away his immortal soul. In spite of all his farfetched efforts, it clings to his fingers like a toffee wrapper. He spent most of his early years in jail, until his crimes were so numerous that he was condemned to life imprisonment. At this point, the existentialist writer Monsieur Sartre staged a Norman Mailer by persuading the authorities to release the culprit on the grounds that he was a genius. If anything more is needed to expose the fatuity of the French nation, it lies in Monsieur Genet's pardon. Obviously a judge with any sense would have said, "Until this moment I was unaware that the prisoner before me had any means of staying alive other than robbery. Now that I am informed that all this time he could have been earning an almost respectable livelihood as a writer, I order him to be shot." Nothing as logical as this took place. Monsieur Genet became a celebrated author and wrote *Querelle de Brest*. It is an interesting book but nothing like as absorbing as Mr. Baldwin's novel *Giovanni's Room*, which is similar in theme.

Monsieur Genet's perpetual quest is for defilement, preferably at the hands of total masculinity—symbolized by vast sexual organs. He seems never to have known anyone of normal proportions. In this current movie, the tyrant is a Mr. Kaufmann, who is (I think) the same black gentleman we meet in *Veronika Voss* and other Fassbinder films. Here, he is perfectly cast—as handsome as the sun, as wide as the screen, with a neck thicker than his head. He is called Nono (but not as in Nanette); he rules the brothel in Brest and hires out his wife to the customers.

Monsieur Genet's moral scheme is worked out so that cruelty is good, tenderness (symbolized by kissing) is bad, and passive sodomy is the ultimate degradation. When even this sexual role does not provide a sufficiently satisfying sense of humiliation, there is always the betrayal of those whom you have led into trusting you. Secretly, I find this elaborate ethical structure quite absurd. I cannot see why it is more ignoble to lend your playmates one part of your anatomy rather than another.

Apart from all this spurious philosophizing and the operatic plot, *Querelle* has very considerable virtues. It is photographed through a gauzy twilight chiefly in shades of mauve and yellowish brown and is beautiful to watch. In this respect, it reflects exactly the prose style of the author, whose genius is for describing disgusting events in such a way that they seem poetic. The acting is universally good and Miss Moreau is outstanding. Abandoning her usual expression of contempt, she looks glamorous and suitably battered. Her powers as an actress can be measured by the fact that even when she goes into a detailed description of the differences between Mr. Davis's penis and that of her other lover, nobody laughed. Unfortunately, she is compelled to sing an absolutely ludicrous song, the words of which are from a maudlin poem by Mr. Wilde, while the tune is like a honky-tonk number that would be appropriate to Miss Tucker.

Readers may be cheered by noticing that everybody, even people in the background, is good looking, but the ultimate message of this film is depressing. If you long for assurance that somebody really cares about you, being buggered can never be a patch on being stabbed.

TOOTSIE

Tootsie is not a gay movie; it is not even a happy movie, but it is highly enjoyable in spite of certain weakness.

The story concerns a struggling actor, played by Mr. Hoffman, whose struggling girl friend fails to qualify for a certain part on television because she does not present to the casting office a sufficiently aggressive image. Her lover dresses up as a woman and wins the role. He falls in love with or, rather, since this is a modern film, begins to lust after the juvenile lead in the TV serial. He also becomes famous, but, after a while, public acclaim no longer compensates him for the complications his deceit has brought into his relationship with the girl and he abandons his imposture.

Nobody wins.

The central idea of pretending to be of the opposite sex is by no means new to Hollywood. Even to my scanty knowledge, it goes back as far as *Where's Charley?*—a musical that starred Mr. Bolger. This was a screen adaptation of a play called *Charley's Aunt*, which, it may amuse you to know, was running in London in 1895 at the same time as Mr. Wilde's *The Importance of Being Earnest*.

In those happier days, sex never was allowed seriously to interfere with our entertainment. There were no ambiguous overtones in Mr. Bolger's movie. Its idea of fun consisted chiefly of the hero darting awkwardly in and out of rooms to avoid detection, with glimpses of sock suspenders seen below swirling petticoats.

The classic, more sophisticated version of this transvestite theme came much later in *Some Like It Hot*. This film was less ambiguous in intention than *Tootsie* but, in many ways, much more daring. When, for instance, Mr. Hoffman—still disguised as a woman—shares a bed with Miss Lange, it is nothing like the romp that Mr. Lemmon enjoyed or endured with Miss Monroe in the berth of a sleeping car. In fact, the entire dialogue of the Jack Lemmon picture was much racier, but, then, it was written by Mr. Diamond, who is a movie star's best friend.

Moving forward from those mists of antiquity to the lifetime of readers of *Christopher Street*, we come to *Victor/Victoria*. Here again, the script is much funnier than that of Mr. Hoffman's film. I went to see *Tootsie* with your very own editor, Mr. Steele, who asked me why, if the film with Miss Andrews was wittier, it was much less popular. The answer seems to me clear but by no means simple.

Victor/Victoria is a gay movie. Everyone in it is gay or part-time gay or erroneously thought to be gay. This instantly makes it a specialized form of entertainment. Furthermore, the only people made ridiculous are Mr. Garner, who is seen to be as straight as Fifth Avenue, and the French police, who must be presumed to be heterosexual, or where will it all end? All this perversity is not really surprising. The movie is a remake of a 1930s German film. At that time, Germany was thought to be a land where every man, woman, and child secretly or openly wore a black garter belt. Such flagrant kinkiness may be distasteful to American audiences.

There is also a deeper reason for the different levels of public acceptance between these two films. Miss Andrews pretends to be a boy, which the world considers to be a step upward; Mr. Hoffman moves in the opposite direction. This is an unalterable law. When Miss Dietrich appeared in a white tie and tailcoat in Morocco, or in *Seven Sinners* in the uniform of a pretty officer of the American Navy, it was seen as a delightful, almost valiant gesture, but when Mr. Kaye and Mr. Crosby sang "Sisters," they were clowning. On a more serious level, consider that episode in *A Chorus Line* that so touched the hearts of gay Americans. I seem to remember that a young man is seen (one might almost say "caught") by his parents playing the part of a Chinese maiden. It was impossible to avoid the impression that Mum and Dad would not have been nearly so embarrassed if their son's first acting assignment had been that of a rapist or a murderer.

There is no sin like being a woman.

Consequently, though *Victor/Victoria* is a murkier tale than Tootsie, it is less comic because nothing is so hilarious to one human being as the humiliation of another.

The real weakness of Mr. Edwards's film was that Miss Andrews never truly seemed like a boy—not even the most homosexual boy in the world. She remained her indestructible self and her two songs were simply beautifully polished Julie Andrews cabaret numbers. Here, I think Mr. Edwards missed a trick; he should have inserted a sequence in which the adorable Mr. Preston could be seen teaching his protégée how to camp. When a drag artiste performs, she flexes her fingers to the utmost extent and twitches her hips like an awakened corpse getting the stiffness out of its limbs, while over her skull, her features slither as though we were observing them in a fair-ground mirror. None of these grotesque exaggerations was present in Miss Andrews's act.

It is quite otherwise with *Tootsie*. Mr. Hoffman becomes a woman before our very eyes. Left to its own devices, his face resembles that of a tired mongrel dog. That is why his appeal is universal. When he changes his sex, his features are totally transformed. He tidies up his face and instead of looking out of it as a man does, he presents it to the world like a shield, as women do. I thought his walk was slightly ill-judged; the paces are too short for the no-nonsense woman he has decided to impersonate. He should have adopted the Rosalind Russell stride. Everything else is perfect.

Everybody in this film acts excellently. Indeed, the work of Mr. Durning, who tries to woo Tootsie, is too good. It becomes distressing to see a man of such noble countenance taken for such an ignoble ride.

Except for a few excess words, the entire picture is surprisingly clean. There were no double meanings about the physical differences between being a man and being a woman, unless I missed them. I should warn you not to see this movie at the Art cinema on Eighth Street. Either its equipment is faulty or it had been given a poor print. Both Mr. Steele and I found some of the words difficult to hear. This mattered less than it might have done because most of the jokes are visual. Of these, by far the funniest is a glossy photograph of Tootsie with her arm around Mr. Warhol as proof positive that she is famous.

Tootsie has a quiet, almost wistful ending, which doesn't mar but also doesn't quite match the rest of the movie. Under the farcical main theme, we seem to hear played softly in the left hand a different melody. The hero confesses that when he was a woman, he felt closer to the heroine than he can ever expect to feel now that he has admitted that he is only a man. That this is at least part of the message of the film is confirmed by an interview in which Mr. Hoffman said that playing Tootsie had given him new insights into the disadvantages that women face.

It is, of course, a self-evident fact that nature made a grave mistake in creating two sexes; there was bound to be trouble. We see that now. Both men and women are abandoning their more extreme postures and, as they move closer together, we shall for a while be inundated by a flood of films about transvestitism and sexual ambiguity in general. I myself did not think that Miss Breckinridge was a true answer to this problem. I wait for the day when Mr. Capote gets his magical hands on the court files of the recent John/Diane Delia murder case.

What I always want from any movie is a saga of human depravity.

BETRAYAL

From time to time, every mature homosexual man should issue a solemn warning to all his young gay friends that they must never adopt, even unconsciously, an exile's view of normality. To this day, in spite of all that gay pride stuff, many of us who stand in the street, knee-deep in the snows of rejection, press our noses to the cold windowpanes of establishment and imagine that the carpet slipper setup that we see dimly on the other side of the glass is permanent, cozy, peaceful.

In fact, those who are on the inside are frantically trying to get out.

Most gay men are at some time asked, "Is it true that homosexuals find it extremely difficult to form lasting relationships founded on sexual attraction?" The reply is often that there are so many forces at work in our society that keep a man and a woman together but that drive two people of the same sex apart. A better answer might be that, owing to our peculiar temperament and our unique position in the world, we are forever free from the torture chamber of eternal love. The sterility of our relationships is, of course, the governing factor. If not for the sake of the offspring, it is very difficult to guess whence the "till death us do part" rubbish sprang. It is a myth hardly discernible at all in nature. As Mr. Porter would have said, "Doves do it," but most animals, birds, and fish remain with one mater for what an impresario would call a limited season only. In other words, an instinct not for perpetuating a personal, romantic dream but for the survival of the species prompts most living things to join forces as well as bodies with one partner until the offspring have learned to live on their own without parental guidance. One of the many things wrong with the human race is that its young take such an unconscionable time to grow up. This state of affairs is improving but it is still not easy to persuade a daughter to leave home before she is thirteen, and even if you succeed, some wretched social worker is likely to keep on bringing her back until she is eighteen. Eighteen years is a hell of long time to stick around with one person.

The three main characters in *Betrayal* (all as straight as arrows but not as swift) fail to stay this arduous course. The wife (Miss Hodge) has an affair with the best friend (Mr. Irons) of her husband (Mr. Kingsley). Never was the boredom of heterosexuality more precisely or more devastatingly enunciated than by these three people.

Mr. Pinter is a highly classical dramatist; he is always working his way toward a smaller, more ordinary area of human behavior into which he will dig deeper and deeper. In this respect, he could be said to be the opposite of the late Mr. Williams, who never stopped heaping more rhetoric onto an ever widening field of experience.

In this latest film written by Mr. Pinter, he narrows our view of the action as much as possible. Except for a waiter who serves the two men an expense-account lunch and a landlady who rents an apartment to the guilty lovers, we hardly catch sight of anyone except the three principals, but we watch them in the utmost detail so that we miss none of the subtle meanings in their eyes, which at all cost must never fall from their lips. The only glimpse of a desire for total commitment from her lover comes when the wife says, "Have you ever thought of changing your life?" She means "your wife." The only sign that the husband is annoyed at finding his best friend in his wife's bedroom is that he leaves the door wide open so that the other guests can see what is going on.

Americans frequently tell me that they consider London to be the most civilized city in the world. Possibly it is, but we must never forget that politeness is a way of dealing with people whom you do not like. *Betrayal* could be called *Channel Thirteen and a Half*. Mr. Pinter puts Englishness to the fullest use; he makes his characters members of the upper-middle-class intelligentsia, and because publishing has been described as a profession fit for a gentleman, they are a publisher, a publisher's wife, and a literary agent. The streets outside the windows that enclose their desperation are tidy and quiet; the books on the shelves in front of which they pace to and fro are by Mr. Auden. The clothes are as well chosen as the locations. Miss Hodge's dresses are expensive but not exciting, because in Britain, style consists of wearing garments no one can remember when you have left the room.

The infernal triangle has been the subject of many Greek

dramas and countless comic picture postcards, but here we have neither tragedy nor farce. This movie is the subtlest possible blend of comedy and pathos. It is so discreet that when Mr. Irons (who in a previous incarnation flung poor Miss Streep to the ground) slaps Miss Hodge's face, we watch him perform this ungentlemanly act through the kitchen window; we do not hear what dialogue provoked it. When, in a later scene, Miss Hodge weeps, we see her grief through the windows of her car.

The acting is uniformly good; that is to say, it is uniformly muted except that the eyes of Mr. Kingsley still smoulder darkly with that fire that prompted him to snatch India from Queen Elizabeth when he was Mr. Gandhi.

The affair that for a few years sheds a wan light on the lives of this trio is without passion and without poetry. The verbal extravagance of the wooing is phony ("Your eyes kill me"); the lovemaking is trite, but none of these remarks must be taken as my criticism of the film. They are the playwright's judgment upon people with small appetites and no real desire—on people who handle talent but do not themselves possess any.

At least, that is how I read this movie, but I walk on tiptoe through Mr. Pinter's mind. I know him slightly. Indeed, it was after seeing my now-notorious abode in Chelsea, London, that he decided to write his first play, *The Room*. I once asked him the foolish question "What do your plays mean?" "Mean," he repeated, with that rising inflection usually reserved for exclaiming "A handbag!" Pressed for further information, he said, "They are just what those people said on that day."

I saw *Betrayal* at Cinema 2 on Third Avenue, where I would like to report that the staff is exceptionally courteous. I was accompanied by Mr. Steele, who remarked that the house was unusually full for a twilight showing and that, after an uneasy start, the audience laughed in all the right places when the dialogue teeters on the verge of parody. He pronounced the film an unequivocal success. I, too, enjoyed the evening, but occasionally I pined for a little zest—perhaps a nude lesbian chariot race on ice.

1984

1984 was written as a political satire and read as a science-fiction fantasy. When it was first published in 1949, few people who shuddered at Mr. Orwell's prophesies thought that any of them would ever be fulfilled—except members of the gay community (at that time known as "The Queers"). To them, the whole horrifying situation described in the book was already happening nightly in British cities.

In January of this year, Mr. Steele and I saw a secret screening of *1984* and for me a certain irony pervaded the occasion. Nine years previously, I had watched Mr. Hurt acting with great intensity the story of my life, walking in terror along dark pavements, finally having his home invaded without warning by the police, and being threatened with eight years imprisonment. Now I beheld the same actor suddenly caught naked with Miss Hamilton in a rented room and being dragged away to prison by the grim servants of Big Brother.

Things don't change much do they?

In fairness to real life, I ought perhaps to mention that, even in Britain, the punishments for being happy are less extreme than the sufferings endured by the hero of *1984*. My brain was never washed (and it shows) and my face was not gnawed at by rats; it only looks as though it had been.

In the movie, the main objective of Big Brother, the absolute ruler of the state in which Mr. Hurt lives, are to suppress the orgasm and eliminate human relationships. His method is to forbid them. This is foolish; it gives them the glamour of all things that are difficult to achieve. The modern way of putting a stop to these follies is less openly sadistic but, in the end, it will be far more effective. Now the state allows us to pursue a life of pleasure with such persistence and such crudity that we must ultimately tire of it. One of the many hideous truths brought to light by the permissive society is that fornication is a bit of a chore.

The story of 1984 takes place in Oceania, a territory comprising what was once known as North America and Britain. It is perpetually at war with one other of two neighboring superpowers, Eurasia or Eastasia. Society in Oceania is divided into a privileged but by no means free Inner Party, a carefully controlled Outer Party, horribly like the English Civil Service, and the Proles, who correspond to the working class as it was in Dickensian times. This lowest stratum of society is more or less free to live in its own squalor, but the Outer Party, of which Mr. Hurt is a secretly subversive member, is under constant surveillance through television screens that cannot be turned off and from which are issued commands that must be obeyed. In spite of these conditions, the hero embarks upon a furtive affair with another Outer Party member. After a brief spell of happiness, they are betrayed by Mr. Cusack and tortured by Mr. Burton until they totally renounce one another. When they meet again, they realize wanly that their relationship is ended.

The film is faultlessly acted by the entire cast and the settings are perfectly photographed in the kind of lighting that prevails on Waterloo or any of the main-line railway stations in London. Any of you who may have seen *The Dresser* know that very little has to be done to English towns to make them look depressing. A tale of unrelieved bleakness is told with relentless accuracy to Mr. Orwell's novel, to which it is a kind of homage.

In 1955, the book was adapted for the screen somewhat more freely. It then featured the rather too-well-fed Mr. (Edmond) O'Brien and Miss Sterling, who never put a foot wrong in any of her movies. In those younger and happier days, the film industry was not prepared to offer its audiences a tale of quite such unrelieved despair. I seem to remember that at the end of his picture, Mr. O'Brien, in defiance of the state, made a public speech affirming his belief in human values and was killed. This version of her husband's work so upset Mrs. Orwell that as soon as she legally could, she withdrew that film from circulation. There is something touching but irritatingly pompous about this kind of gesture. If posterity is interested in Mr. Orwell, it can read his books. Movies are sacred and should never be destroyed. They should be shown from time to time and judged in their own right as good or bad according to the standards of whosoever happens to be evaluating them.

In England, the new *1984* just managed to be shown in the appropriate year. There, it came to the ever-watchful attention of Mr. Ackroyd, who is known and loved by all of you as the author of *The Last Testament of Oscar Wilde.* In his opinion, it is the human element—the love story—that is the weakest part of this picture. He found this section too long and too sentimental. My hands tremble over my typewriter keys as I make so bold as to contradict him, but I cannot refrain from stating that for me the bedroom scenes were not sentimental or, perhaps, merely not friendly enough. The girl, who admits to (boasts of) having engineered hundreds of these secret meetings with other men, seems such a worthless creature. Was it, I ask myself, worth the while of these lovers to risk so much for such diluted passion or even for so little fun?

Two days after witnessing the movie in Times Square, I went to a very discreet hotel called the Mayfair Regent to meet Mr. Hurt, who had been described by the press as coming to New York for some tub-thumping. Never was a tub more urbanely thumped— nay, tapped. By this, I do not mean that the actor does not endorse the product that he is representing. He believes in his latest movie all the way. When I questioned him concerning what I considered might be its weakness, he explained that, as he saw them, the lovers, though still wanly clinging to the notion of love, had been robbed of all but the frailest capacity for expression by their treatment at the hands of the state. I now accept this explanation.

I also asked him—because I thought that you would wish to know—what it had been like to come face to face with Mr. Burton. To my surprise, he said that the great actor was extremely nervous; also that he was in such a poor state of health that in the torture scene where he holds his hand before Mr. Hurt's weeping eyes and over and over again asks him how many fingers he sees, his arm had to be held in place by an assistant. We agreed that Mr. Burton admirably restrained his "public-address system" voice, looked wonderful, and radiated an appropriately commanding presence.

The question that remains is whether or not I can say that you will wish to see this film. Certainly, I dare not prophesy that you will enjoy it. Even in a preview theater (where laughter and tears are forbidden), certain members of the audience slunk out when the rats came on. However, enjoyment, in the lighter sense of the word, is not always the point of moviegoing. Did you enjoy *The Dresser*, in which every character was ignoble without the slightest coercion from the authorities? Can you remember being happy while watching *Battleground* or *A Walk in the Sun*?

I think the answer is this: If you sometimes think that the American government in its present form is not according you your rights in sufficient measure, watch *1984*, because you ain't seen nothin yet.

A STAR IS BORN

As in the famous old song, your Mr. Steele is now sitting on the banks of the Ohio, so I went with a different gentleman of equally refined tastes (he once ruled the Elgin Cinema; you cannot be more high-brow than that) to Mr. Warner's preview theater to see *A Star Is Born*. To my relief, he enjoyed the film and declared Miss Garland to be the very embodiment of American show business. He did not even feel the picture was too long but, then, he once sat through the whole of Mr. Gance's *Napoleon*, which to me was like eating uncut spaghetti; it seemed to go on forever. That epic was screened at Radio City and therefore seemed not only too long but also too wide.

For those of you who have never seen any of the many versions of *A Star Is Born*, the story concerns the girl singer of a small band who is taken up by a fading movie actor and made into a very successful musical star. As her fame increases, he watches his decline until, unable to endure the comparison between his fortunes and hers any longer, he kills himself. There is a famous French novel called Thaïs in which a monk, after a great struggle, converts a courtesan to Christianity. She becomes a nun but he takes to a life of debauchery. Miss Garland's movie has the same plot but translated into English. That is to say, in accordance with national values, sanctity has been replaced by success in the realm of entertainment.

In the new long edition, this sad tale is quite adequately told but with surprisingly little sparkle considering the screenplay was by Mr. Hart, and the fair name of Miss Parker appears on the list of credits. The film also lacks deep understanding of the gradual alteration in the relationship between the two main characters. As Miss Garland's rise to fame puts her in the ascendancy, she would almost unconsciously start to dominate Mr. Mason. He would pass from being her mentor to being a sly and inadequate servant. We needed at some moment to see her surreptitiously adding water to his Scotch or even openly reprimanding him too much.

If somewhat inadequately told, the tragedy is by no means poorly acted. Miss Garland is her eager, tail-wagging self and her costar is good as the ruined cynical actor. Everything about him works in his favor from his sheep dog's teeth to that curious voice, to which has been added a purring sound as though he was speaking beneath a roof onto which soft Irish rain was forever falling. He has by nature the most lightless smile in the business and when he is desperately trying to seem amused at his wife's description of her day's shooting, he is heartbreaking.

When the film opens, the two leading characters seem to be overacting or presenting themselves in such a stereotyped way as to embarrass the audience. For a moment, I thought that perhaps the clichés of the cinema might have changed since the film was made, but I soon realized that this could not be so because Mr. Brickford, as the studio chief, and Mr. Carson, as the publicity expert, are absolutely superb wearing their roles as casually as if they were bathrobes. Gradually, I became accustomed to the mannerisms of the stars; after all, they were playing the parts of stars.

What was harder to bear than anything for which the cast could not be held responsible was the truly awful look of the screen during most of the film. The sets are dreadful and Miss Garland is made up in such a startling way that her eyes seem about to take off from their sockets and her lips, which are by nature too prominent, are nearly always a shrill vermilion. In the few moments when she is not painted in this bizarre manner, she looks quite middle-aged, the lower half of her face full and heavy as though she were a lesser member of the British royal family.

Apart from *Judgment at Nuremberg*, in which she played hardly more than a bit part, this must be considered Miss Garland's most meaningful role. A morbid thrill ran like fire in stubble through the five people in the Warner theater when Mr. Mason said, "Don't let success change you too much," but even if we refuse to allow our curiosity about this film to be intensified by events that have taken place in the outer world since it was made, it remains a triumph. Go and see *A Star Is Born* but watch it without morbid fascination and do not expect any revelation from its increased length. The much-advertised additions consist chiefly of a few monochrome stills accompanied by almost incomprehensible dialogue and a typical clown number in which Miss Garland wears freckles and a funny hat.

Why were these excisions from the first print of the film preserved as though they were fragments of The Dead Sea Scrolls? Why, furthermore, was an opportunity found—nay, contrived—for distributing this very long but hardly improved version. All films (even Mr. Hitchcock's) are cut, but though bit players may weep, as a rule the rest of the world is slightly relieved.

I think we have to regard this weird phenomenon as part of the Judy Garland cult.

This mania did not begin with her death. A pleasant feeling is always generated by the demise of celebrity. The occasion gives us nonentities a lot to discuss and it provides us with a situation upon which to lavish those tears that our sons and our lovers find embarrassing and try to prevent us from shedding. It also proves to the envious that, ultimately, the stars are only our equals or we theirs if we can just find a significant way to die.

The worship of Miss Garland has turned out to be more peculiar and less ephemeral than this customary public interest. It started with her failure. On the first day of shooting *Annie Get Your Gun*, Miss Garland was replaced by Miss Hutton. The world shook. It was not possible to think that the star of so many nice, healthy movies had done anything wrong, so she became a self-evident victim. From that moment onward, she attracted the homosexual vote. These men did not so much champion her cause as wallow in her defeat.

How did Miss Garland race so far ahead of her nearest competition in the Degradation Stakes? Miss Piaff might have been a rival but she was disqualified; she was French and being French is a form of degradation in itself. A more edifying parallel can be drawn between Miss Garland and Mrs. Miller. All rights in the soul of this unfortunate woman have been brought up by Mr. Mailer. One therefore hesitates to mention the name of Miss Monroe, but it can at least safely be said that she, too, was racked by the lust for reassurance. She also became a cause for anxiety among her coworkers but not an object of contempt as Miss Garland did according to Mr. Bogarde, who was her costar in *I Could Go on Singing*. What prevented Miss Monroe from sinking to the lowest level of abjection was her looks. Even when all was lost, she remained beautiful. Miss Garland, on the other hand, totally lacked glamour. When I first saw *The Wizard of Oz*, I was appalled by her lack of prettiness, by her bulging eyes, her short neck. In her later films, she offset her plainness by weaving into her screen image an element of self-mockery, but she never became alluring. Indeed, she was hardly a woman; I do not recall ever seeing her half-naked or even in a transparent negligee.

This disadvantage gradually became one of her assets. She never inspired envy. No one's eyes narrowed or became green when they watched her win the love of Mr. Rooney. In fact, the world *gave* her Mr. Rooney unconditionally.

Miss Garland's ambitions onscreen were exceptionally modest, while in real life the world demanded such a lot from her. I think it was the combination of these two factors that raised this unhappy song-and-dance girl to be the patron saint of a group of men who, however much they differ in other respects, are united in the idea that they are persecuted by a heartless world.

ERNESTO

This movie contains the most romantic love scene ever depicted on the screen. It is more poetic than Lord Tennyson's description of Mr. Lancelot's adultery with Mrs. Arthur, more lyrical than the duet sung by Lieutenant Pinkerton and Miss Fly, more beautiful than the famous kiss sculpted by Monsieur Rodin.

We watched *Ernesto* in the very pleasant 8th Street cinema, where some months previously we had seen *The Hunger*. At that time, the events taking place on the screen did not hold your Mr. Steele's attention completely. When someone stole his briefcase, he was instantly aware of the theft and rushed in pursuit of the culprit, but during the present film, if anyone had asked him, he says he would have given him the briefcase rather than take his eyes from the picture.

The amorous sequence about which I am rhapsodizing takes place during the first twenty minutes of the film. Both aesthetically and for reasons of realism, this is too soon. The story never again reaches such a high level of intensity. Worse, the speed with which Ernesto and his lover arrange to consummate their desire makes the situation seem slightly facile. The boy is so young that he does not need to shave, while his lover is over thirty; the boy is Jewish, whereas his friend is Italian; the boy is middle class but his friend is a manual laborer. These barriers would not be easy to cross even now when all our values have collapsed. Seventy years ago, they would have been impassable.

To some extent, the love scenes depend for their special quality on the photography. The laborer is extremely handsome but does not appear to have been technically idealized by soft-focus lenses and rosy lighting. The incident is also enhanced by the way it is prepared for the screen. The embrace can be seen to be sodomitic but you know what is never shown. However, the essential luminosity of this sequence emanates from the acting of Mr. Placido.

In a sexual encounter, there is a moment, which most people never experience, in which the orgasm is followed by a lull of sad but transcendental peace. It flows out of every pore of the body in a surge of gratitude to the love object. It is this blend of triumphant joy and humility that the actor manages to convey to his audience.

This episode is vastly different from the parallel incident in *Querelle*. There, the divine Mr. Kaufmann was in no way beholden to Mr. Davis, who, in turn, had no wish to gratify anybody but only to undergo that pain and degradation that to Mr. Genet represented the guilt and atonement with which he was so ludicrously obsessed.

To this extent, *Ernesto* is more pornographic than Mr. Fassbinder's work. The Italian picture *does* try to sell sex to us for more than it can ever be worth. Mr. Samperi can be accused of the same sentimentality that weakens Mr. Forster's novel *Maurice*. You cannot go and live forever in an English wood with a gardener (what would your mother say?) and, similarly, there is no such thing as a romantic Italian laborer.

I myself have never visited the Mediterranean but I once had a friend who spent most of his holidays in Sorrento. Concerning the sexual climate of that terrain, he said, "The thing about Italy, my dear, is that you can't make a mistake." He meant that no advance made to a native could ever be unwelcome; at worst, it could be inconvenient. I also questioned a woman about her experiences in Rome. On one occasion, she had gone with a flock of tourists to marvel at the interior of a church. When, for a moment, she strayed from her companions, she was approached by a man whom she mistook for a church official. She assumed that he wished to show her a sacred relic and, in a way, he did. To her maidenly protests against his private exhibition, he only replied, "It won't take long." This my friend told me was no recommendation. From this assorted information we may conclude that Italy is the land of instant sex—not of the Anglo-Saxon stuff you have to peel and bring to the boil.

Ernesto is also involved in a deeper lie than any arising from mere nationality.

The sexual relationship upon which this film dwells is the initiation of a teenager into sodomy. He is seen to experience discomfort, but this surely is hardly realistic. As every schoolboy knows, the first time he is in this situation, it is like undergoing a colostomy operation without an anesthetic. Even women, when initially subjected to sexual intercourse, have a terrible time. In one of Mr. Cassavetes's movies, a deflowered virgin, lying beside her seducer says, "I never dreamed it could be so awful."

The happiest moment in any affair takes place after the loved one has learned to accommodate the lover and before the maddening personality of either party has emerged like a jagged rock from the receding tides of lust and curiosity. Even then, for homosexual men complete fulfillment is very rare. Where only sensation and frequency of sensation are the point, monotony rapidly leads to experimental extremes, in the hope that variety of circumstances will add spice to the chore of several orgasms a day, but, in fact, sex at the back of a classroom or in an elevator between the mezzanine and the second floor is more enjoyable in the recounting at parties than at the time when it was experienced. Those who avoid these smash-and-grab raids are really hardly interested in physical sensation at all. They merely long for a Pepsi-Cola model with whom to be seen arriving at or, better still, departing from some fashionable bar.

People are forever objecting to sexual acts between men on

the grounds that they are sinful or dirty or anatomically harmful, but the real trouble is that they are contrived. In the early stages of an affair between a man and a woman, it can at least be hoped that their union can be taken for granted—that they can merge in it almost by instinct. This can never be the case for two men; before they get into bed, they must have a board meeting. The soul doesn't have a chance.

Apart from the great love scene, *Ernesto* is, I regret to say, an unsatisfactory film because its hero is such a trivial creature. He is a middle-class Jewish teenager employed (more out of pity for his mother than for his usefulness) to supervise the piecework of his boss's carters. He is lazy and impertinent to his benefactors, nags his mother for money and, worst of all, is capricious with the adorable Mr. Placido.

He spends the traditional afternoon with a prostitute who refuses to accept all the money he offers her (how golden-hearted can you get?) and finally becomes betrothed to a girl when it is really her brother that he fancies. At the end of this sordid tale, we leave him socially elevated, financially secure, and invincibly smug.

As this movie is called *Ernesto*, we do not really have the right to expect anything but what we are given. The picture is consistently well acted, beautifully photographed in the green-gold light of a painting by Mr. Vermeer and attractively costumed in the period of 1910. Nevertheless, I couldn't help longing for the narrative to be not about a young bourgeois's ignoble dash for cover but about a beautiful Italian workman's broken heart. Because I was brought up on film's featuring Monsieur Gabin, there were times when I thought the lover might stab his little friend. I would have liked that.

Quite often, when reviewing movies, I have found that apparently my heart was not in the right place and I have known at least one other person who suffered from the same feeling of displacement. I took him to see *King Kong* (the first time round). During a dramatic episode in which a certain Miss Wray lay gibbering across Mr. Kong's wrist, my friend, in a voice shrill with irritation, cried out, "I can't think what he sees in her."

THE BIG CHILL

For this review, I apologize. I write it with the fear hanging over me that I may be compelled to finish it in long hand on an aeroplane. Although my typewriter is portable, if I use it in midair, I may disturb other passengers who are working away at their gin lag before disembarking at San Diego. It is also unfortunate that *The Big Chill* is the weakest film that so far I have witnessed with Mr. Steele.

It starts with a funeral, which is always nice and which places it immediately in the great tradition of *The Third Man*, the only good picture ever to come out of Britain, but it differs from that masterpiece in that it is not the coffin but the film that is full of old bones. After the burial and the tearful speeches, we are left with four men and three women who were at college with the deceased and an extra, younger girl who was living with him and who boasts that she had sexual intercourse with him a few hours before he killed himself. She doesn't seem to have learned anything from this sinister fact. These people spend a lost weekend fornicating and talking in a house where the dead man and his girl friend occupied the basement in the capacity of care-takers.

No suicide note was left.

Some of his friends are as annoyed as I was about this, but one of them seems to feel that this omission should be praised as a gesture of defiance of the conventions.

No mystery unfolds. The film is as disappointing as being alive, but I must hastily add that it is very carefully prepared for the screen; at all times, it looks natural and the acting is superb in that there appears to be no acting at all. If there is a weak link among the members of this house party (which is a cross between a wake and an orgy), it is the man who plays the part of the television star. He looks just right—as cozy-tough as Mr. Selleck, as luscious as Mr. Reynolds, but he blends in effortlessly with his companions. This seems unlikely. In real life, his fame and his wealth would set him apart from ordinary mortals; he would spend hours on the telephone and would be quite incapable of talking for long about anything but show business.

It is time that the cinema and television divided the available material more sensibly than they do at present. *The Big Chill* is an almost-perfect television play. It is very thoughtful but very slight. Without embarrassment, we can watch it with a cup of tea and a piece of toast beside us, while we file our toenails just as we do when listening to the depressing confidences of our friends.

The movies are another matter. They are an outing. For them, we put on a clean shirt; for them, we nag a friend into going to the cinema with us so that their presence will mitigate the sin of a life of wanton pleasure. Above all, they are an occasion for which we are willing to pay. We expect—we deserve—more than we ask of television. Unfortunately, these two forms of entertainment have recently usurped each other's kingdom. Sitting innocently in our own homes, we can now be shot twice and questioned by the police any number of times, while in the cinema we merely watch people sitting around a cluttered breakfast table or wandering hand in hand through the autumnal countryside and uttering half-finished sentences about the past.

This is a general complaint. There is a more specific fault in *The Big Chill*. It tries to give local significance to a universal situation. You may point out that *Betrayal*, which I praised, does the same thing, but there is a difference. Mr. Pinter's play was mocking, critical of its subject. The present film, as far as I could detect, has no irony. There is, in fact, only one moment of humor. The most disturbed member of the cast, while in town, crosses a red light and insults a policeman. He is escorted back to the house in which he is staying. When the local cop catches sight of the television star standing on the lawn, he cannot conceal his amazement and offers to drop all charges if the actor will demonstrate how he jumps into his car on the television screen. If this film is ever shown anywhere else in the world but here, this scene will be regarded as wild parody, but it is not. Recently, when I was walking innocently down Second Avenue, I was beckoned by the occupants of a police car and asked my name. I gave it to them and added, "Am I illegal?" "No," they replied, "we just wondered how the show was going."

Apart from this comic incident, the film is sententious. All the main characters are in their late thirties. It would, therefore, have been in the 1960s that they would have reached late adolescence, experienced their first daunting encounters with the real world, and formed their most censorious opinions concerning it. The film treats the sixties as though they were a specially important time in American history and they were. It was in 1963 that what was then called "the missile gap" was at its widest. That is to say, it was then that American nuclear supremacy was at its greatest. That was the moment when the President could have destroyed the rest of the world with the least fear of retribution—except, possibly, from You Know Who.

Rule now; pray later.

This is not, however, the opinion expressed by this film. Instead, it chooses to regard the sixties wistfully as a time of spiritual hope in which the young would suddenly bring peace to all mankind, when in fact they were all tottering about some campus or other weak with debauchery and senseless with drugs.

It is not only history that repeats itself; it is also historians who repeat one another. In America, they share a passion for decades; they are forever saying that the fifties were like this and the sixties were like that, as though on January the first every ten years, everybody suddenly changed his style of dress or his political posture.

The dim feeling of regret that pervades every frame of this film has nothing to do with any particular decade. Almost all men, regardless of when they had the misfortune to be born, look back on their college days as a time when they might have changed the planet's destiny and they resent the approach of middle age as a period when they will join the world they despise because they cannot conquer it.

I have news for them. The world is cozy.

BROADWAY DANNY ROSE

In order to meet Mr. Steele and be taken by him to see Mr. Allen's latest movie (though, by the time you read these words, he may easily have produced another), I went all the way to Hudson Street, which I discovered is what happens to Ninth Avenue when all is lost. There, as I had been promised, I found a new bookshop called A Different Light. The Manhattan premises are a branch of an emporium of the same name in Los Angeles, where, in a time cutworn, I met a great Mr. Rechy, so I entertained great hopes of this occasion. I was not disappointed. The place was as crowded as the subway at dusk but with a less defeated-looking clientele. I had no idea that there were so many people in New York who can read. When, at a later date, I mentioned this phenomenon to my landlord, he warned me that I should not assume that all the young men who tarry in kinky bookstores are interested in what is displayed on the shelves.

After drinking as much champagne as we could in the time and space available, your editor and I walked to the Quad, which is one of my favorite cinemas. There, by using two of its screens, the management is able to show *Broadway Danny Rose* almost every half hour.

By modern standards, Mr. Allen's latest work is very short. It lasts only an hour and twenty minutes but to make even the briefest movie costs hundreds of thousands of dollars. Therefore, because anything that involves a large sum of money is sacred, something kind must be said about it.

This isn't easy.

The film has only two real assets. One of these is that it is sexless. Sex has been the undoing of present pictures. This I can prove. About a month ago, I was invited by Columbia Pictures to a secret showing of *Against All Odds*. In a way, this is an excellent movie. It has a fast-moving and remorseless plot, but its lurid sexuality is its downfall. It is remade from a long-dead film called *Out of the Past*, to which it is inevitably inferior. In both stories, two men, who used to be friends in a shaky sort of way, reach a state where they are ready to kill one another because of a woman. As was the custom in happier times, the original version did not tell us how far the relationship between the girl and the men had progressed (or deteriorated). It was therefore possible for us to think her alluring and mysterious and we could imagine that her admirers thought of her in the same way. The contemporary edition shows the leading lady in situations so grossly sensual that it is impossible to like the wretched creature—let alone adore her. By the end of *Against All Odds*, almost everybody has been killed, including the glorious Mr. Karras, but who in his right mind would commit murder, would throw away his immortal soul for a girl with whom he has already had sexual intercourse in various decorous circumstances? In my experience, men do not even speak kindly of such women—much less do they care about them.

In *Broadway Danny Rose*, I am glad to be able to assure you that nothing unpleasant takes place. The audience is not told much about Mr. Allen's girl friend and we can only guess how well he is acquainted with her. This makes his interest in her plausible and even bestows upon their story a certain unexpected sweetness.

The other asset possessed by this film is the young woman herself. We are given an entirely new vision of Miss Farrow. Gone is the evasive elegance that she wore like a bridal veil when she was the Great Gatsby's true love and gone is the subtle moral obliquity that she evinced in *Rosemary's Baby*. In that picture, you may remember that she was married to Satan, for which her private life may have provided a significant rehearsal. In her new film, she has humanized—almost brutalized—herself. This makes it possible for us to accept that she betrays Mr. Allen. She is a sort of tough, latter-day Cressida. When she apologizes for her perfidy, the hero forgives her. I did not. It is high time for everybody to learn that rottenness has a certain lure but that abjection does not. It is an unalterable law that no one may apologize for anything that has been done deliberately. It only makes matters worse. It is a transparent attempt, having indulged natural baseness, to avoid paying the price.

At the end of the film, reminding us a little of Mr. Keaton, Mr. Allen makes a long run through the streets after Miss Farrow. If he had done this in order to strike her a blinding blow in the face, the movie would have been a masterpiece. I do not wish Miss Farrow any harm, but I would have liked to see the character she plays punished for her duplicity.

The fundamental weakness of *Danny* is that it lacks singleness of purpose. The story is diffuse to say the least. Because of all the champagne I had been given at A Different Light, I may have dozed while this unlikely tale was being unraveled. What I recall is that Mr. Allen is suspected of betraying someone to a rival gang; he and his girl friend are pursued by this man's brothers. They lay the blame on a convenient ventriloquist and that section of the story ends. Then Miss Farrow betrays Mr. Allen by recommending his only successful client to a more powerful agent whom she hardly knows. Shall I go on? These events are related by someone sitting in a restaurant frequented entirely by men talking about show business. Mr. Steele was of the opinion that this somewhat specious device explained or, at least, excused the improbability and the diffuseness of the narrative. I cannot disagree. After all, he is the editor of an illustrious magazine. It is certainly true that the events in this movie are almost as haphazard as the things that happen to us in real life and considerably more annoying because we do not pay to experience real life—or do we?

Mr. Allen is trying to occupy the heavily mined terrain between comedy and farce. This is a mistake. It means that no situation is taken to its wildest limits. For instance, at one moment, gangsters tie him face to face with Miss Farrow. Imagine how hilarious the incident would have been if in one of Mr. Kaye's pictures, that greatest of clowns had been bound to Miss Mayo! On another occasion, Mr. Allen's best client sings, but either the sequence is too long or else the song is not good enough. Everything is half-cooked. We are never really frightened of the mobsters; we can't bring ourselves to love Miss Farrow; we are only mildly sorry for the hero.

The trouble may be that Mr. Allen makes too many movies. When Miss Davis was asked whether she would make any more pictures, with glaring eyes and mouth upside down she replied, "I may have to." This cannot be true for Mr. Allen. He has never had to buy 365 pairs of nylons a year; his image is painstakingly thrift shop. He could go into a monastery for a year and come back to his adoring public with something out to the last detail.

At the moment, what he has given us is a sketchy chain of events leading to a half-hearted liaison between a helpless man and a not very likable girl.

ARMED AND DANGEROUS

The opposite of a Western is not an Eastern. That word would only describe those dreary movies in which one oriental gentleman thrusts his bare foot into the face of another. The antithesis of a Western is an urban and that is just what *Armed and Dangerous* really is. It has a glib, fast-moving plot with lots of action, less thinking, and almost no kissing. There are easily recognizable baddies, clearly defined goodies, and instead of riding, riding, riding, we have driving, driving, driving. At the end, there is even a stampede of cars at least as thunderous as the last sequence in *Red River*. As the dust clears over this metallic orgasm, many vehicles are seen lying on their sides, their once-bright headlights now glazed in death.

Dry your tears.

At least by then the unfairly discredited sheriff's good name has been restored. He doesn't "get" the heroine (who is allotted to his deputy, a Mr. Eugene Levy), but we all know that is because he is destined (like Mr. Destry) to ride again.

The secret screening that Mr. Steele and I witnessed at the United Artists cinema was what in England is called a "Saturday morning show" in the middle of a Monday night. Appropriately, the audience was made up largely of children, who applauded the triumph of good over evil and cheered Mr. Candy the moment he appeared.

Who, for one reason or another, would not?

To watch him—during the first few minutes of the film— climbing a tree in a policeman's uniform as tight as a coat of paint was an experience never to be forgotten. He is the latest screen- filler—going on where Raymond Burr left off—if he has left off. He is a sly, laughing Orson Welles. If a man is allowed to be a movie star, Mr. Candy is it and this is entirely his picture. In it, he plays the part of a cop brought low by the perfidy of other cops. On leaving the force, he joins a group of security men. Forced to become a member of their union, he discovers it to be a corrupt organization whose boss is planning to steal its funds by hijacking the armored car that is supposed to transfer the money across the city. Mr. Candy, on foot, on a motorbike, or in a truck, and his sidekick with the girl in an armored car race about the streets in an effort to thwart the machinations of the villains.

The rest is hysteria. Never have I seen so much metal impacted, melted, or broken.

Mr. Lester, who directed this picture, indulges his star in every conceivable way. In old Westerns, doors were built low so that Mr. Wayne could be seen to stoop as he entered the saloon. Mr. Candy is given a bike, which he seems to ride as though it were a kiddy car. He changes his costume as often as Miss Dietrich used to. At one moment, like her, he gets into drag in which he looks almost as divine as Divine. On another occasion, for no reason at all, he appears in the gear of a 1920s aviator.

In a way, this is a highly immoral film. It is made for the very young and will undoubtedly give them the idea that they can drive as recklessly and the like without doing anyone serious harm. Not a pint of blood is spilled. Victims climb unscathed out of cars that have been reduced to abstract sculpture. This is bad propaganda, but, like so much that is immoral, it is highly entertaining. It is presented on the screen with quite astonishing skill. The big crashes are all in close-up; their flames scorch the faces of the audience. It is impossible not to feel that the people in the greatest danger must have been the camera crew.

Thinking over a movie like *A & D*, a question arises that requires a serious answer. Until now, I would have said that what distinguishes heterosexual men from human beings is their inordinate and misplaced love of machinery. My father, for instance, spent every weekend of his life in his garage. He would have winced at every frame of Mr. Lester's film, but modern audiences gloat over the dismemberment of vehicles of any kind. The hatred they once directed at screen Germans and later at screen Martians, they now focus on machines; they long to see them die.

Why is this?

Perhaps cars have taken over the role once played by women. Men may have come to resent their complete dependence on them. Perhaps on Sunday mornings, as suburban householders wash their cars, they curse them under their breath.

Could we save the world simply by persuading everybody to walk?

THE FOURTH MAN

The Fourth Man is not hard porn because although the audience is regaled with a glimpse of you know what the very moment the central character staggers out of bed, it is always seen at rest—never prepared for action. The movie is not even soft porn, because pornography is an attempt to sell sex without mentioning the price. Here, the wages of sin are quite clearly death. Furthermore, scenes of sexual activity are not given the nauseating gauzy treatment that is customary in so many modern films. Instead, it is depicted as the nasty, slightly ludicrous pastime that it truly is.

Almost from the beginning of the picture, violent extermination stalks the screen either in the lurid dreams of the antihero, played by Mr. Krabbe, or in the actual narrative. Even the home movies of the heroine, played by Miss Soutendijk, are unflinching records of the various ways in which her three husbands have met their ends.

The first spectacle of extinction comes in the form of a fantasy in which Mr. Krabbe murders his flat mate by strangling him with a bra that just happens to be lying about their apartment. (Who wears this garment is not stated but why should it be? Perversity is in the very air of Holland.) As the boyfriend is practicing the violin before breakfast, silencing him seems a fairly natural act. Indeed, we can say more. Murdering anyone who plays the violin is justifiable homicide. All the same, this entire incident is nothing more than a bloodstained herring. Mr. Krabbe commits no subsequent murders and the young man is never seen again.

This kind of wanton depravity garishly ornamented with symbolism is the main weakness of this picture.

The story tells us about a thoroughly unlikable author who visits a seaside town to deliver to its literary group a lecture peppered with aphorisms. On the way there, he sees a young man to whom he takes a fancy. Later, this object of his desire turns out to be the lover of the treasurer of the literary group, a woman with whom he spends the night. The usual permutations follow. First, there is a scene in which the author copulates with the treasurer. Miss Soutendijk gratifies her appetite for Mr. Krabbe by straddling him. This in movie terms is the new position and possibly marks the industry's acknowledgment of equal rights for women. Next, the heroine is ravished by her more permanent lover in a more conventional posture. This incident is observed by Mr. Krabbe through a keyhole. He becomes so excited that he masturbates. This is such a stock scene in all pornographic movies that I expected to see him dressed in the uniform of a butler. Finally, the two men start on one another. This last abortive meeting takes place in a family vault where the ashes of the heroine's three former husbands are kept. When the author catches sight of the three urns and reads their labels, his erection collapses. He realizes that the girl in the erotic triangle is a witch. This thought might not occur to the average American, but in the Netherlands, witches are as plentiful as photographers are in Manhattan. Mr. Krabbe warns the young man that he will be Miss Soutendijk's fourth victim but, as any fortune-teller can inform you, fate is inexorable. On the way home from the cemetery, there is a car accident and the lover dies. Mr. Krabbe is unharmed because while fornicating with the witch, he invoked the names of Jesus and Mary. When told this, the doctor asks, "Mary who?"—the only joke in the whole movie. The grim saga ends in hospital with the author lying in a mild state of shock beneath a crucifix.

People of my generation have all enjoyed movies (chiefly starring Miss Dietrich) in which the heroine luxuriates in a delicious life of sin for an hour and a half but for a few final minutes, to placate the censor, puts on some very dull clothes and takes to redemption. However, the final scene in *The Fourth Man* is the most sanctimonious copout in the history of the cinema.

All through the film, sex, witchcraft, death, and the Catholic faith are inextricably woven—nay, flung together. Netherlanders seem to have a lot of trouble with their immortal souls. I imagine that this is a sincere national preoccupation that the rest of us find difficult to understand, but in the movie industry, it has begun to be exploited purely for the sake of sensationalism. Now that watching mere fornication has become a form of family entertainment and even the right of perverse sexual activity hardly sells an extra theater ticket, what is left but blasphemy? This film is full of it—the worst instance being a moment in which in the mind of the antihero a figure on a crucifix in a church changes into the body of the young man he so fervently desires. Some years ago in England, a blasphemy lawsuit was brought against *Gay News* by a certain Mrs. Whitehouse. The paper had published a poem by Mr. Mirkup that described the sexual feelings of the men who prepared for burial the body of Jesus of Nazareth. I dread to think what will happen if *The Fourth Man* is ever released in Britain. In the Times Square screening room, the effect was mild. The gentleman sitting next to me laughed heartily while a vast spider killed a fly caught in its web, but he slept through much of the rest of the film. If we are dealing with sorcery, this picture has none of the Gothic power of Mr. Dreyer's classic *Day of Wrath*; it hasn't even the single-mindedness of *The Exorcist*.

If you are in the habit of seeing two films a week, go to this one. It has definite assets. It is short—only just over a hundred minutes—and it is never boring. The photography is good in the sense that the violence is extremely ingeniously contrived. The sound track is acceptable. Music is like a dog; the nicest thing that can be said about it is that you wouldn't know it was there. The acting is excellent—especially that of Mr. Krabbe as the cynical author. If you only go to the cinema once a month, you could still try it in a dry season, but I couldn't say that the story takes hold of you and drags you forward to an inevitable conclusion.

In fairness to the makers of *The Fourth Man*, I must record that it has won awards in Seattle, Toronto, Chicago, San Francisco, and various European cities.

SPLASH

During the years when I was only English, I went to the pictures with startling frequency—sometimes twice in one day. As we are speaking of the prehistoric age of the double feature, this meant that on those happy occasions, I escaped from real life for seven hours in twenty-four. It was during these spells in the "forgetting chamber" that I realized that I was American in my heart.

Now I have taken up permanent residence in Manhattan. You could say that, for the past three years, I have been living the movies. For this reason, I do not need to see them so desperately. I visit the cinema less often.

Nevertheless, on two beautiful successive evenings in May, I went to a movie. On a Monday, in a screening room filled to capacity in Times Square, I saw *The Fourth Man* and, on the following evening, in the half-empty Waverly cinema on Sixth Avenue, I witnessed *Splash*. The contrast between these two experiences could hardly have been greater. The first of these two programs was a highbrow debauch of depravity, destruction, sex, and blasphemy; the second was a cozy idyll about true love. The difference was inevitable. *The Fourth Man* came from the Netherlands, and the voice of Europe is a cross between a scream of frustration and a yawn of despair. The other picture is American and is therefore, if not an affirmation of perfection, at least a message of hope.

Both these productions, however, have things in common. In each the heroine is apparently a normal, attractive, blond young woman but is secretly something quite different. In *The Fourth Man*, she is a witch, bringing doom to any man who tries to win her love. In *Splash*, she is a mermaid who dares to venture on to the dry land of Manhattan in pursuit of a man she rescued when he was a boy.

There have been several movies about these alluring sea creatures. One was called *Miranda* and featured Miss Johns. She spent most of her screen time in a wheelchair, with a rug tucked firmly round her tell-tail, but occasionally she made indiscreet remarks such as "I haven't had a moment's peace since I set tail in this house." Being an English movie, it was a cozy domestic comedy rather than an aquatic poem. Another such fantasy starred Miss Blyth, whom Mr. Powell kept clandestinely in his bath. These films have more in common than a seductive and mysterious heroine. They pander to our fundamental need for an event—even a peril beyond our diurnal routine, however comfortable that may be.

In recent years, flights of fancy have usually taken the form of encounters of a nasty kind with science-fiction monsters. Such films allay, in a half-scary, half-humorous fashion, the genuine terror of the young generation in the face of the grim future that their elders are so busy preparing for them.

Splash is an agreeable diversion from these menacing preoccupations. It is advertised as requiring "parental guidance" before it can be safely seen. I can't think why. It has always been the suffocating influence of our mothers and fathers that has prevented us from hearing the siren's song or in any way extending our imaginative horizons.

The story could hardly be more innocuous. It begins by presenting two young brothers, one of whom represents the flesh and the other the spirit. The former spends much of his time groveling on the deck of a pleasure steamer so that he can look up the skirts of the female passengers. The latter is a solitary child who hates the world. When his parent leave him on his own for a while, he jumps into the sea. Underwater, he meets a young mermaid, but only for a moment before he is rescued.

This brief contact with the life beneath the waves confirms forever his innate "otherness." In adult life, as soon as he is able to take a holiday from his business in a fruit market, he makes a dash for Cape Cod. There, he again meets the mermaid, who follows him back to Manhattan, shocking the corrupt world with her naked innocence.

She only wears her tail when she is in the water. On land, she wears legs and very pleasant ones they are. This device makes it possible for her to pass as an ordinary mortal—at least for a while. Diaster strikes. A young scientist, who has caught a glimpse of the heroine underwater, becomes frantically intent upon proving his theory that mermaids exist. He tracks down his quarry and, by spraying her with water, converts her back into a part-time fish in the middle of a banquet in honor of the President of the United States. In consequence, the poor girl becomes imprisoned in the Museum of Natural History.

I am happy to be able to tell you that her lover abducts her and, after many hilarious adventures, she returns to her natural element.

During the last few minutes of this beautiful film, I must confess with head bowed in shame that I doubted that the authors would rise to the challenge with which the climax faced them. I feared that the lovers would agree to part wetter but wiser and that the hero would remain a mere mortal—but no! Suddenly the movie transcends its Disneyland boundaries and acquires a truly poetic dimension. While a woman in the audience burst into applause, the young man dove into the filthy waters of the Hudson, risking typhoid fever and heaven knows what other dangers for love, and I mean Love. As you know, in their quest for procreation, fish behave with considerably more decorum than mere human beings.

How right they are!

If this picture has faults, they are superficial and mercifully few. The sound track is too coarse; the eardrums are often slapped and banged and generally assaulted by cries and curses. Also the color is less winsome than it might have been. Miss Hannah looks gorgeous with her bright red-gold tail. Indeed, the film might well have been called *The World According to Carp*; but ought she not to have been the palest shade of green? Likewise, the hero, played by Mr. Hanks, is a shy American boy. I would have preferred him to be a haunted poet. The member of the cast whose character fits him like a glove bursting at the seams is the older brother, Mr. Candy; he radiates jovial carnality.

Deep down, this is a cautionary tale like so many other stories of visitants from elsewhere. It warns us not to assume that their natures are as gross and hostile as our own. Though the mermaid is not shot down by panicky troops as is customary in such situations, she is subjected to prolonged and pitiless examination.

When we left the cinema, Mr. Steele recommended a nearby Japanese restaurant, but there the seafare was not just raw but living. After our evening with Miss Hannah, I felt to touch it might be in bad taste, so we went to a delightful restaurant called The Derby on Macdougal Street, where we ate sole discreetly cooked. During dinner, we discussed *Splash* and decided that it is possible to ignore its symbolic values and simply enjoy its sweetness and its often riotous humor. The film is really a modern Doris Day affair reorchestrated for Esther Williams.

PLENTY/QUEEN KELLY

. . . of what?

Presumably of worldly possessions, but the heroine is excruciatingly English. We, therefore, never see her extravagantly dressed. She is tastefully clad and seems to occupy elegant surroundings with ever-increasing disgust. Why she does this, I never fully understood. The symptoms of this woman's mental disorder are evident but her disease is never named.

The film begins with Miss Streep being parachuted into occupied France during World War II. There she has a smash-and-grab sexual encounter with a fellow spy. When she returns to England, she finds employment making television commercials. Why? She obviously doesn't need the money, because she leaves the job with no better excuse than her own impatience.

Somewhere along the way she meets Sting and enlists his services in an effort to become pregnant. Their union is not blessed, so why is this incident included unless to show us what an unpleasant character she is? At another moment in the story, we find her in a mental home, but even madness she does not seem to take seriously.

After a lapse of practically everything including time, the duration of which, as Mr. Steele pointed out, could only be reckoned by a change in Miss Streep's hairstyle, she marries someone (Charles Dance) fairly high up in the Foreign Office. Again why? She doesn't even seem to like him. She ruins this benighted gentleman's career firstly by behaving appallingly at a hilarious dinner party given for Mr. Gielgud, with other assorted diplomats, and lastly by going to her husband's office to demand a promotion for him. At the end of this inconsequent tale, she is reunited with her wartime lover for a brief, fully clothed grapple on a bed in a rented room.

There is a sense in which mad people are more sane than the rest of us. They see things as they really are and cannot play that they are different—cannot rearrange them in some easily digestible order. Are we supposed to regard the heroine of this movie as such a person—as someone unable to return comfortably to smug peace after the life-and-death drama of Occupied France? Is the guilt of a life of ease too great for her to bear?

I would not express my bewilderment so brazenly if I had not watched this picture with Mr. Steele and, as an unexpected bonus, Mr. Patrick (at one time, the Lower East Side's resident dramatist), and been relieved to note that both these distinguished gentlemen were as dazed as I.

As I waited for Mr. Patrick to arrive outside the Murray Hill cinema, I saw in one of its showcases a pair of cuff links. These keep recurring in the film and are to *Plenty* what the word *Rosebud* was to *Citizen Kane*, but without the blinding impact. They were once presumably the property of the heroine's first lover and if this entire story is about a girl who never recovers from the effect of her first sexual experience, we have indeed been sold the mangiest of pups.

The press tells us that this film is an allegory of the fall of the British Empire. No wonder it is dreary!

We must not, however, totally condemn this picture. It is decorated with beautiful interiors; the dialogue, provided that we regard the heroine as mad, is always believable and the acting throughout is marvelously restrained.

There is also Miss Streep. She is a highly accomplished actress playing with complete conviction a variety of parts, but this very ability has its disadvantages. Her public never really gets to know her. Had she been born in happier days, she would have been a star. She would have been assured of a seven-year contract. During that time, unruffled by worldly considerations, she would, like an exotic fish, have swum down, down to the very center of her personality, where she would, forever after, have glowed with an unblinking phosphorescent light, changing only from time to time her hairstyle or her costume. We, in response, would have expected nothing from her but an occasional bland aphorism floating from buttered lips. In those days, we would have accepted without question the odd behavior displayed in *Plenty*; we would have known that she thought the world in which we live so happily was unworthy of her. After all, this was Miss Garbo's permanent posture. That era is past; the movie industry has been badly shaken, but we cannot lay all the blame on the shoulders of the film moguls. Ultimately, they will always give us what we demand. It was audiences who so foolishly asked that women, both on the screen and in real life, should be as boring as people. As Mr. Shakespeare has told us, the fault lies not in our stars but in ourselves.

I must not, however, imply that the star system never made mistakes.

A few weeks before my visit to Murray Hill, I went to the Public Theater to watch what has been called Mr. von Stroheim's lost masterpiece, *Queen Kelly*. Alas, it is no such thing.

Its greatest attraction is now its scandal value. Since its star, Miss Swanson, told all and worse than all in her autobiography, we know that this venture was financed by Mr. Joseph Kennedy, the father of all those politicians, for love of her or perhaps merely to keep her quiet. The movie that was screened on Lafayette Street showed only one third of the tale that its director had in mind. Even so, it lasts about an hour and a half and is consistently and irritatingly slow.

The plot, which is as complicated and as improbable as that of an opera, takes Miss Swanson from a convent where she is a schoolgirl through sundry disasters and to a brothel of which she becomes proprietress. The setting for all this action is a tiny middle-European kingdom tyrannically ruled by Queen Regina (Seena Owen). She is about to marry a debonair hussar called Prince Wolfram (Walter Byron), but he, having once clapped eyes on Queen Kelly (Miss Swanson), has fallen madly in love with her and cannot bear the thought of being wedded to anyone else. For this, he is flung into a dungeon and his true love is summoned to the deathbed of an aunt who persuades her to marry a lecherous cripple (Tully Marshall). That was as much as the film's distributors could stand. The rest of the narrative is given to us in prose printed on the screen by some modern researcher. The whole saga is rounded off with a portrait of Miss Swanson looking exactly like a drag queen. Her clown-white face is dominated by eyelids like mussel shells hanging over flinty eyes, while her black lips nestle in a corsage of orchids the size of palm trees.

The style of *Queen Kelly* resembles a parody of the works of Mr. von Sternberg—especially *The Scarlet Empress*. Banquets are given in which the diners sit at a table the size of a tennis court, with a footman standing behind each chair. In case we miss the point of these sequences, each course is paraded before our starving gaze. Both Mr. von Sternberg and Mr. von Stroheim seem to have been obsessed with lace and with candles, but Miss Swanson, though her face is wonderfully dramatic, is not as beautiful as Miss Dietrich—nor, incidentally, as Miss Streep. She cannot justify all this lingering, gauzy treatment. We begin to notice that her film lacks the one ingredient that every movie needs—variety of pace.

I never thought that I would find myself recommending moderation, but what I think we now need is something between the unsatisfying allusiveness of *Plenty* and the ponderous detail of *Queen Kelly*.

THE TRIP TO BOUNTIFUL

Like Mr. Jefferson, I hold certain truths to be self-evident. One of these is that the four great actresses of our time are Julie Harris, Geraldine Page, Anne Bancroft, and Kim Stanley. In *The Trip to Bountiful*, Miss Page once again gives proof of her place on this list.

In England, when I was in *The Bride*, I thought that I would meet her on the set, but she had completed her small part as Sting's housekeeper and had escaped. All I could do was to question the dressers, who in the film industry are a race apart (if you know what I mean). When I found that behind the scenes democracy prevailed to an unusual—almost shocking—degree, I said, with an inflection rising to a squeak, "You didn't dare to call Miss Page 'Gerry,' did you?" The reply was a delighted boast. "Oh yes, we did. She's a crazy lady." I felt sure that the star in question would have been pleased with this remark.

In the end, some time after I had returned to America, I did meet her. She was lying on the floor of a dim basement room on the East Side of Manhattan. I could hardly, in these circumstances, kneel at her feet. I could only stand before her prostrate form and wait until she rose to greet me. This she immediately did, as though I was more deserving of respect than she.

We had been summoned by our director to do the "loops" —a term that, in my ignorance, I had never heard before and now hope never to hear again. It meant that we were required to reinforce the sound track of our voices by repeating for a microphone many of the lines that on the set had been drowned by rain, the wind, and the thunder. I was hopeless at this and to my amazement, Miss Page was nearly as bad—beginning too late for the image on the screen before us or too soon, or, occasionally, not beginning at all. From this encounter, I decided that she is not a highly technical actress so much as an inspired one.

I first saw her acting more than thirty long, dark years ago in *Hondo*; she was costarred with Mr. Wayne, who in England was called the midday cowboy. It was a wretched film and I didn't understand Miss Page's presence in it. Much later, I saw *Summer and Smoke* and it was then that I was struck by the self-evident truth mentioned earlier. Even when the cameras were busy with Mr. Harvey and Miss Page was slightly out of focus, it was fascinating to watch her preparing to withstand the insults that he was about to heap upon her. I assumed then that she was born to play the role of a victim. This is not entirely true but there is, in all the performances that I have seen her give, a brave acceptance of defeat. Even in *The Pope of Greenwich Village*, though she outfaces the gangsters with hilarious brazenness, one is aware that she is wearily accustomed to being threatened.

In her newest picture, she is defiant for only one day before she allows resignation to close about her forever.

The Trip to Bountiful is apparently an already-famous play. The fact that I have never heard of it means nothing. I am but a twilight American and have held even this shaky position only recently. Furthermore, I never go to the theater unless ordered there by Mr. Steele, who, I am sure you will all agree, must be obeyed. What I now know about this work I learned at a secret screening of the film, where I was given "production information" containing as many pages as an entire scenario.

The Trip to Bountiful was first shown on television in 1953. It then featured Miss Gish. After its showing, Mr. Paley telephoned her and said, "Television came of age tonight." Miss Gish may be accustomed to such compliments but television certainly was not. For this triumph, the author, Mr. Foote, was paid a thousand dollars. By my humble reckoning, he was doing fine. Twenty-two years later, when money had gone out of fashion, I was paid about seven hundred dollars for the conversion of my life story into a television play, and I had been compelled not merely to write but also to live the beastly thing. Mr. Foote has written innumerable plays and many films, the most famous screenplays being *To Kill a Mockingbird* and, more recently, *1918*, which I reviewed here a short while ago.

The new movie is thinner than the previous one. *1918* was about a time and a place and it had the outbreak of Spanish influenza to startle us out of its prevailing mood of dreamy reminiscence. *The Trip to Bountiful* is about an old woman, and it holds your attention completely only if you are a closet actor and can be amazed and enthralled by Miss Page's masterful occupancy of the screen. She plays the part of a Mrs. Watts, who after a lifetime spent with a husband she never loved is compelled to take up residence with her only surviving child, played by Mr. Heard, and his wife, to whom this arrangement is almost unbearable. The old woman longs to go back to the small town where she lived as a child, but this is impossible. Her son must work and in order to do this must stay in Houston. Finally, when she is alone, Mrs. Watts creeps out of the house and goes by bus to her hometown. Her escape is discovered almost immediately and the sheriff is sent to find her. She is only permitted to spend about ten minutes in the house her family once occupied. It is a ruin; the whole village is a ruin. I would happily have lived there forever, except that there were no cinemas within fifty miles, but Miss Page accepts the fact that the past is past. She is resigned—almost at peace. She even agrees to a list of rules compiled by her merciless daughter-in-law; she will never again sing hymns; she will not pout when asked questions she does not wish to answer; she will walk about the house—not run. She promises to comply with all these conditions and so, by his silence, does her son.

The acting in general is very good—especially that of the sheriff, played by a certain Mr. Bradford, whom I had never seen before but who was in *The Mean Season* and *Missing* and many other films. The art direction is also superb. The entire film is made to look like a series of paintings by Mr. Wyeth.

Mr. Steele did not see this picture with me; he had seen it on a previous day. We conferred later and agreed that it was an excellent movie. *The Trip to Bountiful* shows us no machines whizzing across the sky and there is not one hint of sex. The moment you catch sight of Mr. Heard in bed with his wife and you lean forward eagerly, he gets up and sits with his mother. (Mr. Oedipus, where are you?) It is a wistful tale made for people old enough to appreciate that there is no going back—that the present, however wretched, is all we have.

THE BRIDE / DANCE WITH A STRANGER

When it came high time to review a movie for August, Mr. Steele became distraught. As in all good pictures, he rushed about the city consulting his spies—beggars wearing dark glasses and pretending to be blind, newspaper vendors who secretly collect betting slips, and so on. In this way, he uncovered the best-kept secret in town. The following evening there was to be a screening of *The Bride* at the National cinema on Broadway. "Is this true?" Mr. Steele asked Columbia Pictures. The reply was "Yes. Bring all your friends." Mr. Steele has only one, so the three of us sat together in what, if we had been at Ascot, would have been the royal enclosure. Incidentally, the cinema was packed.

As, for old time's sake, Mr. Roddam, the director, was kind enough to give me a part in *The Bride*, the least I can do is to praise this film, and I sincerely can. The three principal actors are fascinating. Miss Beals is perfectly cast. She looks like a woodland creature, shy and savage at the same time. Sting starts as the traditionally obsessed scientist, but as the story unfolds, he becomes arrogant and finally downright nasty. Mr. Brown, who plays the monster, reverses this process. In the beginning of the film, he is hardly more than an animal, but by the time he at last reclaims his bride, his scars have healed and he looks handsome and lovable

—like one of Mr. Steinbeck's glorious oafs. Mr. Steele nearly swooned.

The film is lavish and filled with beautiful visual effects. I greatly enjoyed them all, but a purist would point out that they are digressions. During a wonderful circus scene between Mr. Brown and Mr. Rappaport (a man so tiny that the Monster can carry him all the way to Prague), the audience quite forgets the central theme. The narrative could be said to lack inevitability.

To me, a more important defect was the absence of a sense of sin, although the movie is full of both human and elemental violence. We are not made to feel that Sting is guilty of creating two beings who seem human but have no souls. Though no fault of their own, they are damned and this is what binds them to one another. This weakness is rooted in the dialogue, which occasionally provoked laughter even in an audience composed largely of Columbia hit men. At their ultimate meeting, Miss Beals asks Mr. Brown, "Is it you?" and he replies, "It is." Surely that was a moment when someone should have said more—"We know now that we are only a couple of anatomical patchwork quilts, but at least we have each other," or words to that effect.

In recent years, there has been an attempt to bring a number of myths, legends, and fairy tales into the adult world. *Close Encounters of the Third Kind* made an effort to invest science fiction with a certain poetry; in Miss Derek's version of *Tarzan*, the story ceased to be an adventure book for boys. It was in part successful but lacked a genuine sense of period. To get the costumes right is not enough. Miss Derek did not convey to the audience what in that purer age a well-brought-up girl from Baltimore would have felt upon meeting in the jungle a gentleman straight from Chippendales.

Though far better than either of these two films, *The Bride* is in the same category. Less of a fable than the early vehicles for Mr. Karloff and less of a parody than *The Young Frankenstein*, it is an adult movie and for this it must be unstintingly praised.

I wish I could say the same of *Dance with a Stranger*. I fear that moviemaking is definitely not the folk art of Britain. Even when someone hits on the brilliant idea of remaking the story of Ruth Ellis (I think it has been attempted before with Miss Dors), the project is mishandled. If it were not for the historic irony inherent in the subject matter, this picture would be unwatchable. In other words, if we did not know that we were seeing two people, one of whom would soon be shot and the other hanged, we could not possibly endure their endless sordid bickering.

Every crucial confrontation except the shooting is avoided. When Mrs. Ellis is dismissed from the club of which she was the manageress, we are not there: we only see her leaving. When her son is sent at the age of ten to a boarding school, though this is an experience at least as harrowing as going to the scaffold, we are not made to suffer with him. Worst of all, we do not see Mrs. Ellis hanged. That is the one sequence that could have redeemed this picture. It is a tribute to Miss Richardson's acting that we long to see her in jail, her lips no longer like glacé cherries, her once silver-gilt hair darkening at the roots, and if at last we could have beheld her eyes burgling and her neck distended, oh, how happy we would then have been!

If you compare *Dance* with *I Want to Live*, you realize how poor a movie the British one is. It has only two things in its favor. One is the art direction. Shortly after the Second World War, a certain Frenchman named Mr. Dior invented "The New Look." This was the last time that a mere fashion in clothes ever caught the imagination of the general public. It was also the final desperate effort made by the women of the world to look attractive. Waists were narrow, hips were wide, bodices were low, skirts were full and of ballet length. Faces at that time were masks of makeup and hair was elaborately coiffed and neat. Through Miss Richardson, the film presents this image to perfection.

Its other great asset is the casting—right from the minor characters such as the boy and Mr. Holm, who once again gives a faultless performance, to the doomed lovers. In a delightful interview with Mr. Saban, Miss Richardson described Mr. Blakeley as an upper-class twit and this is how Mr. Everett represents him. He looks like Mr. Stallone but made with water instead of wine.

Above all, of course, there is Miss Richardson as Mrs. Ellis.

Mr. Schiff of *Vanity Fair* (whose opinions I tremble to contradict) described Mrs. Ellis as a vamp. She was no such thing. Miss Bara was a vamp in *A Fool There Was* (Mr. Steele assures me that I haven't made up that title). Miss de Putti in *The Heart Thief* was a vamp; so was Miss Dietrich in *The Devil Is a Woman*. A vamp (contraction of the word *vampire*) was someone who destroyed men by first arousing and then frustrating their desire for her. Her function in movies was to avenge the female members of her audience—to compensate them in dream for all the times they have been stood up, neglected, insulted in real life. Mrs. Ellis was just as much a victim as her wretched lover and this is how Miss Richardson plays her, cruel and bleeding at the same time. A Mr. Williamson in *Playboy* magazine says that Miss Richardson is like Miss Monroe, but she rightly displays none of that legendary lady's sweetness. Really she is very like Miss Davis in *Of Human Bondage*—brittle, trashy, plastic. The sex scenes make this very clear. If we were intended to believe that Mrs. Ellis was in the grip of an overwhelming passion, these should either have been omitted, leaving our imaginations to guess what she felt, or we should have heard her howling like a cat. As it is, we only see that what Mrs. Ellis and her lover felt for one another was a seven-minute itch. If this was so, why the murder? The movie states but does not explain.

KISS OF THE SPIDER WOMAN

June was a month of debauchery.

During it, I watched two films in one week, one wantonly with a movie maniac and the other in the line of duty with your Mr. Steele. The first was part of a small John Gilbert Festival held at the Museum of Modern Art. Many of his pictures were shown on different days. The one that my movie-mad friend chose was called *Man, Woman and Sin*. Before it, Mr. Gilbert's charming daughter (by the silent-screen actress Leatrice Joy)—in order to promote her book about her father, *Dark Star*—told us that the film we were about to see was one of his favorites. An old legend states that he asked Mr. Mayer to finance it, but when the mogul was told the story line, he protested that Metro-Goldwyn-Mayer would not make a picture about a whore. Mr. Gilbert replied, "My mother was a whore" (as though that made things any better), and Mr. Mayer hit him. In fact, by modern standards, if there are any, this stark description of the heroine is somewhat of an exaggeration; she was merely a journalist whose sumptuous apartment is paid for by one of the owners of the paper for which she works. The entire melodrama, which includes Mr. Gilbert's soppy infatuation with this wicked reporter, her heartless treatment of him, a murder, false evidence, repentance, and a mother's abiding love for her son, totters perpetually on the brink of farce and Mr. Gilbert is the worst thing in it, but, out of respect for his daughter, nobody laughed.

After the show, as we strolled down Fifty-second Street, my kind companion put my thoughts into a single sentence. It is embarrassing to watch an actor try to win an audience's love by playing the part of a mature man totally at the mercy of the worldliness of those around him—like a tragic Jerry Lewis.

Two days later, after only twenty-four hours in the decompression chamber, I saw Mr. Babenco's masterpiece, *Kiss of the Spider Woman*. Though this was screened in an upper room on Broadway for the most highbrow critics in the land and is as sordid a tale as you will ever find (however hard you try), the woman sitting next to me laughed delightedly throughout the entire two hours of its showing time.

Kiss has glaring faults but none that, in my opinion, make it ludicrous.

Perhaps we should deal with these errors at once and quickly so that we may dwell at length on the film's remarkable virtues.

The first mistake is the title. Many moviegoers are accustomed to a weekly encounter with a freak from forty fathoms or a comic from a comet and they will imagine that this picture is just another "screamie." It is no such thing. It is the story of two men living in a Brazilian prison. One is a revolutionary and the other has been found guilty of perverting a minor. The latter insists on telling his cell mate the plot of a movie with which he has totally identified himself. Here we come to the film's second weakness. The sequences, of which there are many, showing us the film within the film should have been in pure black and white—always a more glamorous medium than color. Instead, they are in a sort of minimal color that makes everything—even the heroine—a yellowish green like used broccoli. As she is playing a kind of Hispanic Marlene Dietrich in *Dishonored*, this is an effect that cannot be overlooked. The third defect is that the homosexual prisoner is played by Mr. Hurt (Mr. William Hurt, not my Mr. John Hurt, who was my representative of earth in *The Naked Civil Servant*) and he is much too large—taller, if anything, than Mr. Julia, who is playing the man of this odd couple. We all know dizzy gentlemen, six foot high with huge hands and feet, who, at the slightest provocation or none, prance around the room in hats with eye veils, but that's life, which was never famous for its casting. In the movies, if you are going to camp and are going to utter the words "I've fallen in love with you," stay small. To increase the confusion, this character has been accused of pederasty. This makes it very hard for us to feel that he could become romantically attached to a full-grown man. Either the film should have made it clear that Mr. Hurt had been falsely charged or that his physical interest in Mr. Julia is a last resort. Even a prison official uses the phrase "You've fallen in love with him." This seems the last straw of romanticism.

Apart from these rather technical flaws, the film is superb.

At first, it seems to be going to be another dreary tale about human relationships; we spend a lot of time in the gloom and squalor of the prison cell. Then, suddenly, we are in the pure light of day. Mr. Hurt is being interrogated in the governor's office and we become aware that he is being used to spy on Mr. Julia. We have hardly been able to digest this turn of events before it becomes obvious that Mr. Hurt is also manipulating the authorities. By giving them the impression that he can lead them to the headquarters of the underground movement, he secures his release, but by this time, he has become too deeply involved with his cell mate and we know that he cannot try to betray him. From that moment onward, the plot races forward and our hearts race with it. The climax of the film is absolutely stunning; it has become the story of a young man whose very weakness drives him to heroic action, like a Graham Greene novel but kinky instead of sacred.

The acting by the two main characters is faultless. Mr. Julia, whom I thought inadequate in a recent play about Mr. Fellini, is totally convincing—a man who has been in a rage since the day he was born. However, if the picture belongs to any one person, that person is Mr. Hurt. He completely overcomes his physical disadvantage. His need to hide from the real world in his movie fantasies, his secret perverse enjoyment of his incarnation, and his growing dependence on his companion are all portrayed with a pathos I have never seen equaled.

Because homosexual men are pathologically incapable of making love with their friends or making friends of their lovers, it is not possible to write a satisfactory play about their world. The dialogue can only be midday gossip or moonlit grunts. A dramatist tends to sink into the sentimentality of *The Boys in the Band* or lapse into mere pornography. In *Kiss*, for a change, the basic situation is entirely believable. Mr. Julia consents to a physical union with Mr. Hurt partly because no women are available, partly out of pity for anyone so ill-equipped to live, but mostly in the hope of compromising him into delivering a message to his subversive confederates in the outer world. Mr. Hurt, though mortally afraid, agrees to do this partly out of loyalty to Mr. Julia but also because such an action would give him a leading role in a real-life melodrama just as glorious as one of the movies in which he is so wholly involved.

In recommending this film so highly, I feel that I am teasing you, because I do not see how it can ever be shown in a real cinema. It is not too shocking, but it is too serious. Perhaps, if you sit up late enough, it will one night be shown on cable television or, if you wait with sufficient patience, it will be released at an art house in a crooked side street in San Francisco. It is worth waiting a long time and going a great way to see.

OUTRAGEOUS FORTUNE

A movie must be described as good not necessarily because it gives you what you hoped to see but if it delivers what it promises. *Outrageous Fortune* does this and by this standard can hardly be criticized. It is a shameless farce with a thoroughly improbable story that drags Miss Long and Miss Midler by the hair across most of the desert states of America. The two ladies travel at breakneck speed on foot, by car, in trucks, and even on burros, along highways, through cities, into brothels, thieves dens, airports, and sundry other hazardous places.

If this picture has a fault, it is that there is never a pause and the plot is almost too complicated; hardly anybody is what he seems. Furthermore, to increase the urgency of the action, the director, Mr. Hiller, and his photographer, Mr. Walsh, present nearly every scene in close-up. Not only does this film addle the brain but it also dazzles the eye, and the sound track slaps the ear.

Once again, our visit to Mr. Ziegfeld's theater became group therapy; once again, four of us sat within inches of the vast screen. Apart from the pleasure of their company, there is a special benefit to be gained from being with Mr. Steele's friends. They are all movie experts and from them I learned that Leslie Dixon is a woman and that *Outrageous Fortune* is her first script. She is to be congratulated—particularly because, though the plot she has woven is so intricate, it is unraveled on the run. By this I mean that the audience does not have to be kept in after the show has, in effect, ended in order to be given a long, static explanation of what really happened and why.

The narrative goes somewhat like this. Two students, enrolled in the same drama class, find they have something in common beside their passion for the theater; they share a lover. Wishing to find out which of them he truly loves, they set out in pursuit of him, only to find that they themselves are being followed by sometimes two, sometimes three men who at first they think are enemies but later decide are allies. Heavy bodies and vast sums of money fall or flutter through the air during the chase, while it transpires that the lover is really a foreign agent in possession of a vial of liquid capable of defoliating almost all the vegetation of California. As I eagerly await the day when the world will be a vast slab of concrete like a global Grand Central Station, I took this notion calmly, but none of the participants in the movie did. The fiendish fluid is passed from one person to another with ever-increasing rapidity and recklessness until at last it comes to rest in the hands of the American authorities. In a final hilarious tableau, the students who started out as sworn enemies become friends. If there is such a periodical as a *Girl's Own Paper*, this film, except for the shocking language, could be one of its most absorbing serials.

Because the action of this picture is so elaborate and so fast, there is not much time for dialogue, but even so, the script is spangled with some short, cynical, and very funny lines, which I will not quote for fear of diminishing your enjoyment of them in their appropriate context.

The cast is huge and it was pleasant, among the minor characters, to catch a glimpse of Mr. Schuck, who used to be Mr. Hudson's lieutenant in "MacMillan and Wife," but for the same reasons that there is little speech, there is also not much opportunity for acting. People are required merely to run, jump, climb, or fall. Except from the two young women, what is needed is energy rather than artistry.

The heroines are good. By this I mean that they act well rather than play the parts of virtuous women. Miss Long, as an earnest acting student, flings herself with great comic effect into impersonating various types and adopting a number of accents. Miss Midler, on the other hand, represents, throughout all disasters, one invincible character—believing in nothing but sex and money. She is swiftly becoming what I imagine is an antiheroine. As far as I know, this is a phenomenon—something the movies have never shown us until now. By using this term, I do not wish to signify that she is a villainess, going on where Miss Davis and Miss Collins leave off (if they ever do leave off). She is not the female counterpart of actors such as Mr. von Stroheim, whom publicists used to advertise as "the man you love to hate." No. Miss Midler plays the tarnished soul who finds herself on the side of right almost by default, and the audience learns to love her in spite of the sins that she flaunts —crassness, coarseness, and carnality. It is noticeable that she has already begun to adopt certain mannerisms—flapping hands and a wobbly walk. She is wise to do this; no one can consider herself a star until she has become somebody that future drag artists can imitate.

MARLENE

On the south side of Central Park, a movie called *Marlene* was showing in a cinema like an expensive padded cell. When apprised of this fact, I ran all the way there. I am a fan—nay, a devotee, of Miss Dietrich.

The film is insufficiently historical to be called a documentary. It is more in the nature of a long conversation. It is at least less annoying than *My Dinner with Andre*, but, sad to say, it is a feast that promises so much yet leaves its audience decidedly undernourished. The blame for this effect cannot be blamed entirely on Maximilian (empty) Schell, who made the film and whose voice, other than that of the star herself, is almost the only one we hear. Some of the culpability must be attributed to Miss Dietrich. She is no longer the amenable creature she was in Mr. von Sternberg's day. She flatly refused to be photographed even in such discreet lighting as was shed upon her in *Just a Gigolo* (of which we see a fragment). She would also not allow any pictures to be taken of her apartment.

Worst of all, Miss Dietrich is very wordly and not given to gossip. None of her love affairs and very little of her married life are discussed. Of Mr. Hemingway she says, "I loved him and he loved me but our welationship was not ewotic." Concerning Mr. Remarque (who wrote *All Quiet on the Western Front*) or Mr. von Sternberg, she says almost nothing. Even about Monsieur Gabin her only observation is that he was pigheaded.

She admits only two serious aversions. She did not like working for Mr. Lang, who directed her in *Rancho Notorious*—a surprisingly weak film to come from one of the greatest moviemakers who ever lived. Mr. Ferrer (Mel, not José) says that the making of that picture was such a fiasco that whenever two people who were involved in it meet, they start to laugh.

It is also obvious that Miss Dietrich did not approve of Mr. Jannings. She described him as a ham, and in *The Blue Angel*, he certainly was. At the time when this movie was first shown in England it was quite usual for anyone who considered himself artistic to praise Mr. Jannings by saying that he was really acting while his costar was merely showing her legs. It was prophesied that she would not last. It is interesting to note that we were slow to unlearn the way we saw films when they were silent. Only gradually did we come to appreciate the nonacting that makes talkies so secret and yet so vivid.

It is about *The Blue Angel* that Miss Dietrich is most interesting. She says that she never expected to be given the part and therefore took no trouble with her screen test. Later she realized that it was precisely this indifference that excited Mr. von Sternberg. He enjoyed her contempt. Strange to relate, she seems unaware of the subtlety of his direction. She mentions unfavorably the tinny soprano voice that he asked her to use for the early songs, but it is this and her plumpness in the first half of the film contrasted with her later slimness and the famous contralto moan that in this masterpiece gives us the sense of time passing and of hope abandoned.

Although she declines to tell all about them, it is obvious that she has special taste in men. Her husband was a compact German gentleman; Mr. Hemingway was the all-American he-man, and Monsieur Gabin was a chunky Frenchman. She also admired Mr. Tracy and positively adored Mr. Welles, of whom she told Mr. Schell, "When you mention his name, you should cross yourself." Mr. Schell replied, "I do."

We have long ago been told that Miss Dietrich *never* liked making movies, but it is depressing as we watch this movie to hear her disparage almost every clip we are shown. Of *Morocco* and *Dishonored* she keeps protesting, "They were kitsch. They were rubbish!" They were. Even the elderly audience with whom I saw *Marlene* laughed when she made up her lips standing in deep snow before a firing line, but the merit of a film seldom lies in its narrative content and never in its probability. All movies—and hers especially—should be judged as an arrangement of glorious images of love and death.

She must have known that most of this interview and any other that she might grant would consist of clippings from her American films and, whatever she may say, they are still magical. I was sorry not to see her as a petty officer in *Seven Sinners* or momentarily wearing Mr. Brooke's army captain's hat in *Shanghai Express* but was delighted to behold once more the sequence in which, wearing white tie and tails, she kisses one of the female patrons in a restaurant. Above all, I enjoyed her emergence from her gorilla suit in *Blonde Venus*—surely one of the most exotic fragments of film ever devised by the mind of man.

Glimpses of her more recent past are less satisfactory. We are shown a sequence in which, wearing the rhinestone dress that caused such comment when she appeared in London, she sings Lili Marlene and says goodbye to her audience. This clip is in color. I experienced the same reaction as Mr. Perelman (or was it Mr. Marx?) when, at a party in Hollywood, he was introduced to Miss

Garbo. He said later that he was dismayed to see that she was in color. The great dolls of the screen such as Miss Hayworth and Miss Grable look gorgeous in color—like human beings but more expensive. The fixed stars, Miss Del Rio, Miss Dietrich, and Miss Garbo, should remain forever in black and white so that we cannot judge them by terrestrial standards. All of them at some point in their movies sank as low as possible. In *Resurrection*, Miss Del Rio worked in a brothel; as Anna Christie, when she could no longer endure the deception she had perpetrated about her past, Miss Garbo cried out, "What did you think I was really doing in St. Paul?" (I'm happy to tell you that no one had the nerve to reply.) In *Shanghai Express*, Miss Dietrich stated that she had taken "a gweat many men to change my name." She couldn't say more, could she? All these delicious glimpses of depravity are only acceptable even to the immoral majority because they happened to heroines living in the distant dimension of monochrome.

It was not only into her celluloid past that Miss Dietrich did not wish to delve. Her dismissive attitude was maintained even about her real life. When, after the war, she revisited Germany, she did not go to see the house where she lived as a child; she does not have any thoughts concerning her father, who died when she was a baby ("You do not miss what you have never known") and her sister she has excised from her memory altogether.

What Miss Dietrich really wanted was to talk about the present; but what present does she have? By her own admission, she seldom goes anywhere and never meets anyone but, instead, sits in a small apartment in a dim side street in Paris and reads books.

It would seem that she wishes to express opinions. She has many and they are firmly held. Feminism she thinks absurd. (Why can't they accept that they are women?) The afterlife she rejects completely. (You think they are all flying about up there. A bit crowded, wouldn't you say?)

In spite of its faults, *Marlene* is stimulating. It is a shadowy portrait of a very sophisticated and slightly difficult woman. She describes herself as practical and disciplined, and she is.

175

MENAGE

Imagine three filthy Marx Brothers—or, rather, two brothers and a Marx sister and you will have an inkling of how inconsequential *Menage* really is. None of the events that make up its narrative is natural or likely and some of them are downright impossible.

The place is Paris or, at least, a large city in France; the time is recent but not the present because, though some incidents take place in the urinals below a discotheque, we see no drugs being bought or sold or used. There is no plot but this does not mean that nothing happens. The film abounds in robbery, fornication, and even murder.

The story goes somewhat like this. A totally unlovable woman sits with her husband in a dance hall; she berates him because he does not earn even enough money to provide her with a change of underclothes or the opportunity to take a bath; he sits beside her round-eyed, disconsolate and tells her she is beautiful. This hapless pair is joined by an ex-convict, who first hits the girl and then gives her a fistful of francs to keep her quiet. Finally, he takes the couple on a robbing spree. From that moment onward, these three distasteful characters are never separated for long. The main preoccupation of the director, a Mr. Blier, is the sexual permutations through which these three erotic amoebas pass.

Some sixty years ago, there was a Central European picture called *Bed and Sofa*, at the beginning of which their lodger brings breakfast in bed to a husband and wife; later the husband offers the same service to his wife and the lodger and finally the wife sleeps on the sofa and the two men occupy the double bed. That film, which at the time of its English release seemed so ooh-la-la is tame compared with what is currently shown at the Cinema

Studio. For instance, in one sequence of *Menage*, a rich couple, on some disenchanted evening, returns home without realizing that our terrible trio has broken into the house and is eating everything in sight. The lawful owner says, "I'll never go to the theater again." (This is the best line in the entire film but nobody laughed, although, as Mr. Steele pointed out, the audience tittered uneasily through the rest of the movie.) When the presence of the thieves is noticed, they are not ordered to leave nor are they arrested; instead, they are commanded to perform or submit to a whole catalogue of kinky sexual practices. They demur (not, I feel sure, for moral reasons), whereupon they are threatened with a gun. In this film, there is as much unsafe sex and, indeed, unsafe life as in New York. The city bristles with knives and glistens with guns.

When questioned by a Ms. Darnton of *The New York Times*, Mr. Blanc (who plays the downtrodden husband) explained that during his ultimate humiliation, when he reluctantly consents to put on female attire, he tried not to look like a drag queen. He succeeds. He wears discreet clothes and appears just a typical provincial Frenchwoman—sensuous but respectable, greedy but grim.

It is in this spirit that the entire picture is made. In spite of all the debauchery, the direction is prudish. While the girl straddles the supine body of Mr. Depardieu as energetically as if she were riding a horse, she is still wearing her underclothes. When Mr. Depardieu lies on the bed with her husband, whom he longs to seduce, you know what is still encased in the tiniest, jazziest, and, one cannot help thinking, the most uncomfortable briefs ever seen.

During these antics, the person not actively involved is usually standing at the foot of the bed demanding to know what is going on, and no one is ever unwilling to explain. The dialogue is therefore more shocking than the action and the subtitles are worse than both because the human voice is tentative, evanescent, which to some extent ameliorates the hideous truth. The printed word, on the contrary, has permanence, authority, and even a certain scholarliness. Perhaps, at the bottom of the screen, there ought to have been a strip of dirty wall on which the captions could have been misspelled in shaky handwriting with appropriate illustrations. To those of us who, in our infinite wisdom, refuse to understand French, the subtitles of this movie are mere graffiti.

It is impossible not to condemn this film, but I must admit that it is never boring. Furthermore, it is well acted and it stars Mr. Depardieu. He is the European equivalent of Mr. Nolte, though he lacks the golden skin tone, as of a basted chicken, which adds so greatly to the allure of the American star. The color of *Menage* is dreary throughout and renders all nudity as an unappetizing pinkish gray. Nevertheless, Mr. Depardieu is superb. As he pads about naked between classical statues that adorn the home of one of his rich clients, he in no way suffers by comparison with them.

After the show, Mr. Steele and I hurried through the cold night from Broadway to Amsterdam Avenue, where we ate in a very cozy restaurant named for Mr. Fellini (though there wasn't a fat woman in a black dress anywhere in sight). While we dined, Mr. Steele voiced the conviction that *Menage* was filled with inner meaning and it is true that the very madness of the film does suggest much greater work, such as the later movies of Mr. Buñuel. In the midst of farce, we are in pathos. At one moment in *Menage*, the girl says that all she really wants is a home and children. At another, Mr. Depardieu describes a vision of lying in the countryside with a young girl in a white dress, which seems to be a symbol of the years of innocence of which his term in jail deprived him. When the husband prophesies that they will all be arrested, his lover says that we all kill somebody (an enigmatic remark indeed) and adds that all life is a prison sentence from which the only way out is death.

I wish I could have liked or at least have pitied these characters, but I couldn't. I found the lovelessness of their sexuality appalling. However, no parental guidance is recommended. In spite of Mr. Depardieu's monumental beauty, the film is never arousing and it is by no means pornographic. Never has there been a picture that made it more hideously clear that, even without the intervention of the police, crime does not pay and that sexual experimentation does not reward its practitioners with happiness. *Menage* may not be a moral tale but it is certainly cautionary. All three of its principal characters end up in female attire standing at a bitterly cold street corner trying unsuccessfully to make a living by prostitution.

As far as I know, the only foreigner ever to visit France and leave with friendly memories of the natives is Dee Sushi. The rest have less benign reactions and if *Menage* is anything to go by, it would now appear that even the French have a low opinion of the French.

ONE WOMAN OR TWO

Lately, I have spent a lot of celluloid time in the jungle—firstly when I saw *The Mission* and secondly on *The Mosquito Coast*. I now take back all my complaint about my own suffering when in *The Bride* I was sprayed with steam, threatened with fire, and deluged with sand. These misfortunes were but pinpricks compared with the hardships that Mr. Irons and Mr. De Niro must have endured in the first of these two pictures while climbing a waterfall to reach the sources of the Amazon River and the souls of a tribe of Amerindians, or with discomforts inflicted by Mr. Ford on poor Miss Mirren in the latter film.

The Mission is a real work of art photographed with wonderful color consistency in a pinkish golden light. Its only fault was that Mr. Irons was nowhere seen to be deteriorating from religious zeal into absolute madness. There was, after all, no sane need for him to persuade the women and children of an entire tribe to sacrifice themselves for You Know Who. His own martyrdom would surely have been enough to satisfy even the most devout Christian.

The Mosquito Coast, on a less spiritual level, was equally spectacular but less believable. Miss Mirren, who played the heroine, is a very good actress, capable of making even Jacobean tragedies credible, but it was hard to accept that she would have put up with her husband's (Mr. Ford's) antics for so long. Her sons she might have been willing to sacrifice, but she also had two young daughters with her on their terrible journey who might at any moment have succumbed to some tropical disease, been poisoned by a snake, or become the casualties of native hostilities, and yet she did not finally rebel against Mr. Ford until he had tried to kill the entire congregation of a jungle church. I was positively relieved when the crazy, tyrannical Mr. Ford died.

By contrast with these harrowing experiences, I looked forward eagerly to a frolic in the quiet countryside of France, where *One Woman Or Two* is set.

I've terrible news for you. Monsieur Depardieu, whose heights, in some measure, redeemed the lowness of his earlier picture *Menage*, is not as tall as his costar Miss Weaver.

That's not all.

His current movie is unsatisfactory on all levels, but chiefly because it lacks the very quality that was the greatest virtue of *Mission* and *Coast*—style. By this word I mean not elegance but consistency. The fact that *One Woman or Two* is a farce is no excuse. A novel may digress indefinitely but a movie is more like a short story and must possess a unified vision and singleness of purpose.

This film is a very complicated mistaken-identity story, which Mr. Steele hated from the first frame to the last. All comedies in this genre cause him a certain amount of misgiving but that may be because he has difficulty with the real identity of Dee Sushi.

One Woman Or Two starts as a joke about archaeology, lapses into a farce built round one person posing as another, and ends up as a romance between two totally mismatched people—Mr. Depardieu, an unworldly archaeologist (the James Stewart role) and Miss Weaver, an American advertising agency employee (the part that Rosalind Russell might once have played).

The archaeologist finds some bones lying on the surface of a hillside in France. From these, he reconstructs first a complete skeleton and then a clay model of a prehistoric woman. The team of diggers asks for financial support from a rich director of an American philanthropic institute (Dr. Westheimer). When Mr. Depardieu goes to the airport to meet her, Miss Weaver, in order to avoid a persistent admirer, allows herself to be mistaken for the philanthropist.

When her imposture is unmasked, the film ought to end but it does not. Without telling anybody in the film or the audience, Mr. Depardieu has decided that the prehistoric woman he had reconstructed was black. At a meeting of paleontologists, he unveils his dark-skinned statue and consternation breaks out. France is deeply offended, but America, on the other hand, is delighted.

A likely tale!

The story line here makes the essential satire of this situation impossible. In truth, to be black in France is merely not to be French—a sort of bad taste, whereas in America having a dark skin is either a noble cause or a sin, according to what color you happen to be.

When the offending statue has been revealed, this second theme should come to a close but once again it does not; another begins. We move on to the dawning of Miss Weaver's interest in archaeology and the softening of her hostile attitude to Mr. Depardieu. She now discovers more bones and a love scene takes place in a wooden hut on wheels, which has been brought to the excavation site. This contraption, while the lovers are still in it, slides down a mountainside and disintegrates into a thousand pieces. This entire sequence is mismanaged. The lovemaking is positively torrid and involves the inevitable baring of Miss Weaver's breast. Why? The film has not until this moment been a salacious or even a naughty farce. Furthermore, when the hut temporarily housing the lovers falls apart, they merely climb out of the wreck, whereas, to justify this episode, they should have continued their illicit liaison oblivious of their incongruous circumstances.

In a word, the plot is everywhere improbable but the details and the acting, though good, are naturalistic. The dialogue is also tame. When Mr. Depardieu tells Miss Weaver that "Laura" is 2 million years old, she does not merely say, "I've heard that Frenchmen go for older women." She weakens the joke by adding that this seems to be going too far.

What genuine comedy there is in this picture rests in the hands of Dr. Westheimer. I have met her in real life, or at least on television. The immediate and lasting impression that she gives is of efficiency and likability—two attributes that no one else has ever been able to combine. On the screen, she still manages to radiate these qualities and, furthermore, allows—nay, connives at—the exploitation of her diminutive stature in a quite delightful way. On seeing the statue, which is the same height as she is, she says, "So beautiful and so petite!" Her delivery of this comment is at once sincere and sly. In Orion's tiny screening room, the tiny audience, at this point, managed a tiny laugh.

See this film purely for Dr. Westheimer's sake. She has publicly declared that she likes making movies. I prophesy that she will become a kind of Central European Carmen Miranda.

PRICK UP YOUR EARS/ FLESH AND THE DEVIL

It is the weak who destroy the strong.

This is the appallingly clear message contained in both the book and the movie of Mr. Orton's life and in his diaries.

On the ninth of August in 1967, Mr. Halliwell (who was what my brother would have called a drip) hammered to a pulp the skull of the tough, bouncy Mr. Orton, with whom he had been living for seventeen years. It is impossible not to think that the victim deserved his fate. He was popular—even with his agent—but, deep down, he was not a likable man.

He was, however, a minigenius who wrote *Entertaining Mr. Sloane*, *Loot*, and *What the Butler Saw*. In a small way, he was a man of destiny. That is to say his particular talent was what his generation was waiting to receive. By the early sixties, the world had fallen into the hands of the young, who have always been impatient with the establishment. All Mr. Orton's plays make fun of respectability—a viewpoint that was considered fashionable. He also despised discretion, which is less easy to condone.

Mr. Halliwell was somewhat older than Mr. Orton, was well educated, and had a little money of his own. When they first met, the latter had nothing. He came from the lower middle class and, worse, from Leicester. There are two ways of dealing with this handicap. You can either stay there and triumph by becoming even more respectable than your neighbors or you can leave and forever after enhance your enjoyment of life by imagining how shocked Leicester would be if it knew what you were doing. This was the course chosen by Mr. Orton. He went to London and entered the Royal Academy of Dramatic Art. That was where he met Mr. Halliwell, who, at first, became his mentor and collaborated happily with him in writing a novel that no one would publish. Soon, however, Mr. Orton began to blossom on his own, wrote plays that were actually staged, and acquired theatrical friends who thought of his companion as a hanger-on and dreary with it.

That was the moment when the dramatist should have found a way to end the relationship as kindly as possible. Some perverse kind of loyalty that did not include being nice to his flat mate prevented him from doing this and disaster followed.

I doubt that mere envy of his protégé's success was the sole motive for the murder. I think that from the very beginning what Mr. Halliwell wanted was love. He was not a sensualist and, at one moment, even states that he has difficulty in becoming fully aroused. He lent himself to his friend's sexual pranks, which included three-somes with total strangers, but he despised himself for doing so. Mr. Orton, by contrast, lived in a perpetual state of what the English call randiness. There is a sequence that shows him rejecting a proposition that would have obliged him to be the passive party. This gives the audience the erroneous idea that he drew the line somewhere. It is obvious from his diaries that he drew no lines.

He did not subscribe to the old-fashioned notion that one sex act is more effeminate than another. In his judgment, all unbridled carnality was manly. It was the faintest hint of restraint, discretion, or tenderness that was womanish. Thinking in this way, it was obvious that merely indulging in a little light masturbation with someone he had known for years in the privacy of their shared apartment was a complete waste of time. The only occasion when we see him doing this is when he can add to the fun by watching with half an eye the television screen on which Elizabeth II is taking part in some public ceremony. I think it was this heartless, strident masculinity in Mr. Orton that really brought about his murder.

A film that endeavors to present this subtle but turgid relationship deserves praise.

The acting is superb—especially that of Miss Redgrave as the agent who is so intrigued and amused to find that her newest client is an overt homosexual. She even lends him money; there can be no greater love.

Also the script is good. The dialogue is full of bizarre descriptions of sexual behavior interspersed with remarks such as "Please pass the sugar." At times, it is almost Pinteresque.

What the film lacks is unity and a gradual quickening of pace. Although we know from the stunning beginning what the climax will be, we do not feel that we are being drawn relentlessly toward it. *Prick Up Your Ears* is a biographical story set in the recent past. This makes success difficult. All the main facts are known and therefore must be presented more or less truthfully. The result of this constriction is that we are shown a series of events all interesting in themselves but not all aimed at the heart of the drama—the film is patchy.

When, on leaving the screening room, I voiced this opinion to Mr. Steele and some of his merry men, they all replied that life is like that. I consider that as weak an excuse as attempting to justify some instance of obnoxious behavior by saying "It's only natural."

Life is a disease for which the movies are a cure—or they ought to be.

The ultimate question is this: For whom was *Prick Up Your Ears* made? It is the story of a binding relationship, but it is certainly not a romance. It is full of laughs, but it is by no means a comedy. Much that is horrible takes place in it, but it is not a horror film. It is a catalogue of sexual encounters, mostly in public lavatories, but it is never pornographic. Though the dialogue is outspoken (to say the very least), visually the film is discreet—sometimes to the verge of absurdity. Mr. Orton stands in a London street making loud remarks about the physical attractions of various men who pass by, but not a curve, not a bulge is anywhere to be seen. No one does anything within sight of the camera except kiss, which, in real life, is a pastime almost unknown on the "tearoom circuit."

Since it shows homosexual life at its very nastiest, perhaps this film was intended for bored-again reformers.

Only a few days before being plunged into this quicksand of depravity, I had seen the silent Garbo classic *Flesh and the Devil*. Ah, how little, in that far-off time, we knew about either of these two sources of temptation!

I first witnessed this film in 1927. The second viewing was a strange experience. It taught me a lot about movies and even more about myself. In sixty years, the cinema and I have both inevitably lost our innocence.

Flesh is based on a novel by a certain Mr. Sudermann and is typical of romantic German literature before the advent of Mr. Hitler. Mr. Gilbert and Mr. Hanson are a pair of officers (and gentlemen) who, in boyhood, have sworn undying friendship. Miss Garbo (billed below the title of the picture!) is what synopses used to call "the woman between." Mr. Gilbert has an illicit liaison with her that draws him into a duel with her husband, whom he kills. For the sake of the lady's reputation, the fight is said to be over a game of cards. Mr. Gilbert leaves the country for three years and returns to find Miss Garbo has married his best friend.

The rest of the tale is the usual anguish, with Miss Garbo imploring her lover to go away with her but finding at the last moment that she is unable to forsake all her diamond bracelets.

Her indecision plunges the two lifelong buddies into proposing yet another duel, but, at the last minute, they realize that Miss Garbo was a mistake and they fall into each other's arms. At the same time, she is conveniently drowned while trying to cross the ice to reach the island where the fatal confrontation was to have taken place.

In a charming speech before the Radio City showing of *Flesh*, Mr. Brownlow addressed Miss Garbo (in the hope that she might be present), assured her that her privacy would be respected, and thanked her for her contribution to the art of the cinema. I have often been asked what celebrity I would most like to meet and I have always explained that the imagined delights of conversing with famous people are an empty dream. I now realize that that was an untruthful reply. I long to meet Mr. Brownlow. He is the way—he is the door to an era of the silent movies. Alas, at Radio City, he was but a speck in the distance.

Another speaker before the showing of *Flesh* was Mrs. Fountain, who is Mr. Gilbert's daughter. She has written her father's life story, *Dark Star*, and her one increasing purpose is to redeem his reputation, which fell into abrupt decline with the arrival of the talkies. Her filial loyalty is touching, but the terrible truth is that whenever I have seen him, he has been all but ludicrous. His face is made up clown-white with a dark shadow all round the eyes and, in whatever situation he is placed, he looks surprised and slightly sick. This effect cannot be blamed on an outmoded film convention because, in Miss Swanson's silent version of *Sadie Thompson*, all the men, mostly marine, look sufficiently masculine to satisfy even the most demanding reader of Christopher Street.

The films of the late twenties were all informed by a strong moral purpose and so, in a way, were their audiences. When I saw *Flesh* for the first time, I was seventeen and sexologists would assume that I longed to be kissed (or worse) by Mr. Gilbert or Mr. Hanson. In fact, I inferred nothing kinky from a tale in which, when the heroine is safely out of the way, her two lovers embrace. I did not even snigger at a hero called Mr. Harden. I don't remember having any reaction at all to the men in the film. I was in a swoon about Miss Garbo—or, rather, about the accoutrements of her beauty—the sumptuous settings, the huge fur coats, the heavy diamond jewelry. In youth, one's greatest desire is not for carnal pleasure but for the power that foolishly one imagines may be achieved through wealth, through the protection of an influential keeper, and by means of flawless beauty deployed with the utmost deliberation. It is only later in life that one begins to daydream about a romantic encounter with a movie hero. In other words, it is when all possibility of ruling the world is dead that sex becomes a repetitious, narcotic compensation for the irreparable loss of that hope.

ROXANNE

The fact that I contributed nothing to issue number 112 of *Christopher Street* should not be taken to signify that nothing worthy of comment was happening in the cinema during the month of May. I went to London, England, for four weeks, but I've seen my mistake and have now returned to the American celluloid circuit.

In the last week of June, I went with Mr. Steele and two of his companions to the Ziegfeld Theatre. We witnessed *Roxanne*, a modern, provincial American version of a French play by Monsieur Rostand called *Cyrano De Bergerac*.

After the show, the four of us dined in a charming French restaurant, where we sat in the garden and enjoyed a very pleasant meal on a mild summer evening. It was almost as though we were still in the movie, because that is what *Roxanne* is like—cozy, amusing, and, inspite of a lot of slapstick gags, thoughtful.

As we discussed the film we had just seen, our enthusiasm was, I would say, muted.

I should have know that the chief quality of Mr. Martin's latest picture would be its blandness. I had already by chance discovered what another critic had thought about it. I never buy a newspaper, for fear that the person selling it to me might suppose that I like what goes on in the world, but I am a crossword-puzzle addict and become very shaky if I am deprived of the opportunity to solve at least two puzzles a day. For me, they are the aerobics of the soul. My hunger for this form of exercise is so great that it compels me to search the trash cans of the house in which I live to reach their discarded reading matter. In this way, I came across a review of *Roxanne* in *The New York Times*. It was by a certain Ms. Maslin. She stressed the appeal of the picture's setting, which she described as gorgeous and homey-looking. The first of these two epithets I question but the second I totally endorse. Another delightful factor of this film is its weather. Much of its action takes place on a still summer evening.

Mr. Martin, who wrote the script of the picture as well as starred in it, plays the part of a little town's fire chief, and he walks through the streets of his domain with a jauntiness that we soon learn masks a frightening rage at his cruel fate, or, to be more specific, at his nose.

For those of you who never heard of Mr. de Bergerac or, worse, who never saw the original film version (featuring Mr. José Ferrer) of Mr. Rostand's famous play, I should explain that it is the story of a cavalier whose romantic longings are forever frustrated by his having a nose that, as he himself says, "precedes him everywhere by a quarter of an hour." He falls in love with a girl named Roxanne, here played by Miss Hannah, but feels that he is at too depressing a physical disadvantage to court her. She fancies a handsome oaf, acted by a Mr. Rossovich, who is too nervous and tongue-tied to talk to her. This situation brings about the best scene in the current version of this tale because it involves the least clowning.

On learning from the other girls that Mr. Rossovich is smitten with her, Miss Hannah asks Mr. Martin to tell the young man that she is interested in him. At the outset of this conversation, Mr. Martin imagines that she is inviting *him* to woo her. As he gradually realizes he is only being asked to act as an intermediary for another man, his expression changes but so subtly that she does not notice. Only the audience perceives that very quietly his heart has been broken.

Beneath all the buffoonery, Mr. Martin is a very good actor.

To deal with this tricky triangle, the two men agree to combine their talents. Lurking in the shrubbery beneath Miss Hannah's window, Mr. Martin makes verbal love to her until she is ready for Mr. Rossovich to take over and do the hard work. Eventually, of course, this imposture is discovered and, at least in this new edition of the play, the tangled web is unraveled with almost preemptory slickness.

Roxanne is genuinely funny but it has several weaknesses of detail. Most of the visual jokes are shamelessly borrowed from other films. Miss Hannah accidentally locks herself out of her house with her robe caught in the front door as it slams shut, just as Miss Day once did to greater comic effect and without the coy nudity. Fireman climbs a tree to rescue a cat; so recently did Mr. Candy. Worse, almost all the high jinks are done to death and beyond.

Beneath these superficial flaws is a more fundamental imperfection. There is a sense in which the theme of this story cannot be modernized. In the seventeenth century, when love was held to be more important than sex, audiences could easily believe in a poet's view of a woman—in a girl who yearned for a man because of his spiritual qualities rather than for you know what. Now that women have decided to be as gross as men, we are quite unable to treasure this idealized notion.

One of Mr. Steele's guests at the Ziegfeld Theatre was Miss Cameron, who is known to you for the elegant short stories that she has recently contributed to *Christopher Street* and who, I am delighted to be able to tell you, is the very embodiment of sophistication and effortless chic. Furthermore, since the invention of the motion-picture camera, she is the only person of the opposite sex that Mr. Steele has ever accompanied to a movie house. I felt that some advantage should be taken of this unique occasion.

The opinion unanimously held by gay men is that a woman approaches perfection as she becomes increasingly like Joan Collins. It was therefore of Miss Cameron that I sought corroboration of my view that Miss Hannah was miscast as Roxanne. Miss Cameron agreed.

Miss Hannah looks, to use Miss Maslin's epithet, gorgeous—too gorgeous, in fact, and insufficiently ethereal. (She was sweeter when, in a previous film, she was a part-time fish.) The original Roxanne said, "If you would win me, rhapsodize," and Miss Hannah does utter a slangy translation of this important phrase. Furthermore, she wears spectacles to show us that she is serious-minded. To be absolutely fair to this very talented actress it must be admitted that her part is poorly written. She is made to use foul language and finally to punch Mr. Martin in the face. From that moment onward, she has lost our love and even our belief in her character.

Fairness must also be shown to the people who financed this picture. It must be said that the audience, with whom we watched it, enjoyed every frame of it, laughed loudly at all the jokes, and quite obviously fell hopelessly in love with Mr. Martin's very appealing version of the brokenhearted clown.

THE BIG EASY

I have now acquired two new movie companions. I met them at the Robertson Gallery, which I had visited to be photographed in a heap of people who, like me, are in the smiling and nodding racket. Those of you who believe in culture may have attended the opening of this strange place in the middle of July. To others of you, whose interests lie elsewhere, I should explain that the Robertson Gallery is two rooms at ground level on the very edge of civilization on East Seventh Street. There, it is proposed that from time to time artists will exhibit their paintings and writers will read from their books.

My two recently acquired friends are readers to the movie industry; their function is to discover new works of fiction and report on the possibilities of these as film fodder. They watch secret screenings at half-past ten in the morning so as to keep abreast of what is fashionable in Hollywood rather than, like me, so as not to have to pay for their seats. They very kindly took me to see *The Big Easy* (which means New Orleans) and I would dearly have loved to ascertain their expert opinion, but we had to part soon after it was finished.

My own unguided view is that, in many ways, it is an excellent picture.

It begins with a large corpse lying face downward in a public fountain. This is nice and it gets better. Indeed, *The Big Easy* really does become that saga of human depravity that we have so long, so eagerly awaited. Each dead body presented for our inspection is bloodier and more deeply disfigured than the last.

The plot is complicated but seldom obscure; the photography vivid but never arty. The acting is variable. It is delightful to catch one last glimpse of the late Mr. Ludlam, but it cannot be denied that he is giving a stage performance in a film. Only Mr. Beatty is flawless. Some years ago, you may have observed him in *Deliverance* being raped by a lot of farmers in a swamp. Here, his cuddliness is more complicated; it is laced with a sly greed that is totally chilling.

The copious literature that, as is customary before screenings, was handed to us by Columbia Pictures informed us that the film was made with the cooperation of the New Orleans police department. If this is true, then all its members are madmen as well as rogues. Every officer in sight, including Mr. Quaid (from *Breaking Away*), is an extortionist and some are murderers, but more unsettling than any one instance of corruption over which we are allowed to gloat is the all-pervading contempt in which all policemen hold all civilians. It is this quality that makes *The Big Easy* so fascinating.

What fatally flaws this film is the implausible relationship between Mr. Quaid, a corrupt cop, and Miss Barkin, an assistant district attorney, who, using the terms very loosely, are the hero and heroine of this story.

Mr. Quaid acts in a manner so irritatingly self-assured that not even the most unattractive girl in the world would settle for him. A nunnery would be preferable. In spite of this, we are asked to believe that the elegant and high-minded Miss Barkin would at once accept a dinner invitation from him. Furthermore, although on their first date she sees him perpetrate a number of small infractions of the law, she very soon enters into a grossly sensual affair with him. At this point, one of my companions whispered, "A bit soon." To this apt comment, I would add, "A bit absurd." Attorneys do not consort with policemen of any kind. They do not consort. They are brainy, excruciatingly respectable people who wear spectacles and flat shoes. They may occasionally arrange mergers or draw up contracts, but they never, *never* enter into embraces. How could a young lady, who could pass bar examinations, which are far beyond the capacities of ordinary mortals, behave in such a weak-willed and immoral way? Miss Barkin was so good as Mr. Duvall's daughter in *Tender Mercies*, but the part foisted upon her in *The Big Easy* gradually becomes unactable. Toward the end of this picture, we see her and her paramour squatting side by side on the edge of a pavement in the middle of the city. I ask you! Even "L.A. Law" would not stoop this low.

As this unlikely tale unfolds, or, rather, becomes ever more complicated, even the depraved detective cannot help trying to extricate himself from the venality that threatens to engulf him. We are led to believe that he sees the light partly because his girl friend has shown it to him (a likely story!) but mostly because, though he revels in bribery, he draws the line at drug selling and murder. It is not Mr. Quaid's fault that he cannot make this change of heart convincing. Policemen do not have hearts and they never change. Corruption is like garlic; there is no such thing as a little of it.

I dare not guess how general audiences will react to *The Big*

Easy as a whole, but I prophesy that they will hoot—nay, I insist that they hoot—with derision at its ending.

This final sequence shows us Mr. Quaid in formal wedding gear, carrying into a *Vogue*-type apartment Miss Barkin, who is gowned in gleaming white as though nothing unpleasant had ever been inflicted upon her person.

He has tried to compromise her in a deeply unforgivable manner; she, in turn, has attempted to secure a conviction against him in a court of law. The differences between these two characters could not be healed in a lifetime. If the last few minutes of this film had revealed them parting, besmirched, broken, and bewildered, *The Big Easy* could have been a small masterpiece.

A BIGGER SPLASH

There have been four outstanding painters in this century—Mr. John, Mr. Dali, Mr. Warhol, and Mr. Hockney. What makes all these men great is that their personalities touch the world's imagination even more intimately than their work. Pictures are only things, but artists are people. Of course, some buyers acquire a Hockney purely because they hope that in fifteen years time it will be worth twice what they are paying for it now, but others want one so that, in a tenuous way, they may spend time with the painter—may share a fragment of that shamelessly exotic life.

Mr. Hockney is one of the saints of happiness. He looks like a midday owl. Most owls are nocturnal creatures, perpetually wide-eyed and watchful in a darkling world, but Mr. Hockney is never a vigilant predator, partly because his dinner plate is already heaped with field mice or whatever it is on which owls thrive. I think of him forever sitting in a garden that others have tended, his eyes half-closed against the eternal sunlight of Los Angeles, his lips half-smiling at how easy life turned out to be. On the one hand, his success seems to have cost him nothing; on the other, he manifests none of the guilt of inherited wealth.

This is the state of being so many of us wish to experience and when we see a Hockney, we do.

It was inevitable that, as his agent says, Mr. Hockney would become the definitive painter of Southern California. There, everybody is beautiful and everybody is rich. Los Angeles is New York lying down. This is most immediately conspicuous in its architecture. In Manhattan, the buildings stand one close behind another, craning their necks to keep apprehensive watch over what is going on in the rest of the world. In Hollywood, however vast they may be, the homes of the record-industry tycoons are single-story buildings. They lie limp and spread out like stuccoed cats along the tops of the surrounding hills. Nobody cares about anything but pleasure. Mr. Hockney has said that he paints the things at which he likes to look, and that means luxury. This being so, he has naturally depicted a lot of swimming pools, partly because they are the icons of wealth and partly because around them are usually gathered a number of naked or partly naked people. In Mr. Hockney's work, even the boys look expensive. When he paints interiors, they represent the modern version of high living. A hundred years ago, you became aware of your host's riches when you saw how full his home was of things. There were Oriental plates balanced along the picture rails, as well as pictures hanging from them; there were photographs on the piano, ferns on bamboo stands, rose bowls on tables, and even rugs on carpets. Nowadays, a millionaire's setting looks sparse because it covers a much greater area of the earth's surface. His apartment in Beverly Hills contains only a lamp, which illuminates nothing but the ceiling, a cushion to enjoy, which guests themselves must fling on the wooden floor, a book too heavy to pick up. If you cannot find the ruby-encrusted coffee spoons, they are not in another room; they are in the Hamptons.

Why was the artist so powerfully drawn to this Sybaritic milieu and how does he present to us this sunny, sinless vision?

These were questions that I hoped would be answered in a

movie entitled *A Bigger Splash*, now showing in an unknown cinema on the upper reaches of Broadway.

I was disappointed.

For all I know, every incident in this film may be true, but the way in which the picture is made is the exact opposite of the manner in which Mr. Hockney paints. Its style is early Cassavetes—indirect to the verge of incomprehensibility. Faces are forever sliding out of the frame and voices are continually fading from the sound track. Why did not somebody sit Mr. Hockney down in some of the localities that have become his natural environment and question him about his life and work? When he speaks about his paintings, he says such marvelous things.

I was once in his studio in Los Angeles. In the center of the huge room was a huge landscape on an easel. An unknown man stood before the canvas with Mr. Hockney to one side of and slightly behind him. No one spoke for an almost unbearable minute. Then the artist said, "That's Los Angeles. It doesn't really look like that." There were no verbose aesthetics, no psychological explanations, no long words. Directness on this scale amounts to a kind of innocence.

The movie purports to tell the story of the painting of a picture called *A Bigger Splash* and implies that the work was interrupted by the departure of its subject, a young man on whom, at the time, the painter centered his affections. In an interview with the *New York Native*, Mr. Hockney made no bones about his relationship with Mr. Peter Schlesinger but explained that the difficulty he encountered in completing the picture was technical—a matter of perspective. Why was no mention made of this fact? It is impossible not to suspect that this was a less popular explanation.

Some of the scenes in this movie are entirely gratuitous. One such is a sequence showing Mr. Hockney taking a shower. The shower is extremely elaborate, with water spouting out of its wall at all angles, but, apart from that, of what interest can this incident possibly be?

There is another moment when the painter enters a room in which two men have positioned themselves exactly as they are seen in one of his portraits. When he addresses them, they neither move nor reply, so he leaves. What does their behavior mean? All these holes in the fabric of this movie are not due to lack of resources. It is not a picture flung together in a weekend and seen by a hand-held camera. Cameras have obviously been placed in elaborate and quite unnecessary places. There is even a long tracking shot of Mr. Schlesinger on a bicycle. We are shown by what means he left Mr. Hockney and along what street he traveled but not why. We have the right to know—at least your Mr. Steele has; he paid for both our seats.

If you enjoy a lot of male nudity and a pinch of the erotic, see this film, but if you hoped at the end of it for a better understanding of the way a painter works and how his life and his art interact, I fear that you will leave the cinema starving. I find it saddening to be unable to find more to praise in *A Bigger Splash*, for Mr. Hockney is a truly original artist and a fascinating and lovable human being.

The day after I witnessed the film about him, I met the man himself. He was at the profane church on Sixth Avenue, where the damned quiver and twitch among the stained-glass windows, the Gothic doorways, and the commemoration tablets. There, beneath nearly naked men standing on pedestals, I questioned him about the film. I think he had once regarded it as a kind of celluloid rape but was now tired of it. As with all rape, you get used to it. In a slightly tired voice, he said, "It looks nice." And it does. Once again, Mr. Hockney's genius for directness triumphs.

FATAL ATTRACTION/ MAURICE

I was given a day's crowd work on *Fatal Attraction*. The moral of this unexpected piece of good luck is that we should all accept every invitation we are offered. Slightly reluctantly, I went to a cocktail party given as a curtain-raiser to a preview of *Man-hunter*. The film was only a mild success but the gathering before it was a triumph. At it, I met a Mr. and Mrs. Lyne. It was he who subsequently offered me the job of pretending to be a guest at a literary "do" where Mr. Douglas first meets Miss Close in *Fatal Attraction*. During a break in the proceedings, both the stars shook hands with me. I lived a little while. Had it not been for this incident, I doubt that I would have been so keen to see the film.

The moral of the film itself is that we should never accept any invitation offered to us; we may be dragged into an illicit liaison, which, in turn, could lead to emotional havoc, to pregnancy, or, worst of all, to Miss Close. Indeed, this picture might have been called *Too Close for Comfort*.

The narrative is about a lawyer (Mr. Douglas) who, at a publisher's party, takes a fancy to a publicist (Miss Close). During this scene, like the searchlights of a prison camp, my gaze raked the screen for a glimpse of myself. There was none, but I soon recovered from the loss of my last chance of greatness and became deeply engrossed in the events taking place on the screen. So did everybody else. I once heard an audience cheer when, in a movie called *Flamingo Road*, Miss Crawford shot Mr. Greenstreet, but, apart from that occasion, I have never sat amid a crowd of spectators so totally involved in a film. They were almost clawing at the screen to vent their hatred on poor Miss Close. They gibbered hysterically at each new dirty trick perpetrated upon the errant Mr. Douglas and his family and burst into applause as the murderous tale reached its ghastly climax.

The real victims in this drama are the wife (played by Miss Archer) and the daughter, both of whom act superbly, but they are minor characters. Unlike *Wait Until Dark*, this is not primarily a story of afflicted innocence. It is a duel to the death between two sinners.

Now that we are all so sophisticated that we know that the various scenes in a film are not necessarily acted in the order in which we see them, we are bound to praise the subtle way in which

Mr. Douglas passes from amused curiosity, through misgiving, to abject terror and hatred. It would be unfair to say that Miss Close has an easier part. At one moment, she lies at the bottom of a bathful of water, with her eyes open and a thin stream of blood and air spiraling upward from her lips. When you remember that she may have been asked to do this four or five times, I think you will agree that this required dedication. Her task is only simpler than that of her costar in that the character she plays is in no way related to real life. It is impossible not to describe *Fatal Attraction* as an outrageous melodrama. It sacrifices probability to spectacular effects quite shamelessly. How could a woman, sophisticated, well dressed (only her hair is raving), and sane enough to hold a job in a publishing firm fall apart completely after one mad weekend with an unknown man? Women who kill their lovers start out unbalanced, like Miss Richardson in *Dance with a Stranger*. She was a nightclub hostess and would therefore be expected to be a potential murderess. Alternatively, such people devote so much time to an affair that if it ends abruptly, they feel they have been tricked into wasting part of their lives.

Nevertheless, see this film.

It is marvelously prepared for the screen. There is always a hint of danger—a knife lying at the edge of the frame, seen by an audience seconds before the participants in the battle notice it, or some sign, which its occupants have not yet understood, that Miss Close is in the house. Mr. Hitchcock couldn't have done better. In the way in which it plucks at the nerves of its audience, *Fatal Attraction* is almost a masterpiece.

Within days of wallowing in the unbridled lusts of Manhattan, I was floating chastely among the dreaming spires of Cambridge, England. I went with a representative cross section of the contributors to *Christopher Street* magazine to see *Maurice* (pronounced Morris by the English, to whom any word that sounds even faintly French is depraved). This is a surprisingly popular film. Even at the ten-thirty showing, we were only able to sit together in good seats through the kindness of the management of the Paris cinema, who let us into the auditorium ahead of the mere mortals clamoring to get in. I only wish that in return for this courtesy, I could praise the film with more enthusiasm.

The trouble with a homosexual encounter is that by nature it does not provide its participants with the desired illusion of entering the jungle. A heterosexual man or woman mates with an alien, even hostile being—someone of the opposite gender. In happier times, in order to impart this sort of exciting clash to a homosexual engagement, one party acted cute or helpless or bitchy. These antics are frowned upon by modern gay men. Now, in the hope of bestowing interest upon a union of two people of the same sex, it is necessary to cross boundaries either of race or culture. In the England of 1913, before the irreparable breakdown of its social structure, differences of class were a great help in making sexual activities tolerable.

To the British aristocracy, the embodiment of the primitive male was the gamekeeper with a bloodstained rabbit in his hand. *Maurice* might be called *Mr. Chatterley's Lover*.

Where I see class distinctions inflaming desire, Mr. Forster saw love conquering prejudices. His problem was that—at any rate in literature—he was not content with a bit of rough trade; he longed for eternal love. It is here that this story abandons all probability.

The narrative begins at Cambridge University, which has come to represent the life beautiful—a haven where ideas about "The Ideal State" float through the quadrangles, woven with adolescent longings for love. Clive (Hugh Grant) is the true aristocrat and Maurice (James Wilby) is his middle-class friend. They romp and kiss but do nothing worse, on the grounds that they might "regret it later."

When they leave Cambridge, Clive returns to his family, his estate, and his marriage to some nice girl. Maurice takes to the stock exchange, with his inner life still seething. During a visit to Clive's country house, he at last attracts the sexual interest of the gamekeeper (Rupert Graves), who climbs up a ladder to the guest's bedroom. I thought this was taking the novelettish dream to its limit. It may have worked on the printed page, where reality can be kept at bay, but in a movie it is going just too far. This is partly the fault of casting Mr. Graves as the gamekeeper. He acts well but he is not a D. H. Lawrence man—not an overwhelming earthy presence who doesn't care a damn about his job or the law or society. The actor is too pretty, too young for the part. When, later in the film, he turns up at Maurice's office to blackmail him, he looks hardly different from all the other men in the place.

After much wrangling, parting, and reconciliation, we leave Clive, with his wife beside him, looking out of his bedroom window toward the boathouse in which Maurice and the gamekeeper are locked in a passionate embrace. What are we supposed to infer will happen tomorrow? Will the lovers prance into the woods to start an idyllic sylvan life? We all know that this cannot be and this fundamentally is what makes *Maurice* an unsatisfactory film.

As we all walked along Fifty-ninth Street after the show, Mr. Steele hung his head; he was the only one among us who had enjoyed the picture unreservedly. His reason for this quaint judgment was that it represented the triumph of true (though kinky) love over narrow-minded society. It does, but that's not all that is wrong with it. In spite of some very good set pieces—the best of which is the village cricket match attended with pleasant condescension by the aristocracy and with uneasy earthiness by the local yokels—visually the film is without style. As other critics have pointed out, it is a collection of pretty picture postcards and, as a whole, the story is a series of failed efforts at communication. The blackmail scene is a perfect example of this; it appeared to convince neither the audience nor the actors participating in it.

I fear that the movie industry has recently become guilty of an undue reverence for Mr. Forster. *A Passage to India* suffered from the same defect. If the minor masterpieces of literature are to be used as movie material, it does their authors no service to preserve on the screen all their slow, rambling, detailed quality. Their film versions must be boldly—even ruthlessly—translated into something compact, visually coordinated, and animated by a passionate narrative drive.

HOPE AND GLORY / TOO OUTRAGEOUS!

Two movies in one day—what an orgy!

Although everybody knows that I am only masquerading as a film critic, Mr. Wise of the New York Film Festival very kindly allowed me to attend, more or less at dawn, a screening of Mr. Boorman's latest work at Miss Tully's hall.

In describing this picture, I must exercise a great deal of forbearance; it is by no means a Quentin Crisp Production. I will try to judge it in light of its intention, rather than by my reaction to it.

Hope and Glory (the title is ironic) is a long, faintly melancholy look, through the eyes of an eight-year-old boy, at suburban English life during the first two years of the Second World War. The American forces, who later lent such exotic glamour to London in the 1940s, had not arrived by then. The picture presented to our forlorn eyes is therefore of the dreariest place on earth, outside of the South Pole, at the dreariest moment of its history. It is quite remarkably accurate but, of necessity, it has no plot; it is simply a series of disconnected disasters. Those of you who remember this director's *Deliverance* may wish to pause here for a good cry.

What I hope will save this lovingly created film from failure in the eyes of American audiences is its humor, which is completely realistic but at the same time more outrageous than anything that either Ken or Craig Russell could have imagined. In order that he may join the local boys' gang, the hero must be able to swear. When he utters that four-letter word that is beyond television, the leader says solemnly, "That is only for very special occasions." There is also a hilarious sequence in which a girl slightly older than the boys is given a necklace looted from a bombed house in payment for holding her skirt up with her chin and allowing all the members of the gang to line up for a brief look at you know what.

The acting, both by the children and the adults, is very good, and the art direction or, perhaps, the photography, is faultless. To preserve the wall-to-wall dreariness of England, the fires started by the bombardment of London are not red but a sickly yellow.

After the screening, there was a press conference—the first that I have ever attended. A long table draped with a silver lamé cloth was carried onto the stage in front of the screen, and three microphones were placed upon it. It looked almost as though some exotic form of high mass was about to happen. After a moment of spellbound expectation, the celebrant appeared followed by his two acolytes, Miss Miles, who is the star of the picture, and Mr. Boorman. No one was wearing a camel-hair coat. In fact, all three of them looked businesslike—worse, respectable. No speeches were made about how wonderful New York is and how ecstatic anyone was to be present. Questions from the audience began immediately. These were not, as in my dream I had expected, searching queries about the state of the cinema or about waves and trends; they were not even about profit and loss. Their tone was chatty—just as though film critics were ordinary folk (which we all know to be untrue). Miss Miles said little and, though an actress of considerable talent, was often almost inaudible, but Mr. Boorman was infinitely available and most appealing as he explained how much of the movie was autobiographical. He was, in fact, the star of the entire morning, and, in a way, was more worth the money, more lovable, sunnier than any of his works. He could easily stage a Lillian Gish and travel throughout the length and breadth of the States explaining what on earth he is doing.

This odd ceremony was finished just after one o'clock, and by nightfall, I was in Mr. Fox's preview theater watching Mr. Benner's *Too Outrageous!*—a very different proposition from *Hope and Glory*.

It is very noticeable that autobiographies by gay men are crude and monotonously sexual, while fictional works about them are full of dialogue containing loyalty, friendship, and even love. This film is no exception.

It tells the tale of a drag artist (Mr. Russell) who, after years of doing his impersonations in small Canadian clubs, is given his chance to reach the Big Time. For a while, he dallies with this idea and tries to adapt himself to his high-powered agent's ambitions, but finally he renounces the opportunity for fame and wealth and returns to the company of his friends and the cabarets of Toronto. A likely story!

It is just not possible to believe that anyone in show business would prefer the companionship of a bunch of born losers to the adulation of half the world. I cannot speak for Canada, but in America such behavior would be tantamount to treason.

Nevertheless, I think the gay community will love this film, in spite of—nay, because of—its faults. The dialogue is mawkish—almost as gooey as parts of *The Boys in the Band*; the relationships are tortuous, and the mad girl (beautifully played by a Miss McLaren) is appealing.

The picture's chief asset, which compensates for all its improbabilities, is the presence of Mr. Russell. He has an enigmatic personality and veiled eyes that never quite look at anything. This provides a fascinating contrast to his highly concentrated stage image.

Incidentally, he must, in truth, be a very generous man, because the only faultless impersonation in the entire film is the work of an unknown "Jimmy James," who appears for a few minutes as Miss Monroe.

The movie has style, especially visual style, a consistent bad taste. I am not being sarcastic when I say this. Just what the picture needs in order to portray the turgid, almost hysterical view of life that stage homosexuals have is a relentless garishness, and this it has.

What for me was lacking was better theatrical judgment. Mr. Russell's cabaret acts are fun, and it is easy to believe that he has a large and loyal following in Canadian clubs. His imitations of Miss Streisand and Miss Kitt are very good—almost uncanny—

but he should not content himself with singing the songs these ladies have made famous. Instead, he should acquire lyrics that fit the well-known tunes but that make fun of whatever star is in question. At the end of the film, he does a number, written by Lewis Furey, about being oneself—an echo of "I Am What I Am" from *La Cage aux Folles*. The words are adequate, but the staging of it is misjudged. He should not appear on yet another elaborate set with a lot of superfluous dummies; he should sit absolutely still on an otherwise-empty stage with the lights focused so that we see only his face shining like a lonely star in a universe of doubt and darkness, and he should deliver the song with meticulous audibility and absolutely straight.

There the movie should end.

This would have provided a spectacular contrast to all the previous garishness, the spurious emotions, and the camping, and would have concentrated the attention of the audience upon Mr. Russell, his vivid personality and his troubled soul.

IN A SHALLOW GRAVE/ WHITE MISCHIEF

Recently, a man with an Italian name came from England to ask me to explain Mr. Purdy to the readers of a European magazine. He wished me to perform this difficult task without payment. This, I said, was too much, or rather, too little. I've always claimed to be an unworldly little thing, but I never forget that Shelley Winters said, "Act girlish, but not retarded." We came to an agreement and I wrote the required article. Before I started, I telephoned Mr. Purdy and asked him a few questions. One of these was, "Would you say that all your heroes are losers?" Without hesitation, but also without bitterness, he replied, "Yes, because I'm one."

Of all Mr. Purdy's main characters, the hero of *In a Shallow Grave* has lost the most. Garnet Montrose (Michael Biehn) has returned from World War II with his face, neck, and one hand appallingly disfigured by a flamethrower. He lives alone in a small farmhouse in Virginia, where his only employee is a young black man, Quintas Rance (Michael Beach). In spite of his physical condition, Mr. Biehn cannot abandon his courtship of a twice-widowed woman (Maureen Mueller) who lives nearby. He advertises for someone to work for him whose real function will be to write and deliver love letters to this woman. The young man (Patrick Dempsey) who ultimately performs these duties arrives quite by chance, fleeing from his criminal past. He becomes involved with the widow and disasters of various kinds follow. In the final sequence of the film, the turmoil seems to be tentatively resolved; we see Mr. Biehn dancing with Miss Mueller in a ruined dance hall. As this is a movie, the story could hardly end otherwise, but it is not a Purdy ending. In his novel, Miss Mueller begins to send letters to Mr. Biehn, but to no effect. As the hero says, the longing, though more painful, was better than the fulfillment. Mr. Purdy's genius manifests itself in a series of quirky, sometimes coarse events subtly blended with an eternal, all-pervading pathos. This is something a film cannot present.

The visual style of the picture is broken-down rural, which makes it mournfully pleasant to watch, but the camera behaves in a very odd way. The first glimpse of the widow's home makes it look like a doll's house, and elsewhere, the camera moves around so strangely that people seem to be drifting about, when, in fact, they are standing still. At one crucial moment, one of the characters is removed from sight so abruptly that we are left wondering if he was ever there in the first place.

The acting of the hero is good. (Some time ago, you may have witnessed Mr. Biehn chasing Miss Bacall hither and thither in *The Fan*.) And the heroine is suitably beautiful and remote, but, surprisingly, the actor who seems the most at ease in front of the cameras is Mr. Beach. I say "surprisingly" because the synopsis (almost as long as Mr. Purdy's novel) handed to us by Skouras

Pictures tells us that Mr. Beach left his acting school only a year and a half ago. It is difficult to assess Mr. Dempsey's abilities, because he is totally miscast. He looks too urban, too soft, and much too young, and this makes Miss Mueller's attraction to him downright kinky. The only entirely misjudged sequence is the love scene between these two.

Four of us attended the screening of *In a Shallow Grave*, and when it was over, we held a mini symposium in McBell's restaurant. I think I can say that we never found the film boring but that we are the only people to whom it can appropriately be shown. This does not mean that Mr. Purdy is incapable of writing a popular movie; it only signifies that, if he wishes to do so, he may have to adapt his skills to a more formal, clear-cut narrative.

In spite of Mr. Steele's injunction that I must never watch another British film, I allowed myself to be taken to see *White Mischief*. It was a mistake. As is so often the case with English imports, this movie cannot make up its mind whether to be a documentary or an entertainment. It tries to combine that haphazard quality, which makes real life so hard to bear, with the inevitability of a drama. At least *Dance with a Stranger* had, in the incomparable Miss Richardson, a forceful central character and a narrative drive that dragged the audience at an ever-increasing pace toward the preordained murder. The heroine (if that is not too noble a term) of *White Mischief* is Miss Scacchi. In spite of her Italian name, she looks like the beautiful cover of an English knitting magazine of the 1940s; she has a pink and white complexion, round pale eyes, and sculpted dark gold hair. So far so good, but though she provokes a murder and a suicide, she remains a cipher. We are never told whether she conducted her illicit liaison so brazenly in order to annoy her husband or out of sheer empty-headedness. The real center of the story becomes her husband, faultlessly played by a little-known actor named Joss Ackland, who, hovering between chivalry and abject folly, truly engages our sympathy. He is betrayed by Miss Scacchi with a titled gentleman (played by Mr. Dance) by whom we are asked to believe the entire female population of Africa is fascinated. He brings off the effortless elegance of an English aristocrat to perfection but acts with all the sparkle of a sleepwalker. *Details* magazine has rechristened him "Michael novo-Caine."

He is murdered; Mr. Ackland is charged, but, on the ground that no decent jury would convict an Englishman, he is acquitted. As far as I can remember, in real life, the identity of the culprit remained forever tantalizingly in doubt, but here the finger of accusation points with hardly a tremor at Mr. Ackland. Toward the end of this film, when Miss Scacchi, in a dazed state and with her white silk blouse bespattered with blood, arrives at a party in a graveyard (I am not making this up), she is offered a consolatory glass of champagne, but no one evinces the faintest concern or even curiosity. This, surely, is taking Englishness to the verge of parody, if not beyond it.

The film has a large cast of medium-range actors (Miss Chaplin, Miss Miles—not *our* Miss Miles—and Mr. Hurt, who, as you all know, is my representative on earth). They all extract every ounce of significance from their roles, but, in a sad way, this is one of the film's defects. They seek and deserve our entire attention, but they have little to do with the central theme. Their chief function appears to be to personify the decadence of British Colonial society. Over this, the director lingers unduly. Today, even in the lightest of family entertainment, the shortest words are repeatedly used for the longest things, and in Hollywood, the bared breasts of women grow on trees. Any endeavor to shock a modern audience is bound to fail.

At the end of *White Mischief*, a caption appears on a black screen telling us that ultimately Miss Scacchi married Mr. Hurt. Abruptly, we are yanked back into the documentary mode. This is as annoying as was the announcement at the end of *Dance with a Stranger*, giving us the date of Miss Ellis's execution. Some one must write to Mrs. Thatcher begging her to enact a law that would forbid this method of concluding a film. Movies are pictures—not literature; their medium is images—not words.

Perhaps *White Mischief* should have begun with the marriage of Miss Scacchi to Mr. Hurt, attended by a host of whispering guests, or with a sinister absence of anybody but a few impertinent journalists.

When I was last in England, I was taken to a dinner party at which Mr. and Mrs. Hurt were present. They showed us photographs of a house he was causing to be built in Africa at the foot of a mountain. I was amazed that they were proposing to live in a place so far from everywhere. I envisaged that they would spend the rest of their days in a stuffy British colony singing the national anthem on Christmas Day. Though I do not anticipate that Mr. Hurt will commit a murder, I now know that their fate will be worse than I had suspected. *White Mischief* makes clear what viciousness flourishes in a community where the women can find nothing worthwhile to do. The quintessential moment of the film occurs when, surveying a glorious African sky, Miss Miles says, "Another fucking perfect day!"

D.O.A.

While waiting in a snowstorm to enter the Plaza cinema, I found myself standing on line next to a film critic from New Brunswick. He asked me whether I was who he thought I was and I, who understand less than anybody what is in the hearts of men, said that I did not know. He had an invitation for two to the secret showing of *D.O.A.*, but was alone, so when, after moving forward at the rate of an inch every five minutes, we had arrived at the entrance and your Mr. Steele still had not appeared, he very graciously offered to escort me into the auditorium. "You don't have to sit with me," he said, and added, "My mother taught me that if I struck up a conversation with a stranger on a platform, I should not try to enter the same carriage as he when our train arrived." Nothing in the film we were about to see equaled the charm—the Americanness—of this brief encounter; nevertheless, I recommend it.

Recently, we have seen a number of movies about which our

chief complaint has been that in them so very little happened. No one could possibly level such a charge at *D.O.A.* It has two plots, separate but equal in complexity. One is about a wealthy widow (Miss Rampling), who, to the amazement of all concerned, seems to be putting through college the son of the man who murdered her husband. The second plot involves a professor of English (Mr. Quaid), who is on the verge of being divorced and whose doctor tells him he has been poisoned and will live only another forty-eight hours at most. During his strenuous efforts to discover who has murdered him, Mr. Quaid, either directly or inadvertently, causes the death of a quite spectacular number of people.

This picture is not a thriller; its guiding principle is not suspense. That is to say that at no time are we led to hope that if he can find out who has poisoned him, our hero will regain his health. *D.O.A.* is purely a murder mystery. Satisfaction for the audience lies only in knowing whodunnit and why. As it turns out, the motive for the dastardly deed is more specious than any found even in the works of Mrs. Christie. The murderer's overwhelming desire is to claim authorship of a novel that is in fact the work of a gifted pupil (played by Mr. Knepper), but, as everyone knows, students never write good books; they produce promising ones. At the very end of the film, as he sits in the police station waiting for death, Mr. Quaid says, "It was all over somebody's homework." It was an error of judgment on the part of the scriptwriter to allow this remark to be made. No one on any screen should ever voice an opinion that may echo unfortunately the view of the audience. In a science-fiction epic, for instance, when insects the size of omnibuses are trampling some sleepy American city to dust, no actor may utter the words "They're never gonna believe this."

However, *D.O.A.* will not be judged by its probability but, rather, by its ingenuity and its pace, and of these qualities it has an abundance. Its two plots interweave or rush forward independently at alarming speed and accompanied by a deafening amount of noise.

In any picture of this nature, the players are not required to act so much as to carry out the intricacies of the narrative. Even so, there are a number of ways in which they can persuade an audience to care about the sufferings of their characters, and here everybody suffers most of the time. It is these personal details that are so conspicuously lacking. A very pretty female student (Miss Ryan), with whom Mr. Quaid becomes involved, has several square inches of flesh abruptly torn from her wrist, but, during the subsequent action, she never once looks at, touches, or licks her wound. A woman who has shot herself is last seen lying on a billiard table. This is ludicrous melodrama. Did she climb onto the table for effect? Worst of all, the hero, though he must be in incessant pain and has only a short time to live, says nothing about life and death, though he is a teacher of English and they, even when in robust health, never do anything but make speeches about eternal things. Damn it, he doesn't even take an aspirin.

These omissions and incongruities are not the fault of the cast; they must be blamed on the screenwriter or the directors, of which this piece has two—a Mr. Morton and a Ms. Jankel. Perhaps (as in Mrs. Burton's ill-fated *Cleopatra*), one took over from the other—an arrangement that is always deleterious. If both stood on the set at the same time and bickered about what should be done, it is a wonder the film ever got made at all.

The best acting is done by Mr. Quaid's screen wife (Miss Kaczmarak), who succeeds in conveying to us that she still loves her husband but can no longer bear the aridity of their marriage. If this Mr. Quaid is the same gentleman who so improbably won Miss Barkin's love in *The Big Easy*, it must be stated that he deals far better with adversity than he did with success.

Miss Rampling lends dignity and her beautiful voice to the part of the rich Mrs. Fitzwaring, but she never quite suggests a secretly desperate and violent personality. In extenuation of her inadequacy, it must be remarked that she is asked by the script to say lines such as "Terrible words were said, like *bigamy* and *blackmail*," at which the audience tittered. Moreover, she is put into clothes that look as though they had been hastily pinned onto her rather than designed for a powerful and very worldly woman.

The rest of the cast is adequate.

The Plaza Theater on Fifty-eighth Street is so esoteric that it is not even listed in the Manhattan telephone directory. Whoever arranged this gala even was as ignorant of human nature as the man who wrote the original story of the film. They evidently supposed that not everyone who received an invitation would use it. Even I know that no American ever skips a free movie. Everyone, including Miss Miles, was there, and the place was full to bursting. The occasion was only slightly less disastrous than the preview of *Psycho 2* (or was it 3). Mr. Steele and I were compelled to sit in the front row of the auditorium, where the blood, tar, and broken glass poured onto our upturned faces. This was nice but may have clouded our judgment of the film's true worth.

One thing, however, stands out clearly. The movie's crowning glory is its violence. Destruction takes a multitude of forms, always within inches of the camera's lens; victims fall from rooftops, sink into tar pits, shoot themselves or one another. If the hazards encountered on an evening stroll through New York seem tame to you, this is your movie.

BIG BUSINESS

This is easily the most enjoyable film that we have seen since *Down and Out in Beverly Hills*.

Hollywood's greatest talent used to lie in the making of thriller and gangster movies. Recently, it seems to have lost that particular knack. As technical skills in depicting violence proliferate, pictures in this category have not improved; they have only become longer and rowdier. Furthermore, now that sex seems to be here to stay —at least on the screen—directors deem it necessary to include in all their works long erotic passages that decrease the tension of almost any kind of narrative. It is not easy to find ways of making one's own sex life fascinating and it is well nigh impossible to infuse interest into watching the bedroom antics of others (I have never, in any film, seen a copulating couple do anything truly startling), but, though it is hard to make sex exciting, it isn't difficult to make it funny. Perhaps it is for this reason that, during the present decade, the greatest triumphs of the American movie industry have been their comedies.

Down and Out in Beverly Hills was a comedy with a rather shaky underlying moral; *Big Business* is a shameless farce. In the earlier picture, Miss Midler was what publicists used to call "a featured player." In the new one, she is a star—better still, two stars. As this is an identical-twin spree, we are able to enjoy two Miss Midlers and two Miss Tomlins, but the two women played by Miss Tomlin have less clearly defined differences of character; she is therefore sadly given less opportunity to shine. Who is who of the two Miss Midlers is never in any doubt, and she doesn't waste a moment of her very considerable screen time.

She has become to comedy what Miss Garbo was to tragedy, and Mr. Abrahams gives her the same treatment that was lavished upon the Swedish lady by Mr. Goldwyn. When she is her rich self, she is even allowed a typical Garbovine first entrance. For a moment, her face is concealed by an outrageously large hat, just as in *Anna Karenina* Miss Garbo's face was hidden by a few wisps of steam from the train in which Mr. Vronsky first catches a glimpse of her.

As her humble alter-self in *Big Business*, Miss Midler is initially seen milking a cow and singing—nay, yodeling—a Dolly Parton-type number. Although we watched this picture at the Ziegfeld Theater with a host of hardened preview addicts, at both her urban and her rural entrances, the entire audience burst into applause. I half-expected Miss Midler to pause and take a bow before proceeding with the film.

As we entered the theater, the organizers did not hand us a long synopsis explaining the plot of the film we were about to see. No one could explain it, but I will try.

Big Business works somewhat on the same principle as Mr. Shakespeare's *The Comedy of Errors*. In that play, twin gentlemen with the same name come from two different cities, attended by twin manservants of the same name (I ask you!). In this movie, two women, one of high degree and the other a mere farmer's wife, both give birth on the same day in the same hospital to twin girls. The nurse who assists at these two (or four) blessed events is so scatty that when we first notice her, she is confusing a sample of urine with the soft drinks to be given to the patients. Inevitably, she mixes up the two newly born babies so that one Miss Midler grows up in opulent surroundings imagining that she is the sister of one Miss Tomlin, while the other Miss Midler is paired with the second Miss Tomlin in a setting of rustic simplicity. After this initial error has been perpetrated, as a writer of captions for silent films would say, "Many long years pass."

We next meet Miss Midler One as a tycooness, running a vast corporation in New York City, with Miss Tomlin One as her ineffectual sister. The company they rule is planning to buy up a small factory in the country, throw all its employees out of work, and to strip-mine the entire territory (whatever that may mean). Miss Midler Two and Miss Tomlin Two, who live and work in this threatened community, decide to go to New York and try to prevent this monstrous takeover. Finally, all four ladies meet.

That Dauntless Duo, who every week on television bicker about the merits of the latest movies, pointed out that at this moment of long-awaited revelation, none of the ladies seemed to care or even to notice that, so far, they have spent their entire lives cross-twinned, so to speak. This omission appeared to sour both critics' view of the entire picture—almost of life itself. In the vortex of improbability that was at that point engulfing everybody, I cannot truthfully say that it mattered much to me.

As each of these twins has a suitor who chases her along the corridors of an expensive hotel and through the streets of Manhattan, it will not be difficult for you to imagine what pandemonium ensues. My advice is definitely to see this film but not to bother unduly with the plot. Sit back and enjoy the jolly chaos. The clothes are blinding, the lines are witty, the editing is as sharp as in a Marx

Brothers' movie, and the visual exaggerations are hilarious. There is a black chauffeur who is almost as big as the limousine he is employed to drive.

I need hardly say that, in a farce as sweeping as this, where every aspect of human folly is ridiculed, there are the obligatory two gay men in Miss Midler's employ, but have no fear. The sequence in which their sin is revealed to the audience is in no way offensive and is genuinely funny.

The greatest of the many virtues of this picture is that, in spite of the slapdash nature of the story, it is told with quite astonishing attention to the details of moviemaking. For instance, a car ride includes a view of the outside of the vehicle, glimpses of the occupants through one of its windows, of the street as seen by them, and even of the eyes of the chauffeur reflected in his rearview mirror.

I went to the Ziegfeld Theater with a coach party of your editor's friends, and everyone seemed to enjoy himself enormously. The only pleasure lacking from this gala occasion was the sight of Miss Miles in the preview audience. Expressing his utter bewilderment at her absence, Mr. Steele murmured sadly, "I thought she was a *ciné qua non.*"

I rate that as the joke of the season

BIG TOP PEE-WEE

The story of *Big Top Pee-wee* tells us about a person (Mr. Herman) who lives in a village somewhere in America, and who occupies a houseful of farmyard animals, which he treats as though they were his children. He is unpopular with the villagers—all three of them—but is managing to sustain what I believe is called an ongoing relationship with the only pretty girl in the entire neighborhood (Penelope Ann Miller). When a traveling circus comes their way, Mr. Herman is delighted, but the rest of the community is not. Initially, the circus owner (Kris Kristofferson) embraces defeat; later he decides that all that is needed to overcome local hostility is a gimmick; he chooses to present his show with a farm-yard motif. Mr. Herman, at the very first glimpse of her cleavage, falls madly in love with the trapeze artiste (Valeria Golino). (He cannot be blamed for that, as she is as pretty as the television lady who invented Grape-Nuts.) Delighted that Mr. Kristofferson has decided to stay, Mr. Herman transforms all the villagers by magic into children who adore the circus and everybody lives happily ever after.

In reducing its narrative to the merest skeleton, I am not being unfair to *Big Top Pee-wee*; in fact, I am doing it a favor. Its weakness lies in its innumerable digressions and its lack of any clearly defined intention—its absence of a consistent style.

The setting has a kind of gaudy rusticity, like a calendar il-lustration for July. The sky is very blue and the grass screaming green, but nowhere does the art direction achieve the humor or the beauty of *Li'l Abner*, a movie which perhaps only I of all cineasts still living ever saw. There the contour of the hills was like scenic railway, the healthy glow on Mr. Abner's cheeks was applied with a visible swirling brushstroke, and Miss Daisy Mae wore a bra so uplifting that there was a shadow above as well as below her breasts. By comparison with that small masterpiece, the current film seems to have no art direction—only a few optimistic improvisations.

The animals in *Big Top Pee-wee* have not been Disneyfied; we behold them arrayed in all that grossness with which we are well aware that barnyard denizens are cursed. In the case of the pig, this nastiness works perfectly. A porcine voice (Wayne White) has been found for it, and it is very cleverly made to look as though it is speaking. The pig is called Vance. (I tried all the anagrams of this name that I could think of, but came up with nothing that would explain why it had been chosen.) None of the other animals utters a word.

Why?

The villagers are not, it is true, as revolting as the animals, but they have a Dickensian hideousness. They are consistently hostile to Mr. Herman, but the irascible storekeeper seems compelled to obey him.

Why?

There is dialogue, but there are no jokes. There are songs, but one can hardly say that they are sung. The circus lyric is jolly, but even that has nothing like the catchiness of, say, "When Temptation Comes Along" as rendered by Mr. Cricket.

Why not?

It was not, however, until I caught sight of Mr. Kristofferson that my tears really began to flow. What, I cried, is this superb being—so manly, so handsome, so positively noble—doing here? I felt ashamed for him as, when I was a child, I beheld an uncle who I thought could be trusted, dressed in a Santa Claus suit and bellowing "Ho. Ho. Ho." That was the moment when I prayed that I would never become an adult, and I'm pleased to be able to tell you that I never did.

The rest of the circus performers are the usual motley throng—a giant, a bearded lady, a hermaphrodite, several midgets, and so on. There is also Mr. Kristofferson's wife (Susan Tyrrell), who is a Tom-Thumb-sized lady—the only person in the entire cast on this diminutive scale.

Again, why?

The movie is littered with these unexplained anomalies, the most perplexing of all being Mr. Herman himself.

What is he supposed to be? Though he treats the animals as if they were people, he is by no means a child. With Miss Golino, he engages in a kissing sequence so prolonged that it becomes disgusting—bordering on adult, but he is not a mature man. He seems at times blandly innocent, but his relationship with his first girl friend is cynical in the extreme. It is obvious that he hates her gilded furze-bush hair and her slovenly eating habits, but he would have raped her before our very eyes had not decorum been restored in the nick of time by the arrival of some subhuman children. When he meets Miss Golino, he abandons Miss Miller without explanation. He is in no sense the hero of this dubious tale except in that he is its central character.

Even his magical powers appear to be more or less accidental.

His appearance is as ambiguous as his morality. He wears a skintight suit, but he has no "figure," if you know what I mean. His legs are the same thickness from hip to ankle; his arms, the same thickness from shoulder to waist; even his torso is tubular. What he most resembles is a British pre-World War I newspaper comic strip—one of those marionettelike creatures that presents the minimum of difficulties to a draftsman. His hair looks like a piece of carpet very skillfully cut and gummed to his scalp, and his face, more made-up than that of his true love, is without lines or irregularities of any kind—almost without form. His movements are energetic but neither graceful nor comic, and, though he prances about the village, he is not effeminate. In short, he is ageless, sexless, and characterless, except for a certain heartless eagerness.

Trying to place him in relation to the other great funny men of the screen is not easy. Though he is worldly, he is not a pseudo-child like Harry Langdon. In spite of his elementary interest in girls, he does not display the manic lusts of Harpo Marx. He avoids the nauseating sentimentality of Mr. Chaplin but also lacks his physical elegance. He does not evince the stoicism in adversity of Mr. Keaton, nor the lethal social criticism of Danny Kaye. Of all the cinema's deliberately funny men, he is most akin to Mr. Lewis, to whom he is at least superior in that he does not suffer from the Jerry Lewis syndrome. Miss Ball said, "Never *act* funny." This is the warning Mr. Lewis did not heed. Whenever he found himself in a genuinely comic situation, he immediately crossed his eyes, blubbered his lips, and sagged at the knees, thereby forfeiting the interest of his audience. In other words, with these tricks Mr. Lewis reduced himself to a clown, and a clown is a horrible thing to happen to anyone.

Of course, all this somewhat negative criticism can easily be converted to praise. It is all another way of saying that Mr. Herman is completely original, but if, as Mr. Steele explained, true Hermanism is a cult that has swept like Spanish influenza throughout the land, certain basic questions must be answered—certain doubts laid to rest.

For instance, for whom was *Big Top Pee-wee* made, and what does Mr. Herman's screen image really represent?

A HANDFUL OF DUST

This is a very British movie made from a very British novel by a very British writer. It is, therefore, extremely misanthropic. It is about the marriage of an aristocratic English couple, which at first appears to be an idyllic relationship, but which soon ends with the threat of divorce and plunges everybody concerned into disaster.

Mr. Waugh, who wrote the book, hated everyone and was hated in return. As he himself might have said, What are friends for? He was the only author I can call to mind who was being savaged by the press within hours of his death. I would have written "before he was cold in his grave," except that Mr. Waugh was never really warm.

His dazzling skill lay chiefly in his ability to express his contempt for the entire human race without recourse to invective—without ever raising his literary voice. Some of this elegant spite is present in the film of *A Handful of Dust*. For instance, when there is a discussion about the likelihood of the hero's being compelled to sell his beloved country estate in order to pay his wife's exorbitant alimony, her brother tells him, "Pity the place isn't Gothic; schools really go for that sort of thing." As I saw this movie in a preview theater, I am unable to say whether or not American audiences will appreciate this rather specialized kind of wit. On the evening when we watched the picture, only Mr. Steele laughed.

The acting is of a high standard. The wife is played by a Miss Scott Thomas, who, though she has two very British surnames, lives, we are told by the provided synopsis, exclusively in France. Nevertheless, she manages to drift with consummate English grace into a trivial affair, regardless of the shattering effect that her behavior has on others, and to drift out of it into a limbo so bleak that she takes to going to the cinema alone. (How low can you sink?) Her paramour is played by Mr. Graves, who was so hopelessly miscast as the gamekeeper in the movie made of Mr. Forster's *Maurice*. Here he is just right, and so is Miss Dench as his mother. The specifically "movie acting" is done by a handsome gentleman, unknown to me, called Mr. Torrens. He is the only member of the cast who knows how to present his wonderful face to the cameras and allow the audience to read into it whatever it desires.

Unfortunately, Mr. Wilby, whom you last saw in the title role of Maurice, is here seriously miscast as the wronged husband; he looks too young—not a day older, in fact, than he looked in *Maurice*.

This will not do.

Rich Americans use their wealth to keep themselves looking youthful, but, until very recently, members of British aristocracy regarded that sort of thing as rather vulgar. It was admissible to be a child, and even, at that age, to be deliciously naughty (in *A Handful of Dust*, the little boy, played by Jackson Kyle, calls his nanny a silly old tart), but, as soon as those few carefree years were past, it was not considered good form to remain conspicuously young. One grew old as quickly as possible, and if one lived in the country, one became weather-beaten the moment one stepped out of the womb. The word *adult*, which on Eighth Avenue means filthy, in Berkshire or Hampshire denotes a willingness to shoulder responsibility. Mr. Wilby, in a scene in which he tries to hint at this to his son, acts with exquisitely tender gravity, but unfortunately, he looks like the child's elder brother.

Mr. Wilby's character is one of the few for whom Mr. Waugh ever expressed sympathy. Some of this emotion is present in this picture; there is a very moving shot of him eating alone at a long table in a room as big as a cathedral.

Then there's Sir Alec Guinness. At the very sight of him, I became worried.

A woman whom I do not know but with whom I enjoy hour-long telephone conversations argues that all English actors are good and all American actors, bad. She even goes so far as to suggest that this is the reason why British players do not succeed over here. This, though I do not tell her, I hold to be nonsense. In my (by no means humble) opinion, British actors fail because they still do not understand that movie acting is not about disguising but about revealing oneself. Nowadays, in the United States, film stars are welcome in all strata of society—nay, they have become sacred and because of this, any director can without effort avail himself of the eager services of an entire nation. No one is required to wear a wig or put on a false nose or speak with an assumed accent. Central Casting will produce someone with exactly the right hair, the right face the right voice. In Britain, where, in any case, there are fewer people and where almost nothing is socially acceptable, there are inevitably fewer actors. This means that over there, in a sense, all acting is repertory acting. In the provinces, during the pretelevision era, there was a tradition that a plump middle-aged leading lady, wearing nothing but a tablecloth, would appear as Tondoleyo in *White Cargo* one week, and the next would put on an Italianate costume and become Mr. Shakespeare's Juliet. She was applauded less for her gifts than for her gall. That view of what was needed on stage spilled over into the cinema.

I personally prefer the American method of acting; I consider the wearing of a false nose to be an un-American activity. But from my conversations with The Unknown Woman, I gather that there are a lot of people in the United States who will see *A Handful of Dust* chiefly to find out what Sir Alec has got himself up to look like now.

I think it was a particularly bad mistake for him to appear in the Amazonian jungle toward the end of this film. Sir Alec is somehow comically familiar. (It's a wonder the role didn't go to Comrade Ustinov.) The impression that after a long and lonely illness, we have awakened in an unknown world among unknown faces is completely destroyed.

The elegant Miss Cameron, who writes for *Christopher Street* and who accompanied us to this movie, could remember all sorts of telling details in the novel that had been needlessly omitted from the film. This was an amazing feat of memory, but it was also a naughty thing to do. As a good American, it was her duty to regard the whole of world literature as but a vast file of potential screen treatments. (To me, it has always been strange that the Bible is not advertised as "the book of the film.") Above all, it must be understood that the better the novel and the more closely it is adapted, the worse the picture that results; there is so much in a masterpiece that can go wrong on the screen.

Though the photography in the beginning is too beautiful, making the world look like a transcendental lemon meringue pie, and though the music has everywhere an inappropriate swooning style, there is much to recommend in *A Handful of Dust*—impressive manorial interiors and chilly English landscapes, faultlessly articulated lines, shafts of ironic wit in the dialogue—but it remains a misguided venture; it has been impossible to impose upon the plot a cinematic shape. Worst of all, the jungle scenes, which I do see cannot be omitted, introduce a new location and new characters much too late.

BEACHES

In olden days, when there was a marked difference between the sexes, Hollywood frequently used to manufacture products that were known as "women's movies." This description warned us that they would be about love and would be sad—not to say mawkish. *Beaches* (which Mr. Steele prophesies will universally be rechristened *Bitches*) is just such a tale. It is adapted by one woman from a novel by another and it is made exclusively for a female audience.

As I am writing at the behest of *Christopher Street*, perhaps I should mention at once that this film contains only one reference to lesbianism, and that is oblique. The first time that Miss Hershey is reunited with Miss Midler after a long absence, the latter, not immediately recognizing her childhood playmate, rejects her forward greeting with the words "You're not my type."

All the men in this story are the merest ciphers. Miss Hershey's husband is a rich, stuffy lawyer; Miss Midler's spouse is an Off-Broadway director with not one interesting thing to say about experimental theater, and the only other man with whose affections she trifles is a surgeon so stupid that when she says she wants to become a nurse, he believes her. I know nurses are a wild bunch, but that is ridiculous.

The story only deeply concerns two women. One of these (Miss Hershey) is well-born, well-brought up, well-heeled; the other (Miss Midler) has emerged from the lowly origins and is completely eaten up with the notion of being a star. They first meet as children on a beach. It is well known that children are a mistake—especially in pictures—but the little girl who plays Miss Midler (a certain Mayim Bialik) is so like her in both her appearance and her behavior that her choice for the part seems almost miraculous and constitutes, as far as I know, the only instance in the history of the movie industry of witty casting. Oddly enough, this opening sequence is, in some ways, the most enjoyable part of the movie.

The rest of the narrative pursues the not entirely successful careers of both women. Miss Hershey tries to escape the confines of her strict upbringing by becoming a lawyer, marries, is betrayed by her husband, and becomes seriously, nay, fatally ill.

There is no such thing as costarring with Miss Midler. Inevitably, more screen time is devoted to Miss M's career than to that of her friend. We never see Miss Hershey plead a case in court, but we do watch Miss Midler performing various numbers in various circumstances. Sad to say, none of these is as effective as it might have been. At an audition, she performs with her customary showy energy, but our pleasure would have been greatly increased if she had been singing a song about the hazards of auditioning. Soon after this incident, we find her in the offest-Broadway production ever, a typical German Expressionist drama, with her supporting players wearing masks and making semaphore gestures on a set like an air-raid shelter. This joke also misfires. It would have been so much funnier if we had watched this scene in rehearsal with ludicrously high-flown instructions from the director. Finally, and least appropriately of all, she appears in a cabaret setting wearing a subdued evening dress and giving the full Peggy Lee treatment to a jaunty ditty from the thirties called "That's the Glory of Love." Our hearts are supposed to be touched by this because it was the number she sang as a child. It doesn't work. What was needed here was some wonderful climatic lyric that we could have interpreted as expressing Miss Midler's love for Miss Hershey and her grief at the loss of it.

The parts of this movie which serve the star better are those that do not take place on a stage or a film set. She is a superb actress who combines despotic command of the screen with rare subtlety of expression; on her face audiences can read every nuance of human emotion.

We saw this movie at the Gramercy cinema on Twenty-third Street. It is so conveniently situated that both Miss Cameron and I arrived and stood in a well-ordered enclosure marked TICKET HOLDERS. Mr. Steele appeared only a few minutes later and, in order to join us, stepped nimbly over a tatty piece of string that divided us from the ordinary mortals passing by. At this moment, an elderly gentleman in uniform materialized from nowhere and reproved Mr. Steele for his unruly behavior. When Miss Cameron politely explained that she already held his ticket, she, too, was severely rebuked. I could not decide whether this man was a member of the cinema's staff or one of New York's foulest. I was prepared to deny that I had ever before seen either of my companions, but fortunately the incident ended as abruptly as it had begun.

If you decide to go to the Gramercy cinema, watch your step.

After the performance, the three of us went to a nearby restaurant as French as the Eiffel Tower, where I asked my friends what the film we had just seen meant. Their answers were evasive to say the least. I am therefore compelled to offer an opinion unaided.

Beaches is about a mysterious disease known as "my best friend." It only affects women; they seem to have an incurable need to confide. Men either go out with "the boys" or sit at home and glare at their wives. Women, when they are not glaring at their husbands, write letters—often at the rate of one a week and sometimes for a lifetime—to some girl friend with whom they attended school. In spite of, or, perhaps, because of the intensity and the duration of these relationships, they tend to be subjected to quite startling changes of mood. This phenomenon has been the theme of a number of movies. In a play called *Old Acquaintance*, the heroine says, "It's surprising how much you can sometimes dislike your best friend," and in the movie of the same name, Miss Davis actually shook Miss Hopkins. (It is true that Miss Davis might shake anybody, but that does not blunt my point.) In *The Turning Point*, Miss MacLaine tore the hair from Miss Bancroft's head. These confrontations were climactic, but in *Beaches*, Miss Midler and Miss Hershey wrangle, forgive, embrace, part, and reunite until I found their antics difficult to comprehend, difficult to believe, and finally difficult to bear. In the end, Miss Midler undertakes to look after her best friend's child, or at least to allow it to stand in the drafty corridors of questionable nightclubs. I took this to signify that the meaning of the film is that in spite of the terrible things we do to friendship, something ragged and bespattered survives.

I cannot lay my typewriter aside without mentioning a tiny, entirely gratuitous sequence in *Beaches* in which, at an audition, a totally unknown man sings the fatalistic ditty "Que Sera Sera" with such deliciously and deliberately inappropriate enthusiasm that the incident became the one moment in the entire film when the Gramercy was unanimous in its unconditional delight.